World, Self, Poem

World, Self, Poem

Essays on Contemporary Poetry
from the "Jubilation of Poets"

edited by
LEONARD M. TRAWICK

The Kent State University Press
Kent, Ohio, and London, England

© 1990 by The Kent State University Press, Kent, Ohio 44242
All rights reserved
Library of Congress Catalog Card Number 90–4516
ISBN 0–87338–419–9
Manufactured in the United States of America

Library of Congress Cataloging-in-Publication Data

World, self, poem : essays on contemporary poetry from the "Jubilation
   of poets" / edited by Leonard M. Trawick.
    p.   cm.
  Papers presented at the festival held Oct. 23–26, 1986 in
Cleveland, Ohio, in celebration of the 25th anniversary of the
Cleveland State University Poetry Center.
    ISBN 0–87338–419–9 (alk. paper)⊗
    1. Poetry—20th century—History and criticism. 2. Poetry—20th
century. 3. Self in literature. I. Trawick, Leonard M.
II. Cleveland State University. Poetry Center.
  PN1271.W67   1990
  811'.5409—dc20

90–4516
CIP

British Library Cataloging-in-Publication data are available.

Contents

World, Self, Poem

Introduction

Because of the way they originally came together, the essays in this collection provide a revealing sample of approaches to contemporary poetry in the 1980s. Their occasion was the Jubilation of Poets festival, in October 1986, at which more than three hundred poets and scholars assembled in Cleveland, Ohio, to help celebrate the twenty-fifth anniversary of the Cleveland State University Poetry Center with poetry readings, panels, workshops, and academic sessions.[1]

The festival organizers sent announcements to English departments throughout the United States and Canada, and to the 2,130 members in the MLA Poetry Division, calling simply for papers on contemporary poetry in English. Since we specified no particular topic or approach, the papers that came in reflected whatever subjects and methods the authors themselves chose to pursue. The festival committee selected what seemed to them the best papers, regardless of their focus, and grouped them into eighteen panels and sections according to topic—e.g., politics, women's issues, poetic media, plus a few on individual poets including Robert Duncan, William Bronk, and Galway Kinnell.

I have selected for this collection the papers and talks that seem to be of most permanent interest and to be most representative of the concerns that surfaced at the festival. Many of the papers focused on single poets or even single works; my choices favor those that, other things being equal, not only illuminate the particular author but also cast a broader light on current trends and approaches.

Because the festival was organized from the start as a coming together of poets and scholars, the participants were on the whole closer to the pulse of current poetry than those at most academic conventions. It was an encouraging sign of the convergence of scholars and practitioners of literature that fully half of those presenting papers were also published poets—some of considerable merit—who signed up to take part in the open poetry readings.

It would be unrealistic, of course, to regard this collection as a statistically impeccable sampling of current poetic interests. For one thing, the geographical location of the festival meant that a majority of participants came from east of the Mississippi; if there really is a distinct West Coast poetics, it was underrepresented. Indeed, it may be that only critics of a certain stripe choose to participate in such conferences at all. For whatever reason, there was little interest here in "Language" poetry, and the excursions into deconstructionist and other post-structuralist approaches were not very strenuous. Predictably, the critics dealt most often with poets who came into prominence in the late sixties and the seventies—Kinnell, Stafford, Levertov, Rich, Ashbery, Hughes, Hill, and their coevals. It usually takes several years for a writer to establish a wide enough reputation to attract any academic attention.

Still, granting all of these reservations, this volume probably reflects, more accurately than any other available, the central concerns of poets and of critics of contemporary poetry in the eighties. What emerges here is an intensified questioning of the nature of poetry itself—its relation to the "real world" and to the mind or "self" that has produced it.

It is instructive to compare these essays with Robert Pinsky's influential book *The Situation of Poetry,* published a little over ten years ago. Pinsky shows at considerable length the extent to which postmodern poetry is a development from modernist poetry and in turn from the entire nineteenth-century romantic tradition. In the present collection there is a generational advance: we are now looking at the "generation of 2000" (to borrow the title of a recent anthology) and at *their* debts to the earlier postmoderns. Pinsky's excellent analyses concentrate largely on questions of poetic style and voice; he proceeds under the assumption that he and his readers share a clear idea of what poetry should be and do, and asks only how or whether the poems he treats achieve these ends. In contrast, the critics in this book seem to question more searchingly the role of poetry in the lives of poet, reader, and society; in short, they repeatedly ask, in Hugh Kenner's words, what a poet is for. Such increased concern with social questions as well as with poetic form reflects the directions of more recent studies such as Cary Nelson's *Our Last First Poets* and Majorie Perloff's *The Poetics of Indeterminacy*.

Using a version of the textbook diagram, we may picture the concerns of literary criticism as the apexes of a regular tetrahedron: subject matter, author, work, and reader, each interacting with the other three elements. For some reason—perhaps because many of the critics are themselves poets—these essays do not deal extensively with the impact of the work on the reader. Rather, as the three section titles suggest, they focus almost equally on the other three apexes: the objective world, the poet's self, and the poem mediating between them. In actuality none of these aspects of poetry is separable from another, any more than one pole of a magnet can be isolated; while each essay in this book has its special emphasis, all in some way deal with the interaction of world, self, and poem.

The critics represented here, like most of their contemporaries, reject the ideal—attributed to New Criticism—of treating a poem as an autonomous object. Jeff Gundy attacks such an ideal in his passionate plea for social and political involvement. But neither he nor the others in the first section make the mistake, so common in the sixties, of treating a poem as a vehicle for a social or political program. Even the most politically conscious essays, such as those by John Gery and Diane Kendig, retain an awareness of the aesthetic qualities unique to poetry. In a different approach to the poet's encounter with the objec tive world, Alan Golding investigates the "non-referential," mythologized treatment of history in Edward Dorn's *Gunslinger,* and Rand Brandes traces Ted Hughes's failure to deal successfully with history. All of these essays, of course, overlap with the concerns of the other sections; David Lloyd's discussion of Geoffrey Hill, showing how the personal and the historical merge in *Mercian Hymns,* almost perfectly bridges the categories of "world" and "self."

The relation of the "I" to the "not-I" has preoccupied poets and critics off and on at least since the romantic era; the critics in this collection are interested in investigating, one way or another, where the voice of the poem is coming from, how the poem conveys this self, and how it engages experience from without. As Peter Siedlecki's essay and others here point out, the confessional mode prominent in the 1960s still has its practitioners, but there is also an important "proprioceptive" strain in which the "I" tends to disappear. Alan Golding, in the first section, notes the character in

Gunslinger named "I" whose name takes a third-person verb; Kenith Simmons in the middle section examines the "missing I" in a group of poems published in *Kayak;* in the third section, Mary Lewis Shaw, Fred E. Maus, and Stephen Matterson show how "border-line" poetry—found poems and works that approach visual art and music—involve "disappearing I's." The essays by Lynn Keller, Lionel Basney, and Thomas Byers consider three poets' works where the "I" does not disappear; they examine the nexus where the self engages the "other"—one's own body, one's work, and the expectations of one's society.

There was a good deal of discussion at the Jubilation of Poets festival about poetic form, a topic that would have been unlikely fifteen or twenty years earlier. Lewis Turco made an impassioned defense of the use of traditional forms—rhyme, meter, and stanza patterns—proclaiming the advent of a new era of neo-formalism and refuting the identification of traditional poetic forms with political conservatism. The recent appearance of anthologies like *Strong Measures* (1986, edited by Philip Dacey and David Jauss) and studies such as Frederick Turner's psychological analysis of line lengths in the poetry of various languages bears witness to the current willingness of poets and critics to accept formal patterns as a viable poetic resource and contrasts strongly with the widespread hostility of the sixties to any such external restraints.

The critics in the third section of this book deal with poetic form in a larger sense. Lorrie Smith analyzes the use by Rich and Levertov of dialogue to achieve both self-discovery and political ends, and Thomas Benediktsson studies William Stafford's use of the conventions of pastoral. Three essays explore the outer limits of what we call "poetry": Mary Lewis Shaw examines some French concrete works to show their unexpected similarity to the impersonal strain in French and American poetry; Fred Maus finds striking parallels with music in Ashbery's poems; and Stephen Matterson investigates the essence of the found poem.

Other papers at the festival also examined the forms of poetry: one by Kevin Stein treated James Wright's prose poems, another by Frederick C. Stern defined the genre of Thomas McGrath's "long poem with epic features," *Letter to an Imaginary Friend.* Such a degree of interest in genre, form, and poetic convention is a discernible characteristic of criticism in the eighties.

In an appropriate final essay for this collection, Burton Hatlen discusses Robert Duncan's use of poetic "magic" in *Roots and*

Branches to draw together opposing forces, "with the goal of healing and renewing the self and the world." Duncan's "magic," a response to "Moloch, the state armored in dogma," comes in part from the Kabbalah, and it depends on formal poetic elements—"rime" in the extended sense of patterned ideas and sounds. Thus Hatlen applies a traditional scholarly approach, the source study, to the same concerns that the other critics in the collection have been exploring.

The scope of these explorations is staked out in the very first essay. In "How Poets Learn" Hugh Kenner starts with a consideration of the poet's role in the world—his extreme example being the bard proficient in the use of a spell against rats—and he ends with Yeats perfecting his craft by studying the satirical verse of Ben Jonson. Ranging from involvement in practical politics to the magic of vowel patterns, these essays share at least a belief in the vitality of poetry—in the literal sense that it arises from real life and nourishes a fullness of life in each of us.

Leonard Trawick

Cleveland State University

World

HUGH KENNER

How Poets Learn

It's thirty years ago now since I had a fling at being Poetry Editor for a national magazine. The prospect of mail from Parnassus was exciting. Such mail ought not to tumble through the same slot as mail from the bank, from Sears Roebuck, from other points close to mean sea level. So I rented a post office box; whereupon for a while the mail from Parnassus was scanty. And suddenly one day Box 150, Goleta, California, was filled to bulging, and day after day after that it bulged anew. It seems that another magazine—perhaps *Writer's Digest*—had gotten word of my box and published its number. All at once I was plugged in to the network. I was hearing from what we'll call Poetry America.

Month after month I found myself scanning the submissions of correspondents by the hundred. They observed, on the whole, the protocols. By that I do not mean that they wrote fine poems. No, they did not; but they enclosed stamped return envelopes. The editorial procedure was about as follows: ripping open each cover, I unfolded sheets, scanned them, refolded them, stuffed them into the S.A.S.E. provided, and threw that on the outgoing pile. It took up to a half hour, unpaid, each evening, and eventually we shut the whole thing down. Box 150 was closed; mail addressed there got stamped RETURN TO SENDER. I stopped being a Poetry Editor. The magazine stopped publishing poetry. And that was that. We'd been overwhelmed by Poetry America. It's almost accurate to say that nothing whatsoever addressed blind to Box 150 ever got published, ever got close to being published. I could reject it at a glance, and it was 99 percent rejectable.

We did publish, though, some pages I am not ashamed of: pages by William Carlos Williams, by Ezra Pound, by Robert Duncan, by Charles Tomlinson, by Louis Zukofsky, by Robert Creeley. I mention just a few. There was also a correspondence with Denise Levertov, and another with Charles Olson. Though in neither case did we end up agreeing on something to publish, I remember that we were taking each other seriously.

The poets I've just named did not send blind submissions to Box 150. They responded to letters of enquiry from me. Before you protest that I simply sought out big names, reflect that of the names I've named only Williams and Pound were by any definition "big" about 1956. I was conscientiously trying to publish poets the readers of *National Review* would not have encountered. What the readers of *National Review* by and large made of poetry was perhaps uncertain, but was not my concern. For that matter, I was unsure, and am still unsure, what the readers of *Poetry* magazine make of poetry. I simply wanted my readers to see, by my lights, the best. Someone here, someone there, might experience something fresh. And of course deserving poets would receive checks (seventy-five dollars was our rate; and inflation by a factor of nearly four makes that some three hundred dollars in today's money).

But enough of justifying the enterprise, and back to all those submissions to Box 150. They came from across the continent, from people who'd heard that the boxholder was looking for poets. They were therefore, in their own esteem, poets. And Lord! I remember a man every third sentence of whose long covering letters ended, "within reason, of course." "Here are some poems which I hope you will want to publish, within reason of course. They are not all I have. If you like, I can send you many more; within reason, of course." There was the young Canadian whose letterhead listed his several métiers: Poet, Scholar, Draftsman, Thinker, Genius. There was the man whose return envelopes had all been filched from motels, and most of them had already been used before they came to me. His habit when an envelope boomeranged was to turn it inside out, reglue it, restamp it. That was thrifty of him, seeing he went in for mass mailings. His poems, too, were dog-eared and much thumbed by much refolding. He'd economized by not retyping them. His model was the mother codfish, when she drops into the deep her million eggs: who knows, she thinks, a darling may somewhere hatch.

These and hundreds more were poets by their own anointment. And none of them exhibited the least sign of having ever read a poem in his life. (This is not a moment to say "his or her life.") There was a vague consensus about leaving the right margin unjus-

tified. There was an affinity for words like "fraught" and "lo."
There were sporadic rhymes, like "kissed" with "List!" Such was
Poetry, as defined by Poetry America—by poets who'd not learned
a thing, not even by reading the *Saturday Evening Post,* which in
those days sometimes published decent light verse. So you see how
I'm starting a discussion of How Poets Learn at, so to speak, Absolute Zero. The random movement of a few sluggish molecules,
that is about what we should expect out there, in the spaces between the stars.

A way to put the problem is this: that my hundreds of perfunc-
tory correspondents had no idea what a poet is, of what poetry is
for. I don't mean they'd a wrong idea; they had *no* idea. Let us
move, for contrast, to an opposite extreme. Here is a poet who
knew he was a poet and knew too what that meant. His name is,
more or less, Michael O'Govern—"more or less" because I'm
translating from the Irish—and he offers us what Maire Cruise
O'Brien calls "a scientific experiment" to confirm the authenticity
of his calling. As he tells us in a poem he wrote in Irish, he was out
walking and a tribe of rats surrounded him, meaning to attack.
That appears to be the habit of Irish rats. As for what happened
next, here is a bit of his Irish in Mrs. O'Brien's translation:

> They were no melodious words I spoke . . .
> But the psalmody of sorcery
>   which I did not learn at school.
> When I lifted my head from the book
>   The rout fell silent . . .
> Whatever power was in that quatrain
>   Which was as ancient as the rock
> I saw them flee in terror
>   Under the overhang of the stones.

What O'Govern spoke from "the book"—which would have been
a manuscript, not something bound—was the rat charm, *Artha na
bhFrancach,* words I'm hesitant to pronounce for reasons that will
appear. "This charm," Mrs. O'Brien advises us, "if recited in the
proper manner by a properly qualified person, has the effect of ban-
ishing all rodents from the immediate vicinity." But "if spoken by
an illegitimate operator . . . not only will it not work, but the rats
will turn upon the would-be exterminator and tear him limb from

limb!" So when his rats left, O'Govern had demonstrated his poetic credentials beyond doubt.

Now reflect that what you have just heard me narrate is not a piece of remote folklore. It happened in the twentieth century. Maire Cruise O'Brien lives at this moment—I have spoken with her myself—and Michael O'Govern was someone she knew as a child. So late did one clear definition of the poet's role linger: the role of the poet is to speak efficacious words. By long tradition, one of the tests is rats; when the bard Senchen Torpest spoke quatrains against rodents who'd eaten his dinner, ten of them dropped dead from the rafters. That was about AD 600, in Gort, in the west of Ireland, and we know Shakespeare heard of it from *As You Like It* (iii.2), where Rosalind speaks of an Irish rat "berhymed," the way Browning heard of the Pied Piper of Hamelin, who had similar powers though his charm wasn't worded. We are stirring among deep Indo-European roots.

Notice that the charm needs two things. It needs "a properly qualified person," and it needs the efficacious words. The qualification, by Irish usage, tends to be hereditary. The words, however, need to be learned, and there was a provision for learning them.

They were learned by careful and long apprenticeship. The young bard learned the charm against rats, and the charm that makes antlers spring from someone's head, and the one that brings offenders out in blisters, and the one that makes their cattle sicken. He learned—or *she* learned, inheritors of the gift being not infrequently women—the many intricate systems of meter and assonance, and ways to tense those against natural rhythms of speech, and the art of singing it all to stringed music. These matters were even learned in bardic schools of which we know little save that they existed and were likely not much like State U. Poetry Workshops. There they learned, too, something akin to the language of the gods—the *Berla na bhFiled,* the poets' tongue—which put them in touch with power but could bewilder such mortals as the king who said, "That is a very good poem, for the man who could understand it."

The bard's job, put simply, was to praise the king's friends, curse the king's enemies. Those the bard praised prospered; those the bard cursed sickened. People correspondingly esteemed the bard, who wherever he went was fed and honored and looked after. In the remote West, where they grow up speaking Irish, they esteem the bard to this day—such a bard as Michael O'Govern.

Before you rush off to Ireland to get yourself esteemed, I'll add that Michael O'Govern, who wasn't after all a bard of great talent despite what the rats thought, lived in primitive conditions amid what Mrs. O'Brien calls "the essential charmlessness of poverty." He composed his rat-poem to establish that he was nonetheless *somebody*. We may connect his plight with a long-standing absence of kings. I'll add too that although the face of W. B. Yeats today adorns the Irish twenty-pound note, the highest compliment a state knows how to pay, Yeats when he was alive preferred to spend most of his days in England and sought his deathbed in France. And AE and O'Casey died in England, and Joyce in France, and Gogarty in New York; while, to speak of the living, if you're looking for Seamus Heaney your best place to catch him is Cambridge, Massachusetts.

Bards had schools, anyhow, and a system of education and apprenticeship, leading to at least something like our Ph.D. That all went, I emphasize, with a consensus about the poet's importance, shared by folk and ruler and poet alike. Poetry was sorcery; old Irish poets were pretty much the same people whom Caesar called Druids when he encountered them in Celtic Britain. The connection of poetry with magic is ancient and ought not to be forgotten; an old rhyme that is seldom written down and begins "Thirty days hath September" still has power over the Chase Manhattan Bank, where accountants can be heard mumbling it.

Two extremes, then: the *fili* of Ireland, knowing how and what they were and learning formally; the stamp-lickers of Poetry America, with no idea what they aspire to, learning nothing. I hope my point about Poetry America is coming clear. It is not that they were trying to write good poems and not succeeding; that is something the very best poets have from time to time done. It is that they hadn't a glimmer of what they were trying to do, save get published. I can think of no way to convey the nullity of what they hoped someone would publish. Now and then I did think of Xeroxing some especially null specimen prior to returning it, but always I restrained myself. It would have been too indecent an act, like photographing someone's miscarriage.

Let us say instead that we need Poetry America to designate a negative infinity. Then we can postulate that all poets whatsoever have been situated somewhere along a continuum of self-knowledge, of vocational knowledge, knowledge of what a poet is put in the world to do. Of that continuum Poetry America marks the minus end, the Celtic cult of bards the positive end. In between we find Shakespeare, Whitman, Julia Moore the Sweet Singer of Michigan, John Ashbery. Near the middle we find John Milton, very sure what *he* aspired to do, less sure whether poetry was a fit medium for doing it. (Hence to poetry as understood by Spenser he administered a severe purge.)

How poets learn, then, is a topic embracing great variousness, conditioned by what different poets think a poet is for. If you think that a poet can talk to the gods and get rats killed, that's a very positive thought; from it flows a system of education to which the aspiring poet subjects himself willingly. It's inherited lore, and he's happy to let others impart it: others who know it, and on whose death it will be gone, unless he and his generation master it wholly while there's time. That's not the spirit of the Poetry Workshops.

From somewhere in mid-continuum, let's take a specific poet: William Carlos Williams is a good one, because we have more information about him than we have about, say, Shakespeare. The first thing Williams learned was to write bad sonnets, and that he learned by imitating Keats. To put that more exactly: he began by falling in love with the verse of Keats, thence with the idea of being someone with Keatsian power. Most poets resemble the Celtic bards in this, that it's power of some sort that they aspire to: not power over rats and enemies, but the power to make things as moving as things by which they've been themselves moved. The natural way to do that is to study the ways of a maker you've been moved by. Williams studied the ways of Keats.

After he'd published his pseudo-Keatsian *Poems,* he came slowly to realize that they didn't work at all. When he was past the flush of composing them, they lay dead on the page, contrived of tushery. Yet the mannerisms, one by one, were Keatsian. What was wrong? Well, John Keats was an early nineteenth-century English Cockney. Bill Williams was an early twentieth-century New Jersey . . . what? Part English, part Spanish, part Jewish—if wholly anything, just wholly American, whatever that meant.

Whatever that meant. It could be defined by contrast with Keats. Keats had cottages, and the English weather—an autumn that would "bend with apples the moss'd cottage-trees"; also the British Museum, and Milton and Spenser for compatriots. A rose for Keats was what a rose had been for Chaucer; so was a daisy. Williams had none of these; his common flowers included Queen Anne's Lace and the yellow mullein, neither of them names of any resonance. Jersey springtime was cold, with anonymous twiggy stuff struggling to foliate. Shacks were more likely than cottages (which were summer places). Trees weren't moss'd. If a poet used Keatsian words, every word was a lie. Williams learned by slowly coming to terms with such facts.

The "free verse" of the French and of his friend Pound freed him from facile rhyme and from the pentameter. He learned by reading it, and once freed, he wasn't drawn toward Hellenic Poundian cadences but toward rhythms he listened to in the daily speech. He was defining what it might be, to be a poet in America: that became his vocation, as an Irish bard's vocation had been learning the charms to kill rats and blight crops. No one else, really, has to learn that the way Williams did; it's there to be learned from Williams.

Though I've hastened through that story, it's paradigmatic; poets learn in learning what they are for. And what a poet is for, that is for each poet a personal, unique decision. Hence much perplexity. Poetry America thinks it's for something predefined, and it's not; and it learns not at all.

Poets learn in learning what they are for, because for centuries they have had no socially appointed role. That is not a byproduct of our consumer society. That has been true in every society in which they couldn't do something that was wanted: kill rats, enhance the lives of the fortunate.

Doing something that's wanted is to be regarded as sacred. Just by being a poet, the Shakespeare of the sonnets could confer immortality on Mr. W. H., who I hope in turn helped with the printer's bill. "Mr. W. H. All Happinesse"—that has the ring of a formulaic charm. Our vestigial belief in such formulaic charms is still strong enough to make the fortune of the Hallmark Company. The only poet I can think of who took stock of this fact is Louis Zukofsky, for whom, over and over, the valentine was a "form." His valentines, kept within the family, were explicitly unpaid for, and that's an ironic part of their meaning. Had he been a Hallmark hack he'd have been paid. Zukofsky learned by reading dictionaries, but also by examining the usages of commerce.

Doing something that's wanted. Shakespeare's dramatic verse was wanted, because actors could learn it quickly and then make a sensation by speaking it just as its inbuilt cues directed. Tennyson's *In Memoriam* was wanted, because readers, for reasons too intricate to explore, liked protracted ritualized melancholy sentiment. On a stone in the city of Quebec there's an epitaph:

> If Virtue's Charm had Power to save
> Her faithful Votaries from the Grave,
> With Beauty's ev'ry Form supplied,
> The Lovely Ainslee ne'er had died.

Who wrote that we don't know, but someone wanted it. An excursus into literary history would tell us part of how the person who wrote it learned. Do not say "the style of the period." A style writes nothing save through some person who has learned its ways. There's a Hallmark style, too, and no one in this room could sell four lines to Hallmark save at the cost of learning it: a fearful cost.

But if you're not doing something that's wanted, you're not sacred. Then you have to define for yourself, as Williams did, what it is you propose to do, and learn how to do it. Whitman is a salient case. So is Wordsworth, who proposed explicitly *not* to gratify the public taste. What he did propose to do is instructive. He proposed to offer "an experiment," which should ascertain "how far the language of conversation in the lower and middle classes of society is adapted to the purpose of poetic pleasure." From that phrasing in the 1798 Preface we learn part of how he's been learning, by listening with analytic attention to what poets hadn't listened to except satirically, the diction of the middle and lower classes. That's like Williams listening to the speech of Polish mothers. We learn something else too, that he's aware of a public who'll want what he'll not be giving, and he hopes to fend off their scorn with words like "experiment." Who, in an age that had just been assimilating Newton, could object to being part of an experiment? Paying money, even, to be part of one? Alas, most readers reported a negative result, and *Lyrical Ballads* was a long time getting canonized.

Wordsworth learned, too, by reading his precedessors. All poets learn that way, though they often hide it. The great passage on the crossing of the Alps—the "woods decaying, never to be decayed, the stationary blasts of waterfalls"—learned its tricks of antithesis from Pope, whom the Preface seems to obsolesce; and as for Wordsworth's governing meter, the pentameter, it suffices to point to his evident saturation in Milton and in the eighteenth century's meditative Miltonists: again, poets of whose other mannerisms the Preface is dismissive.

Poets who've decided what they want to do—poets liberated from Poetry America—read other poets intently, intensely. That is a prime mode of learning. Ezra Pound exemplified it, saliently in the eclecticism of what he read intently. For he famously didn't confine himself to the vernacular. He looked carefully at Arnaut Daniel, at Dante, at what he could make out (via Fenollosa's scribbles) of Li Po. His notion was that attention focused on procedures could bring him increments of enlightenment; people and languages were enough alike essentially for an American poet to learn from an Italian one. The sum of these incremental enlightenments was what he called "technique."

Learning, I've been arguing, is directed by self-definition. Here I don't know a better example than that of Yeats, in the decade when he learned from Ben Jonson. That was the first decade of this century; and we should remember that no poet using any kind of English had learned anything from Ben Jonson for over two centuries. If one thing was perfectly clear about Ben Jonson, it was that his so-called poems were curiosities merely. By standards Yeats himself had inherited and mastered, they were not poetry at all.

Yeats seems to have turned to Jonson originally for dramaturgic help, when he was struggling with *The Shadowy Waters* and found he needed an antidote for adjectival lushness. But there was something else he wanted to do and didn't know how to go about doing. He wanted something Irish, the old power of bards over public events. That would have to be gained not in the old magic way, by uttering charms phrased in the language of the gods, but in the secular way, by using the language of men with an uncanny authority that would shape opinion and influence conduct. For that, the language he had at his command, the language of "Innisfree," was quite unsuited. It was just at that juncture that he commenced to learn from the Jonson of the *Epigrams* and *The Forest* and *Underwoods*. The Jonson of those poems can sound like this:

> Say that thou pour'st'hem wheat,
> And they would Akornes eat:
> 'Twere simply fury, still thyself to wast
>   On such as have no taste:
> To offer them a surfeit of pure bread,
>   Whose appetites are dead:
> No, give them Graines their fill,
> Husks, Draffe to drinke and swill:

> If they love Lees, and leave the lusty Wine,
> Envy them not, their pallat's with the Swine.

There's nothing early-Yeatsian in such verses, no "tune," no sensuous "mouthful of air"; no pretty words either, *boughs* for *branches, wend* for *go;* no veils, no gold, no thrill of loneliness; no drawing out of the sense variously from line to line. No, Ben's hard rhymes with abrupt consonants go to work as with ball-peen hammers, and a populace that dislikes the sound of it all gets itself crisply likened to swilling pigs. ("Draffe," by the way, means exactly "hogwash.")

I hope you will join me now in being impressed by Yeats's ability to admire an order of performance so different from his own; so different from ways "poetry" had come to be defined that no one else anywhere had admired it for centuries. Yeat's own best notes had been of a different order entirely, notes sounded so as to woo, not repel: "Impetuous heart, be still, be still, / Your sorrowful love can never be told, / Cover it up with a lonely tune." In a few years he learned from Jonson how to go about admonishing middle-class Dublin:

> What need you, being come to sense,
> But fumble in the greasy till
> And add the halfpence to the pence
> And prayer to shivering prayer, until
> You have dried the marrow from the bone?
> For men were born to pray and save.

Doing that helped define the famous Later Yeats; one thing he learned, incidentally, was something Jonson had learned from his schoolmaster at St. Paul's, to write out his sense in prose before putting it into verse. After about 1910 Yeats always does that.

I've dwelt on that story at length because it exemplifies so much. If there are perhaps as many ways for poets to learn as there are poets, there's a principle at work too, and it seems to be that effective learning is guided by some clear sense of what one's poetic accomplishment is going to be *for.* Every poet these days, it seems, must individually define a role, a theater of operations. There's the story of the young Stephen Spender saying to Eliot that he wanted to be a poet, and Eliot rejoining that he couldn't understand what that meant. A wise rejoinder, which amounted to this: that before

Spender could either learn or be taught he would have to separate himself from the British equivalent of Poetry America and set out to accomplish something in particular. For people who want to be poets I'm afraid there's no hope, no way that they can even begin to learn. Still, they do impinge on the American postal deficit, almost as directly as the charms of Michael O'Govern impinged on those Irish rats.

JEFF GUNDY

Arrogant Humility and Aristocratic Torpor: Where Have We Been, Where Are We Going?

We were the ones we intended to bomb!
Therefore we will have
To go far away
To atone
For the sufferings of the stringy-chested
And the small rice-fed ones, quivering
In the helicopter like wild animals,
Shot in the chest, taken back to be questioned.
(Bly, *Light Around the Body* 37)

I cannot decide in which direction to walk
But this doesn't matter to me, and I might as well
Decide to climb a mountain (it looks almost flat)
As decide to go home
Or to a bar or restaurant or to the home
Of some friend as charming and ineffectual as I am
Because these pauses are supposed to be life.
(Ashbery, *Self-Portrait* 17)

It is hard to realize that twenty years have passed since Robert
Bly's *The Light Around the Body,* with its passionate attack on the
society that produced the Vietnam War. With some notable excep-
tions, American poetry since the early 1970s has become much less
politically and socially charged, less concerned with public morality
and more concentrated in the minutiae of private lives. By 1975,
only two years after Bly's *Sleepers Joining Hands,* John Ashbery's
Self-Portrait in a Convex Mirror—cool, impermeable, and oblivious
to almost everything except art history, New York City, and epis-
temology—won both the Pulitzer Prize and the National Book

Award for poetry. As the Reagan years made greed once again respectable, critics claimed that poetry must avoid moral claims and judgments, abandon sincerity and the "deep image," and concentrate on form, irony, and wit.

Let me give a few examples of the new aesthetic conservatism, and try to suggest some of its social overtones and implications. Robert Pinsky's *The Situation of Poetry* (1976) has been perhaps the most influential book of the last decade. In it he attacks poets like Bly and Snyder, both actively critical of their society, on what seem to be aesthetic grounds: for fuzzily mystic "bardic hush," for "uncertain and confused" imagery, for "more-imagistic-than-thou" boastfulness (71–77). He favors the cool, surface-concentrated surrealism of poets like Ashbery and Mark Strand, saying that "the vigorous comedy of the self can be adapted so as to avoid making a big deal . . . of the individual and his imagination" (86).

Politics play no explicit part in Pinsky's argument, but clearly his celebration of the "vigorous comedy of the self," though proposed as an antidote for spiritual inflation, also discourages poems on social and political issues that claim any degree of moral urgency. All too quickly, however, the comedy of the self tends to lose its vigor, to degenerate into the windy, gratuitous ramblings of Ashbery at his worst. His witty depiction of his "charming and ineffectual" state, amusing at first, soon turns wearisome and self-indulgent. Has anyone, with the possible exception of Harold Bloom, read all the way through the title poem of *Self-Portrait?*

Paul Hoover's essay "Moral Poetry" (1984) also attacks the "Moral Poet" who "believes in feeling alone," who feels only ecstasy and grief and maintains a "missionary earnestness" that is fundamentally (and somehow unfortunately) middle class in its elevation of sincerity over irony. He praises "ironists" such as Ashbery, the fortunate possessors of an "aristocratic hauteur, or at least upper-middle-class self-confidence, which rarely displays itself as earnestness" (14).

Hoover is, no doubt, right that the opposite term to moral earnestness is some kind of aristocratic hauteur or sense of privilege. Certainly that privilege allows a poet to concentrate on form as Hoover suggests, even "perhaps the more arbitrary the form the better" (15). And certainly no poem, and no poet, is bound to engage social issues or indeed anything outside the sphere of the poem itself; the pursuit of "pure" formal beauty, like Flaubert's novel of pure style, is a noble search if one doomed to frustration.

Yet those of us whose allegiances are at least nostalgically democratic might be forgiven for wondering just where Hoover's allegiances are. Any careful attention to the work of Bly, or to other clearly "moral" but less personally demonstrative poets, such as William Stafford or James Wright, will show that Hoover's assault on "feeling" is based on caricature. His claim that Moral Poets can be comfortable in their righteousness because they represent the dominant attitudes of the middle class dissolves immediately when brought down to cases; one need only imagine Bly reading "The Teeth Mother Naked at Last" at the Elks Club.

The deeper objection here seems to be to the claim that poems can make value judgments, carry moral authority that reaches beyond the personal and into the social. Of course we should always, certainly in the post-Vietnam era, be skeptical of anyone who claims too much righteousness. Yet we must not forget that aristocratic hauteur is itself a moral position, based on implicit judgments about the relative worth of human lives. Those judgments rest largely on privilege; peasants in El Salvador or Afghanistan, for example, do not have the aristocratic luxury of separating the personal and the political. Hoover's insistence on the "need" to "restore music, abstraction, and structure," to provide "the necessary alertness and openness" through "the generosity of inorganic form," looks rather pale beside David Ignatow's bitter response to the news of a poet getting an award for "the perfect form of his poems":

> Hello, dead, napalmed man, can you become a poem of
>   perfect form?
> Hello, incinerated Jew, can you become a poem of perfect
>   form?
> If you can't, then you don't deserve to live.
> You're dead, don't exist,
> we want clean earth; get out, get going, get lost.
> We have built a house for ourselves called the Perfect Form
> and we're trying to live in it, and if you can't take
> your napalmed body and your drug addicted brain
> and make them into a poem of perfect form then you don't
>   belong. . . .
> If you can't make yourself a poem of perfect form
> then you have no right to be in this country.

You're here without a passport. You've lost your
   citizenship
rights. You're an alien, you're a spy.   (83–84)

As Ignatow realizes, the concentration on form all too easily turns sterile and isolationist, in its extremes arrogant, xenophobic, and ugly. His speaker ends in an orgy of solipsistic, masturbatory pleasure:

Fuck me, poem of perfect form.
Let me fuck you. We'll fuck each other.
We have each other, right, so let's do all the nasty
things we dream about and we'll have fun and nobody else
will know about it but you and me and me and me and me
   and you.   (84)

Ignatow's work is as successful as any I know in maintaining at once a profound engagement with the social world and a humility that refuses self-righteousness. His poem #89 in *Tread the Dark* recognizes that his poetry distances him from the world, that even in its engagement it is a means for separation:

Finally, I'm sitting here at my desk because I'm afraid to venture into the street to be accosted by a person asking for help that would mean my whole life. I have only myself to spare and I need it to help me. Those who cry out for help have somehow lost themselves, given away or simply been robbed. I have to stay at my desk to keep myself as I am, though it's little enough, but it gives me my presence and place to be.

It is a selfish act, if I can read your thoughts, and I am ashamed, but I am fearful too to act on my impulse to love. . . . They may knock on my door and ask to be let in. I may let them see me crouched over my typewriter, fearful, showing them my back, but glad that they have come to see me writing of my love, my one way to express it without losing myself in their arms.   (85)

A poem worth comparing with Ignatow's is Louis Simpson's "On the Lawn at the Villa," which Jonathan Holden has celebrated as "a truly excellent political poem" ("Poetry" 23) and which is filled with the aristocratic irony and concern for form that Hoover advocates:

> On the lawn at the villa—
> That's the way to start, eh, reader?
> We know where to stand—somewhere expensive—
> You and I *imperturbes,* as Walt would say,
> Before the diversions of wealth, you and I *engagés.*
>
> On the lawn at the villa
> Sat a manufacturer of explosives,
> His wife from Paris,
> And a young man named Bruno.
>
> And myself, being American,
> Willing to talk to these malefactors,
> The manufacturer of explosives, and so on,
> But somehow superior. By that I mean democratic.
> It's complicated, being an American,
> Having the money and the bad conscience, both at the
>   same time.
> Perhaps, after all, this is not the right subject for a poem.
> We were all sitting there paralyzed
> In the Hot Tuscan afternoon,
> And the bodies of the machine-gun crew were draped over
>   the balcony.
>
> So we sat there all afternoon.   (24)

Holden applauds this poem's concentration on awareness rather than program, its analytic detachment, its judgment "impaired by neither ideology nor excessive emotion" ("Poetry" 25). And there are surely many things to admire in it. Yet the poem's awareness is surely also weakened by that same detachment, by its categorical, distant, and theoretical nature. No one actually gets hurt, except far off stage, and the "bad conscience" of the speaker seems little more than a dim awareness that he should feel more guilty than he does.

Czeslaw Milosz defines poetry as the "passionate pursuit of the Real" (75), but here the speaker's ennui and paralysis prevent any more than a token wave at the real. The mild, distant guilt he feels is all too clearly nothing that will disturb the rest of the largely poetic crowd who may someday happen upon it. It seems incredible to me that Holden calls this poem "realistic" and "ruthlessly honest"; perhaps indeed modestly successful American poets in middle age spend afternoons in this manner, and if so one is grateful that they manage to realize the ethical difficulties of hanging around with explosives manufacturers. But his realization of paralysis seems to come much too late to do any good. It has, if anything, the sickening lethargy of the second when you realize your car is not going to miss the child in the street.

I do not mean to generalize my critique of this poem into one of Simpson's work as a whole, especially since in a recent interview he takes a position quite close to my own, criticizing James Merrill and others for writing poems that are merely "elegant word play" that avoid "dealing with any reality at all" (Simpson and Poulin 337). Yet it seems doubtful to me that a poem like "On the Lawn at the Villa" can generate much more than wistful regret, an "awareness" uncoupled from any possibility of action. Is there a ground between propaganda and the genteel sigh about the cruelty and resistance of the world? What kind of poetry might be written that would be honestly committed without lapsing into propaganda or sentimentality?

Two ways of claiming such a voice seem credible to me; neither guarantees success, but one or both are usually present in successful poems on social issues. One is direct experience. Holden deals extensively with Carolyn Forche's *The Country Between Us,* but unaccountably avoids the best poem in it, one that begins with a situation much like Simpson's, but far more intense:

> What you have heard is true. I was in his house. His wife carried a tray of coffee and sugar. His daughter filed her nails, his son went out for the night. There were daily papers, pet dogs, a pistol on the cushion beside him. . . . There was some talk then of how difficult it had become to govern. The parrot said hello on the terrace. The colonel told it to shut up and pushed himself from the table. My friend said to me with his eyes: say nothing. The colonel returned with a sack used to bring groceries home. He spilled many human ears on the table. They were like dried peach halves. There is no other way to say this. He took one of them in his hands, shook it in our faces, dropped it into the water glass. It came alive there. I am tired of

fooling around he said. As for the rights of anyone, tell
your people they can go fuck themselves. He swept the
ears to the floor with his arm and held the last of his wine
in the air. Something for your poetry, no? he said. Some of
the ears on the floor caught this scrap of his voice. Some
of the ears on the floor were pressed to the ground.
(Forche 16)

In "The Colonel," the human suffering that takes place far offstage
in Simpson's poem, recalled only by an act of will and imagination,
is placed squarely before the poet and before us. The mingled culture and brutality of the colonel provide an unforgettable image of
our own contradictions, and the reportorial stance suffices; the few
"poetic" touches are almost unnecessary.

The second strategy—stance may be a better word—is implicit
in "The Colonel" and explicit in Ignatow's poem. It begins in the
acceptance of complicity, the refusal of easy moral superiority. As
Galway Kinnell notes, the persona, that beloved device of modern-
ists, can all too easily give the poet a way to shift guilt, to protect
himself from admitting his own venality, fear, and participation in
collective evil (205–06). But even a simple recognition of complicity
is not enough.

In his essay "Leaping up into Political Poetry," Robert Bly discusses the example of Franz Jagerstatter, one of the very few Aus-
trians to refuse cooperation with the Nazis during the Second
World War. Everyone around him advised him "not to be serious,"
to be ."Christian in regard to his domestic life, but not to his political life." His "problem," Bly suggests, was that he had "extended
the range of his sensibility. . . . He had extended his awareness far-
ther than society wanted him to, and everyone he met, with the
exception of a single parish priest, tried to drive it back again" (96).

I am arguing in this essay that the extension of awareness must
go far beyond the inability to decide where to pass an evening, even
beyond the lackadaisical recognition of our complicity with evil,
into the mourning and the renewal that comes only with the acceptance that the suffering of others is truly our responsibility. To do
so we must outgrow our childish egocentricity, as Albert Goldbarth recognizes:

it was easier to hurt people
in 8th grade: everywhere we stared we found a bounty we

thought made for us alone, so pain in everybody else was
  peripheral
and, in any case, healable by their own rich monogrammed
  cosmos. I
believed our griefs were effortlessly given consolation by
the text in any brick or cloud or bough. But then History
showed us some photos—mass bulldozered graves—and
I'm not sure I believe that now.   (73)

The temptation to aestheticize our own suffering and peripheral-
ize everyone else's is hard to resist. Subsumed in history as we are,
we want to abandon it, to take refuge in the cheerful, comfortable
rooms of the palace of art. But the time of kings is past, and so is
the time of retainers. Auden's tyrant, like Forche's Colonel, pursued
"perfection of a kind"; we must remember that the impulses of life
are not toward perfection but toward plenitude and diversity. The
most perfect forms we have lie waiting in silos and submarines and
hangers, dreaming of making everything in the world simple, hot,
and pure. If their dreams do not trouble our waking, we have not
yet awakened.

DAVID LLOYD

The Public and Private Realms of Geoffrey Hill's *Mercian Hymns*

In his essay "Poetry and Politics," the lead piece of a recent *Tri-Quarterly* special issue, Terrence Des Pres makes a call for poets to produce writing "strong enough to handle history and not stay cowed within the halting world of self" (17). Des Pres values poetry "not so much grounded in ideology as in the concrete reactions of men and women who find themselves in history's path" (18). Since the 1970s, a number of British poets have begun producing works growing out of rootedness in a particular locality's history, topography, and mythology. Dissatisfied with discrete lyrics bounded by Des Pres's "halting world of self," these poets, including Irishman Seamus Heaney, Scotsman George MacKay Brown, Welshman R. S. Thomas, and Englishman Jeremy Hooker, have been working on extended structures: sequences and narratives focusing on history, culture, and politics. Among English poets today, Geoffrey Hill, in his sequence *Mercian Hymns,* has gone farthest towards placing the self within the historical and political life of his culture. Even though *Mercian Hymns* weaves in material from Hill's personal experience, the self does not exist in isolation in the sequence. Instead, the various speakers of these hymns[1] interact with past and present elements of English culture. Hill achieves this interaction by creating an idiom that allows a public voice to take on the intensity and immediacy of a private consciousness, and a private voice to gain the breadth, resonance, and authority of a public persona.

Mercian Hymns is a record of the growth of a poet's mind[2] and of the development of a culture. It is a self-portrait, particularly of Hill as a child growing up in England in the 1940s; but it is also a portrait of a potent British myth: Offa, the king who stands at the beginnings of English nationhood. As the most powerful Anglo-

Saxon king of England before Alfred of Wessex, Offa was instrumental in forging a national identity among the early English.[3] Essentially a single poetic technique—the unearthing and examining of fragments of memory—creates both the private and public portraits in Hill's sequence. While Offa is a historical figure, the relics of his rule are meager—a few coins, the remnants of his dike against the Welsh, and some fragmentary contemporary references. As a subject, Offa therefore does not lock Hill into a great number of constraining facts and dates. Besides allowing Hill special entrance into the history and cultural life of the English West Midlands, where Hill spent his childhood, Offa is an enigmatic figure, and thus a fit subject for Hill's poetic sensibility, which has consistently found expression in a language of paradox, irony, and modernist complexity.

When Hill comments on the "power" of Swift's poetry to "move with fluent rapidity from private to public utterance and from the formal to the intimate in the space of a few lines" (*Lords of Limit* 68), he could well be speaking of *Mercian Hymns*. As he appears in Hill's sequence, Offa might be described as a fluid mixture of private and public attributes. His character sometimes combines elements of Hill's life and consciousness (mostly his childhood years) with what we know of the historical Offa, but it also sometimes includes the public elements of legends, traditions, historical forces, and the environment or topography of the English West Midlands, site of the ancient kingdom of Mercia. *Mercian Hymns* opens with a voice singing or chanting for King Offa a list of sometimes incongruous and anachronistic titles or accolades, many of which derive from West Midlands topography. In Hymn I, "The Naming of Offa," Hill uses colons so that one accolade generates the next:

> King of the perennial holly-groves, the riven sand-
> stone: overlord of the M5: architect of the his-
> toric rampart and ditch: the citadel at Tamworth,
> the summer hermitage at holy cross: guardian of
> the Welsh Bridge and the Iron Bridge: contractor
> to the desirable new estates: saltmaster: money-
> changer: commissioner for oaths: martyrologist:
> the friend of Charlemagne.

'I liked that,' said Offa, 'sing it again.'

Both the content and overall tone of the opening stanza identify the speaker as a scop of the dark ages who would traditionally sing a king's praises.[4] In subsequent hymns, however, we hear a variety of different speakers, including the voice of an adult (whom we might identify as Hill) remembering his childhood (III), an unidentified modern observer (XXI), King Offa (VIII), and, in at least one hymn, a figure who can definitely be identified as Hill himself (XXV). But the speakers are much more complex than these sample categories would indicate. The scop of Hymn I mentions a twentieth-century creation, the M5 super-highway, and so cannot be purely a scop of the eighth century. The adult remembering his childhood in wartime Britain of the 1940s uses a diction that brings to mind Anglo-Saxon battle literature, and other modern voices show attitudes and speak phrases one associates with the eighth century; most obviously, King Offa many times speaks and acts in this sequence like a twentieth-century man. It is largely through the sequence's peculiar mixture of idioms that Hill achieves interaction between the public world of historical events and the private world of individual relationships in contemporary time.

History in *Mercian Hymns* is not chronological; instead, the present moment is enriched by all the past simultaneously. From the first hymn, the events of Mercia over the last twelve centuries are never treated as a linear development; there are no pure "moments" of history. Hill shifts freely between historical periods as well as between public and private experience. Three poems in the sequence—Hymn III ("The Crowning of Offa"), Hymn XI ("Offa's Kingdom"), and Hymn XXV ("Opus Anglicanum")—provide good examples of Hill's use of this strategy.

Hymn III, "The Crowning of Offa," describes a group of twentieth-century English children let out of school to celebrate the coronation of a king, probably George VI, who was crowned in 1937, when Hill was five years old:

> On the morning of the crowning we chorused our re-
>   mission from school. It was like Easter: hankies
>   and gift-mugs approved by his foreign gaze, the
>   village lintels curlered with paper flags.
>
> We gaped at the car-park of "The Stag's Head" where a
>   bonfire of beer-crates and holly-boughs whistled
>   above the tar. And the chef stood there, a king in

his new-risen hat, sealing his brisk largesse with
"any mustard?"

While the scene is obviously set in modern England, certain details—
the ritualistic bonfire, the holly boughs (associated with English
landscape and folklore from very early times), the chef-king's "sealing his brisk largesse," and the hymn's title ("The Crowning of
Offa")—all point back to archaic ceremonies. These flickerings
from the past cause us to hear characteristics of a chronicler or his-
torian in a voice we initially identify as a modern adult describing a
childhood memory. When describing his people's most important
ritual, their king's coronation, the speaker of Hymn III begins to
echo the scop's voice we heard in Hymn I.

Hill initially seems to deflate the ancient, once-vital ritual by humorously "crowning" the chef at the pub and by placing the events
in a modern environment where crowds sentimentally wave
hankies, merchants peddle tacky, stencilled gift-mugs, and the cele-
bratory bonfire is fueled by beer crates burning on tar. For the children, recess from school for the occasion is a "remission," as from
an illness, and they are much more fascinated by the chef than by
the real king, who is physically removed from them, a "foreign"
presence. The children see the chef's "largesse" of generous mustard on a sandwich as more relevant to their lives than any largesse
offered by a real king. Yet while the speaker may at first seem to be
using echoes of archaic rituals to compare a glorious past with a
degraded present (as in many of the historical references of Pound
and Eliot), we should recall that the hymn's setting is the car-park
of "The Stag's Head" pub and that pubs are primary centers of
social, communal life in modern England. In a sense, the speaker of
Hymn III portrays an actual, viable community ceremony, substi-
tuting the pub for the mead hall—and that substitution is not fully
ironic. Instead, the interaction of past and present in this hymn
highlights a cultural continuity that Hill celebrates throughout *Mercian Hymns*. The chef parallels the chief, or "ring-giver," of the
Anglo-Saxon meadhall: both distribute "largesse" to their people
amid drinking and eating. Because the speaker of Hymn III embodies public and private experience, he is able to mediate between ancient and modern coronation rituals.

The speaker of Hymn XXI, "The Kingdom of Offa," fuses ancient border battles and the excursions of some West Midlands tourists to Wales:

> Cohorts of charabancs fanfared Offa's province and
> his concern, negotiating the by-ways from Teme
> to Trent. Their windshields dripped butterflies.
> Stranded on hilltops they signalled with plumes
> of steam. Twilight menaced the land. The young
> women wept and surrendered.

> Still, everyone was cheerful, heedless in such days:
> at summer weekends dipping into valleys beyond
> Mercia's dyke. Tea was enjoyed, by lakesides where
> all might fancy carillons of real Camelot vib-
> rating through the silent water.

> Gradually, during the years, deciduous velvet peeled
> from evergreen albums and during the years more
> treasures were mislaid: the harp-shaped brooches,
> the nuggets of fool's gold.

On one level the action is mundane: busloads of tourists are driven
to Wales on summer weekends, their buses overheating on the
mountainous roads and breaking down. They sightsee, drink tea,
fantasize about the misty Celtic past of Camelot and King Arthur,
and finally return to England with souvenirs and new pictures for
old photo albums. But this speaker's language, heavy with archaic
military double-entendres, conjures up suggestions of eighth-
century military forays from Offa's kingdom, beyond the "dyke,"
to enemy Wales.

The first word of the Hymn, "cohorts," can refer either to a
group of companions, such as the tourists, or to a military unit, a
"cohort." When the sightseeing buses, or "charabancs," overheat,
the tourists signal "with plumes / of steam," as if using a military
code. Also, these buses "fanfared" Offa's Mercia: a word accurately
describing the movement of modern sightseeing buses, yet also de-
noting a flourish of trumpets in an ostentatious military display.
More word play of this nature occurs at the end of the first stanza,
when the young women losing their virginity "wept and surren-
dered." The language carries on the military parallel established by
the preceding sentences, making those women the traditional spoils
of warfare. Once again the speaker's language does not simply create a contrast between public and private experience, or between a
glorious, heroic past and a diminished present: the emotional up-
heaval accompanying the contemporary young women's first expe-

rience of love is not diminished or ridiculed, but subtly acknowledged.

The multiple meanings conveyed by the language in this section yield deflation and satire, as in the description of tourists bringing "treasures" back from Wales: "the harp-shaped brooches, / the nuggets of fool's gold"—not valuable booty of course but tacky souvenirs from modern Welsh tourist shops. It is not only the English tourists who are satirized, however; by linking the eighth-century military forays with tourist excursions, those forays are themselves portrayed not as heroic adventures but as petty, treasure-seeking aggressions.

Besides the comedy and satire, Hymn XXI also reveals a continuity or commonality of attitude that blends the apparently different excursions of the eighth and twentieth centuries. Tourist bus expeditions to Wales constitute a kind of cultural attack, which if less brutal than Offa's invasions, is ultimately more destructive. Offa's eighth-century attitude towards Wales as a land to be exploited for cattle and slaves finds its modern equivalent in the attitude of "heedless" tourists "dipping into the Welsh valleys." While we initially respond to a perceived distance between the poem's language and its ostensible subject—tourism—we later see that the language is in one sense not ironically distant from, but appropriate to, its subject. Hill is serious in asserting that the predatory nature of Offa's border raids lives on in the excursions of Birmingham and Wolverhampton tourists to the Welsh valleys.

The speaker of Hymn XXV, "Opus Anglicanum," differs from the speakers of Hymns III and XXI in that he can be identified with Hill himself. While the poem serves as an elegy for Hill's grandmother, it also uses literary and historical references to charge the poem politically, creating an impassioned attack on industrial exploitation and its human cost:

> Brooding on the eightieth letter of *Fors Clavigera*,
>   I speak this in memory of my grandmother, whose
>   childhood and prime womanhood were spent in the
>   nailer's darg.
>
> The nailshop stood back of the cottage, by the fold. It
>   reeked stale mineral sweat. Sparks had furred
>   its low roof. In dawn-light the troughed water
>   floated a damson-bloom of dust—

> not to be shaken by posthumous clamour. It is one
> thing to celebrate the 'quick forge', another
> to cradle a face hare-lipped by the searing wire.

> Brooding on the eightieth letter of *Fors Clavigera,*
> I speak this in memory of my grandmother, whose
> childhood and prime womanhood were spent in the
> nailer's darg.

The precise language and understatement do not belie the speaker's
outrage; instead, they allow the reader to grasp the intensity of that
outrage. In a similar way the repetition of the first stanza (a strategy occurring nowhere else in the sequence) provides a subjective
context for the two stanzas in the middle and reinforces the speaker's emotional urgency.

In addition to providing a personal tribute to the life and sufferings of Hill's grandmother, Hymn XXV undertakes a far-reaching
indictment of the nineteenth-century capitalist celebration of indus-
trialization, the "quick forge," which resulted in profitable exploitation of the British working classes. Hill introduces this cultural
criticism through the literary reference in the first line: "Brooding
on the eightieth letter of *Fors Clavigera.*" The explanatory note to
this line refers the reader to John Ruskins's "Letter 80" of *Fors Clavigera,* where Ruskin describes two women "nailing"—laboring with
hammer, pincers, and anvil: "Four strokes with the hammer in the
hand; one ponderous and momentary blow ordered of the balanced
mass by the touch of the foot." Ruskin explains that the women
labored from "seven to seven—by the furnace side" for eight shil-
lings a week (174). Overall, "Letter 80" presents a condemnation of
what Ruskin calls "the main British modern idea that the master
and his men should belong to two entirely different classes . . . the
one, on the whole, living in hardship—the other in ease" (172).
Hill's careful use of literary allusion infuses the elegy with the
historical context of industrial exploitation in nineteenth-century
England, broadening the poem's reference and transforming Hill's
private grief into public outcry. This brief hymn captures a moment
when historical circumstances impinge, through a written source,
on a private consciousness.

Hill's epigraph to the English edition of *Mercian Hymns* is a quotation from poet and critic C. H. Sisson. (This epigraph does not
occur in the American edition of Hill's earlier works, *Somewhere Is*

Such a Kingdom, which includes *Mercian Hymns.*) One portion of the epigraph asserts that "the conduct of government rests upon the same foundation and encounters the same difficulties as the conduct of private persons: that is, as to its object and justification" (n.p.). The prominent position given the Sisson quotation reveals that from the outset Hill's sequence will treat "samenesses" between government, politics, and history and private, contemporary experience.

In an article first delivered as a lecture, then published in *Poetry Nation Review,* Hill expressed admiration for Sisson as a poet and as "an administrator of public 'practical affairs' at a high level of accomplishment and responsibility as a principal under-secretary in the Ministry of Labour" (11). Hill's discussion in part focuses on what he terms Sisson's "distinct anti-solipsistic bias, if 'solipsism' is the 'theory that self is the only object of real knowledge' (*OED*)" (12).

> [Sisson] has said: "It is too readily supposed that there is a 'personal experience' which can be conveyed in words. In fact, the consciousness we have is a product of history. . . . When it comes to the feelings of a woman abandoned by her lover, the whole force of a civilization is in play."
> (11, Hill's ellipses).

Going on to paraphrase Sisson, Hill comments: "Our personal experience is not pure experience; it is acted upon by various contingents, of some of which we may be ignorant. Among the least acknowledged of these contingent powers are those of language, and of history effective through the language that we know, the language of which we are capable" (11–12). Hill's paraphrase of Sisson suggests the primary structuring technique of *Mercian Hymns:* in these poems, contemporary personal experience is infused with the "contingent powers . . . of language and of history effective through language. *Mercian Hymns* strives to set the private consciousness against and within "the whole force of a civilization."

By merging private and public realms, *Mercian Hymns* asserts that very archaic elements of history and myth underpin and partially direct the consciousness or cultural life of the twentieth-century English individual. While escaping the "halting world of self," Hill explores a great variety of experience in *Mercian Hymns*— the past, the present, mundane actions, heroic actions, private

memories, public ritual—in an effort to understand the direction
his culture has taken since the concept of English nationhood first
emerged during King Offa's rule. Imperial privilege, economic oppression, and the use of violence to achieve political or economic
ends, to cite a few thematic threads of *Mercian Hymns,* form a pattern in English history from Anglo-Saxon to modern times. In
Hill's West Britain, valued ancient rituals and ceremonies persist,
and contemporary men and women can feel as deeply connected to
the inherited communal life as they can to their region's distinctive
topography and language. But while celebrating the close-woven
tapestry of elements that persist down the centuries to form the
entity "Mercia," Hill yet attacks destructive forms of human behavior which also form part of that tapestry.

RAND BRANDES

Ted Hughes in and out of Time:
Remains of Elmet and
Moortown Elegies

In 1957, at the outset of his career, Ted Hughes asserted that his poems exist because "they are the only way I can unburden myself of that excess which, for their part, bulls in June bellow away" ("Ted Hughes Writes" 1). Hughes's bulls represent his early attempt to claim an imaginative territory outside the ironic understatement and domestic preoccupations of the mainstream of British poetry represented by the Movement in the late 1950s. Although one must take the young Hughes's excessive bulls with a tolerant grin, one must also see the bovine analogy as his attempt not only to distance himself from the affairs of everyday human existence, but also to place his poetry outside the limiting constructs of history. In what approaches self-parody if not blatant mockery, Hughes envisions the poet and his poetry existing in the immediate physical world of the bulls' realm, unencumbered by human time and oblivious to the demands of social or political relevancy. The bulls live according to the rhythms of biological time; their bellowing is an uncontrollable part of the larger creative process. In *The Use and Abuse of History*, Nietzsche argues that the beasts in the field are content because they live "unhistorically" and are not plagued by the "'historical sense,' that injures and finally destroys the living thing, be it a man or a people or a system of culture" (7) or, Hughes would add, the creative vision. Thus, like the bulls that bellow because they live unhistorically, Hughes instinctively writes from an unhistorical perspective.

Hughes in a later and more sober statement (*London Magazine*, February 1962) clarifies his position on the relationship between historical events and the creative impulse, which he calls the "gift" (44). He argues that it is the poet's responsibility to follow his "gift" and not to look "for his satisfaction among more popular

and public causes" or to "mix his poetry up with significant matters or to throw his verse into the popular excitement of the time"
(45). Hughes justifies the orientation of his creative impulse by arguing that it is innately apolitical and unhistorical.

Throughout his poetry Hughes uses a number of strategies to get
outside of time by disengaging his poems from historical and temporal contexts. His dominant strategy is myth; he would agree with
the early Roland Barthes that myth "evaporates history" and is
"depoliticized speech" (151, 142). *The Hawk in the Rain, Lupercal,
Wodwo, Crow, Gaudete,* and *Cave Birds* all draw upon Hughes's preoccupation with mythic structures. Only recently have critics such
as Terry Eagleton begun to challenge the validity of Hughes's
mythic approach because of its apparent lack of the historical sense
and the absence of a readily recognizable interest in contemporary
issues ("Myth" 238). These critics see in the bellowing bulls a
thinly disguised bovine Zeus or Horus singing of a golden world.
They distrust the bull in Hughes's canon and want it sacrificed in
the name of a sociopolitical/historical awareness, arguing that
Hughes's mythopoeics exist in a bubble of irrelevancy outside of the
complexities of recorded time. Perhaps in response to this criticism,
Hughes has more recently attempted to write from a historical perspective instead of his standard mythic approach. In *Remains of Elmet* (1979) Hughes locks an entire volume in a specific landscape
and in a specific historical problem: the Calder valley in Yorkshire
and its decline since the fall of the Celts. Another alternative approach appeared a year earlier in the Rainbow Press first edition of
Moortown Elegies (1978). This volume focuses on immediate action
and the unhistorical moment; its style resembles what D. H.
Lawrence calls the Poetry of the Present, "the poetry of the incar-
nate Now" (183). While *Remains of Elmet* fails because of its indiscriminate use of history, *Moortown Elegies* succeeds because of its
resistance to history.

Remains of Elmet and *Moortown Elegies* were written simultaneously from 1975 to 1978. Individual poems from both volumes
were published concurrently in various magazines and journals—in
fact, they were occasionally mixed in one submission. Hughes must
have felt the almost schizophrenic nature of the dual writing.

In *Remains of Elmet,* Hughes was bound not only to Fay Good-
win's black and white photographs, but also to particular landscapes and a specific historical program: the heroic vitality of the
valley's original settlers and industrialists and the destruction of that

heroic (and capitalistic) breed. The imagistic style that dominates the book is bare-boned and terse. In sharp contrast, *Moortown Elegies,* though written about Hughes's farm, is not tied to a particular farm; we never know exactly where it is, nor does it matter. Hughes never discusses the history of the farm; its origins and previous owners are not part of his vision. The farm is action in the present tense. The verse is full, fleshy, and vibrant. The "verse farming diary" (xii) structure (as Hughes identifies it in the Foreword to *New Selected Poems*) allows him to cover the entire page with long-lined, brimming verse. Though the *Moortown* poems are elegies, their direction is forward into life. Conversely the orientation of *Remains of Elmet* is backward into death. Hughes's nostalgic search for a primeval paradise buries his verse in an isolated time capsule, in historical time but out of life.

Hughes has an innate inclination toward nostalgia; the focus of *Remains of Elmet* exacerbates this disabling historical perspective. The book fails from Hughes's inability to manage satisfactorily the complexities of history. For example, in poems such as "Lumb Chimneys" and "Mill Ruins," Hughes appears to lament the loss of the commercial and spiritual vitality that appeared at the inception of the industrial revolution, and to gloss over the hardships and brutalities of this era. He assumes what Nietzsche calls the "antiquarian" historical mode: "the mad collector raking over all the dust heaps of the past . . . [with] a mere insatiable curiosity for everything old" (20). Hughes appears at his weakest when he forces his vision into the historical domain of chronological events and contemporary problems. Perhaps we may see a reaction to the nostalgic and limited historical perspective of *Remains of Elmet* in the unhistorical orientation of *Moortown Elegies,* where, ironically, Hughes returns to the realm of the bull and escapes from what Nietzsche calls the "Malady of History."

In *Remains of Elmet* the landscape of the once beautiful, now ruined Calder Valley is "heavy with the dream of a people"; "Everywhere dead things for monuments / Of the dead," litter the terrain. In the degenerative process from a powerful beauty to an impotent deformity, the land was the first to suffer. The valley and hills are often described as "wounded," "bleeding," "emptied and seared black." Hughes gazes at the "broken spine of a fallen land." Hughes looks back to the antediluvian world by metaphorically describing the land in terms of "Kings" and "Queens," but he makes few references to the atrocities and injustices enacted by this aristocratic class. One of the most nostalgic phrases, near the end of the volume, sums up his vision of the land: "How young the world was! The hills full of savage promise." This is Hughes's Merrie England, a land of eternal youth without suffering and hopelessness, the land of the glorified savage.

In contrast to this idealized world, the title poem "Remains of Elmet" argues that now all we have is an empty skull:

> Now, coil behind coil,
> A wind-parched ache,
> An absence, famished and staring,
> Admits tourists
>
> To pick among crumbling, loose molars
> And empty sockets.

At times, Hughes reacts to the past like a modern tourist himself. In "The Ancient Briton Lay Under His Rock," Hughes claims that the Briton, whom he calls "the Mighty Hunter," was happy "no longer existing" and being part of "nursery school history." But exacting readers will not accept "nursery school history"; they want Hughes to approach history critically instead of romanticizing the cruelty of the Mighty Hunter's world.

In addition to the dead heroes of Arthurian England, Hughes finds what he considers to be the living relatives of the ancient bards, the old pensioners of the valley. "Crown Point Pensioners" looks nostalgically back in time and history more than any other poem in the volume. The pensioners are the last of a dying race that knew the power and splendor of the Calder Valley and the victories and conquests of its explorers. In the opening line, the "old faces" of the men are equated with "old roots"; thus men and landscape immediately merge into one historical dimension. Hughes also establishes a correlation between the memories and function of these last survivors of a heroic age and the images and function of the poem: the reminiscing old men are "attuned to each other, like strings of a harp"; they are "singers of a lost kingdom." The allusion to the "kings" and the harmonious interaction between the pensioners and their experiences places them in an idealized "lost kingdom" of "wild melody," the heroic age of Merrie England. Hughes, like the pensioners, is a singer of a "lost kingdom." History becomes one-dimensional and glamorized, a process that ultimately limits the potential sociopolitical power of the poetry.

The weatherbeaten, tortured, industrialized landscape of *Remains of Elmet* stands in clear opposition to the soft, rural—one might say pastoral—terrain of *Moortown Elegies,* which is not part of the world of history nor part of the world of myth, but part of the immediate world of action and experience. Hughes stresses the immediacy of the Moortown realm of experience by often (atypically) writing in first person. The world of *Moortown Elegies* runs on natural and biological rhythms and not on commercial human time. That is, not only are there few, if any, allusions to a historical frame of reference in the narrative elements of the poems, but also Hughes rarely mentions exact measurable units of time—seconds, minutes, hours, times of day (four o'clock), days of the month, or months of the year. The references to time are unspecific. Typically, the events of the poem happen in "midafternoon," "dark," "before dawn," "yesterday," or "two days ago." Such general references free the poet from conventional time and the implications of recorded history, yet they are prominent enough to keep the narrative action from slipping into mythological timelessness.

For the first time in his career Hughes makes a significant attempt to create a time frame in which the action described in the poem corresponds to the actual writing of the poem. Thus, the poem's central orientation is toward the "new" life that appears in the poem's diction in the repetition of "now" and "suddenly" and "as I write." In the *Moortown Elegies* everything is in Heraclitean flux—birth, playing, suffering, death. Organic processes are the units of measure in this world. Even though Hughes is immensely preoccupied with the nonhuman, unhistorical life of the land and the sheep and cows, he also explores the place of human action in relation to this realm. In "Coming Down Through Somerset," a poem that describes the death and decay of a badger and the narrator's reaction to this experience, Hughes considers the lessons the nonhuman world can teach the human world about time:

> I want him
> To stay as he is. Sooty gloss-throated,
> With his perfect face. . . .

> I want him
> To stop time. His strength staying, bulky,
> Blocking time. . . .

> A badger on my moment of life.

Not years ago, like the others, but now.
I stand
Watching his stillness, like an iron nail
Driven, flush to the head,
Into a yew post. Something
Has to stay.

The badger becomes an emblem of immortality. Outside of time, the badger paradoxically (not ironically) is time itself. The temporal focus of the narrator's desire is "now," this brief moment. The attitude is not a longing for the past; it is a longing for the present where "something has to stay." Hughes reverses the traditional value placed on immortality and argues that the unhistorical present is the means and the end of the creative process.

Hughes's commitment to both a private and a public unhistorical view appears in the volume's closing poems, the actual elegies to Jack Orchard, Hughes's working partner on the farm. He does not mythologize or sentimentalize Orchard's life, but succinctly describes the rough, hardworking, and stubborn farmer in "A Monument": "burrowing, gasping struggle / In the kneedeep mud of the copse ditch . . . Under December downpour, mid-afternoon / Dark as twilight, using your life up." The farmer is described in a moment of pure action, selfless and oblivious to time. This sense that action or work exists in direct opposition to permanency and time in history appears in "Now You Have to Push." The word *now* embodies the at-this-very-momentness of Hughes's vision in *Moortown Elegies*. He asserts that Now, at the existential moment between life and death, Orchard must push his entire life "into a gathering blaze" since "Now you have to stay / Right on, into total darkness." The tone is confident. Orchard, a man of present-tense action, remains in the moment, harmoniously joined to the rhythms of the nonhuman world; he does not enter the annals of the past. The "Elegies" do not lament the death of Orchard; they attempt to keep him alive in the Now.

"Hands," the final poem of *Moortown Elegies*, is Hughes's ultimate testimony to his faith in the power of the present, in action and work, to move Orchard outside the clogs of time and historical process and to align him with the cyclical motions of Nature. Orchard's hands are described as "strange—huge" and as "nerveless [as] crocodile leather," yet "monkey delicate." Orchard's hands serve as a synecdoche for his entire life: powerful and sensitive. In the poem's final stanza, the reader imagines Hughes looking into Orchard's massive, weathered hands:

> Your hands lie folded, estranged from all they have done
> And as they have never been, and startling—
> So slender, so taper, so white,
> Your mother's hands suddenly in your hands—
> In a final strangeness of elegance.

"Suddenly" the moment becomes revelation. The poem and volume conclude, not nostalgically or sentimentally but committed to the present, to the final strangeness of existence as experienced in this world—a world evolving at its own pace, oblivious to the demarcations of commercial time and recorded history.

Moortown Elegies represents a significant advancement in Hughes's vision. One wonders whether Hughes could have committed himself so fully to the immediacy of existential experience if he had not felt the heavy constraints of history in *Remains of Elmet*. Those critics who want a more historically aware and politically vocal Hughes will probably not get their wish. They will have to go to Geoffrey Hill or Seamus Heaney for that. Hughes's first volume after *Moortown Elegies, River,* though significantly more dependent on myth than *Moortown Elegies,* reveals that he is still not willing to confront what he has called "the excitement of the time." The most recent volume and his first as poet laureate, *Flowers and Insects,* occasionally combines the mythical beauty of *River* with the unhistorical narrative immediacy of *Moortown Elegies;* but overall the volume lacks the mythic intensity of earlier works.

Undoubtedly, Hughes's isolationist attitude—his refusal to enter the world of historical human affairs—and his nostalgic approach to history are significant limitations of his vision. But he is shrewd. He knows that his voice is most distinct and his vision most clear when he is "out of time."

ALAN GOLDING

History, Mutation, and the Mutation of History in Edward Dorn's *Gunslinger*

The dominant, though certainly not the only, tradition of the American long poem has been that of the poem "including history," in Ezra Pound's words, "the tale of the tribe" (*Essays* 86, *Guide* 194). This tradition is represented in different ways by Whitman, Pound, Williams, Crane, Zukofsky, Olson, and Lowell, to mention just a few of the best-known examples. Despite the various degrees of subjectivity or idiosyncrasy involved in many of these poets' projects—Whitman's and Crane's cosmic visions, Zukofsky's opaque transliterations of foreign and ancient languages, Olson's mythologizing, Lowell's attempt to impose his personality on history—they share one common feature. They refer to a historical reality that, as they acknowledge in their texts, has a substantial presence outside of, independent of, the texts.

Many of these poets have also seen their long historical poems as coterminous with their own lives. Once they started their epics, Whitman, Pound, Zukofsky, and Olson worked on them for most of their creative lives; indeed, for all but Zukofsky, only death brought closure. Williams, though he started *Paterson* late in life, could find no way to finish it. In theory Lowell could have continued the contemporary political commentary of *History* as long as he chose, and certainly he had trouble with closure, revising obsessively and publishing three variations on the same book, *Notebook 1967–68, Notebook,* and *History.*

And then we have Edward Dorn's *Gunslinger.* Superficially it seems to continue this tradition of the American long poem by including the history of both frontier and contemporary American culture—its language, its intellectual and political concerns, its myths. At the same time, however, *Gunslinger* represents a new kind of nonreferential historical poetry insofar as Dorn seals the poem off from the history on which it is commenting and of which it is part. And unlike the many American poets for whom self and history intersect, Dorn sets history and biography at odds through his objectification of "I" as a character in the poem, his treatment of "I" in the third, not first, person. *Gunslinger*'s opening confronts us with this trope: "I met in Mesilla / The Cautious Gunslinger" (3). We do not yet know that this "I" is a character named "I" or that the verb is third person singular. The poem begins not in personal statement as, say, "Song of Myself"—"I celebrate myself, and sing myself" (Whitman 28)—but rather in a deceptive parody of such statement. This deception is permitted by a feature of language that helps make subject and object one, namely, that the first- and third-person singular past-tense forms of most English verbs are the same.

Dorn takes this oblique approach to his historical subject, which is nothing less ambitious than the state of the nation, because, between completing the 1967 volume *The North Atlantic Turbine* and beginning *Gunslinger,* he "had become very convinced that the direct onslaught in that sober sense of the political poem was not only very boring but completely valueless" (*Interviews* 26). Furthermore, unlike a modernist historical poet such as Pound, or even a late modernist such as Lowell, he does not cling to the hope of recreating a usable past. He finds Western history in irrevocable decline and the usual ways of understanding that history futile—as futile as searching for the elusive Howard Hughes, the quest that gives *Gunslinger* its initial raison d'être but that is soon dropped. Hughes is a non-presence, not to be found: *"this Howard is kinda / peculiar about bein Seen / like anywhere anytime"* (*Gunslinger* 10). He is a shape-shifter, living "in the dangerous disguise of Nobody" (92), first becoming the character Robart, who is also called Rupert, and then even taking on aspects of his antagonists, I and the Slinger. As Charles Olson argued to Dorn in the letter-essay "A Bibliography on America for Ed Dorn," "the real *power* contemporary to one is *kept hidden*" (*Prose* 14).

If Hughes "aint never bin seen" (*Gunslinger* 91), however, his power is tangible enough. Hughes represents for Dorn, as the poet says in a 1973 interview, "a rather pure metaphor of a kind of primitive, entrepreneurial capitalist take of what America is, which is still embedded in the political and social instincts of a lot of American activity" (*Interviews* 51). He embodies "the most crucial thing we know, money" (27). In his novel *By the Sound,* a revision

of the earlier *Rites of Passage* published in 1971 while he was working on *Gunslinger*, Dorn has one of his characters comment on the
relationship between immense wealth and power in a way that clarifies Hughes's role in *Gunslinger:*

> No, there are two levels and two levels only on which
> money declares itself. The highest of course, is that in
> which there is such an amount that its "activity" is what
> makes money interesting, what it can do, like a toy train
> that can be switched, and made subject to elaborate
> signals.   (63)

As Dorn writes in a later poem on Hughes's death, "his [Hughes's]
control is not to be seriously / questioned" (*Lola* 50). But if his
control is not to be seriously questioned, other ways must be found
to undermine it. And if Hughes and his cronies control also the
terms for understanding history—"it's far out   how / He cons the
present to hustle the futchah / By a simple elimination of the data-
data" (*Gunslinger* 108–09)—then new terms, or new possibilities of
understanding, must be created. Michael Davidson summarizes
Dorn's view of Hughes well: "Clearly Hughes' power defies the
laws by which ordinary citizens conduct their daily business and
demands an entirely new view of history" ("Archeologist" 173).
    Throughout his career Dorn has examined history only rarely
through significant events and individuals, and much more often
through forces. As Donald Wesling writes in distinguishing Dorn's
response to public affairs from that of politically concerned poets
like Lowell, Ginsberg, or Bly,

> Dorn's analysis of the way things work . . . moves very of-
> ten on the level of world-systems and commodities as well
> as the level of personal experience; to a greater extent he
> situates the psychological and individualist possibilities
> within a larger frame of reference.   ("Bibliography" 146)

Unlike Lowell's Alexander, Stalin, or Che in *History*, Dorn's
Hughes is more a metaphor than an individual. He is an "unseen
symbolic Body" (*Gunslinger* 90); "I really don't mean the specific
person" (*Interviews* 51), Dorn has said. Indeed, Hughes is so unim-
portant as an individual in *Gunslinger* that he eventually disappears

from the poem. But as a metaphor, he represents an ongoing theme of Dorn's work, the power of capital to exercise an oppressive, mechanical control over people's lives. As early as the 1964 poem "The Pronouncement," Dorn sees history in terms of a mechanistic pattern being played out to its end: "not a damn thing / ever changes: the cogs that turn this machine are set / a thousand miles on plumb, beneath the range of the Himalayas" (*Poems* 77). In "Oxford," from 1967, he sums up this view succinctly in "the idea that civilization is static" (*Poems* 206). The tool of this stasis is trade, metaphorized in the title poem of *The North Atlantic Turbine* as a gigantic engine. In that poem, while "men rot," "trade revolved and revolves / it remains the turbine." "Unalterable and predictable action" (*Poems* 187) is the turbine's main characteristic: it "turns clockwise. It is that simple minded" (191). By the time Dorn gets to *Gunslinger*, "it looks to me Jack / like The Whole Set is Sinking" (121). The only solution (to go back to "The North Atlantic Turbine") "is / to reverse the stream" (189).

Dorn writes further of the turbine, however, that "as long as its base / stays—solutions . . . / can come . . . / to no effect" (*Poems* 188). That "base" is the mind itself, so that for Dorn a significant shift in historical direction requires not material "solutions" but a shift in consciousness. As he writes in the oft-quoted conclusion to the prose piece "Driving Across the Prairie": "that crippled stem of this country is made with the mind" (*Business* 65). In a 1980 interview with Tom Clark, Dorn puts the issue this way: "The mind . . . is going to have to think of a whole different set of configurations to perpetuate itself. The ways it has perpetuated itself are coming to an end" (*Views* 24). *Gunslinger* dramatizes Dorn's own vision of that "different set of configurations." In it he tries to provide what he says, in "Oxford," Western culture needs: a "guiding hand / to dismount the old model" (*Poems* 201).

Consistent with his interest in mind forms rather than social forms—he calls his cast of characters "our psychomorphs" (*Gunslinger* 130) and states his goal as "the Inventory / and then the Overhaul of the fucking mind" (94)—Dorn emphasizes metaphysics over material history in *Gunslinger*. Marjorie Perloff rightly notes in reviewing *Gunslinger* that "his central concerns are metaphysical and have, finally, nothing to do with his chosen region, the American West" (22). Dorn demonstrates the opposition between the metaphysical and the material explicitly in Book II. There the owner of a runaway horse

              discharged
ten rounds with such ferocious rapidity
the bullets got stuck back to front
crowding each other out of the barrel
and fell to the boardwalk
as two segmented slugs 12345
each about 2½ inches in length.

Slinger comments thus:

    this can only be
    materialism, the result
    of merely *real* speed. All
    the smoothest gunnies Ive known
    were metaphysicians and of course
    no jammonings of this sort
    were ever associated with their efforts

Then the poor materialist is transformed into a statue, a monument to a bygone mindset:

          the Owners hulk
settled into a sort of permanence
as if a ship, gone to the bottom
shifts several ways into the sand
while finding her millenial resting place

      It has become an Old Rugged Statue
of the good ol days, Everything gasped.   (74–75)

Dorn uses various strategies in *Gunslinger* to displace material history, to avoid making the poem refer to a concrete historical reality. The only historically real person in the poem, Howard Hughes, is characterized by his absence. All the other main characters are cartoon characters or stereotypes, generically defined as either roles or pronouns: the Gunslinger, the Poet, Everything, the cabaret madam Lil, the Horse, I. And just as the poem has no "characters" in the traditional sense, so too it has no external place setting. Certainly places are mentioned and even stopped at: Mesilla, Truth or Consequences, Four Corners, Cortez, Colorado, and so on. But none of these places is concretely rendered. They remain labels, signs, verbal creations in this poem in which location, *"Here,"* "sounds like an adverb / disguised as a place" (65), and the site of "the big Ascension Day Burn" "aint no place, it's an Idea" (160). Unlike his mentor Olson, Dorn is no poet of place: "I'm not a localist at all, and I don't take much interest in Locality by any definition" (*Interviews* 79). The real action of *Gunslinger* takes place on an inner, imaginative landscape, its terrain "pseudo-historic" (*Gunslinger* 72)—"pseudo" because it is both fictional and metaphysical. Dorn's Poet calls the story "the fabulous accounting / of our coursing / the country of our consciousness" (50), a journey "Across / two states / of mind" (41).

Along with this absence of a material place setting, *Gunslinger* lacks both a specific time setting and chronological unity. It moves episodically, as its group of travellers "wander estranged" from all those time-bound citizens "who implore this existence / for a plan and dance wideyed / provided with a schedule / of separated events" (45). Further, despite the turbulent times during which *Gunslinger* was written, the late 1960s and early 1970s, Dorn makes very little reference to public affairs. Such topics, he suggests, make poetry not more serious but merely more salable: "Into the system came the muse / Singing   Used War for Sale" (109). He banishes any talk of Vietnam, referred to at one point as "the war / in, well you know where the War is" (79). And finally, *Gunslinger* incorporates via allusion, but pointedly does not align itself with, literary history. Shakespeare, Keats, and Eliot, for instance, all appear frequently, but they are present merely as alternative forms of language, to offer a good line or two. Unlike Pound or Eliot, Dorn does not use allusions to connect himself with a tradition; he denies any precedents.

In all these ways Dorn ignores history and envisions in the Slinger, as Michael Davidson puts it, "a completely ahistorical figure in whom resides a new consciousness" ("Narrative" 122). Whatever the "different set of configurations" Dorn seeks, it cannot be found in or learned from a history in decline. As Robert von Hallberg has shown ("Accidentalism" 67–71), Dorn dramatizes this new consciousness through the motif of mutation—a motif that has considerable implications for a historical poem. If history is usually discussed in terms of causation or system, linear theories, progressive theories, cyclic theories, mutation is a phenomenon that, by definition, violates all notions of causality or predictability. The mutant is thrown up inexplicably, randomly, by chance, breaking the chain of causation that, if it derives from an intellectual and cultural wasteland, can lead nowhere anyway. The Slinger does not deal in causation, logic, or explanations.[1] When I, who functions as a kind of surrogate reader early in the poem, ponders "the inexplicability / of all that had, in this half / hour passed," Slinger mocks his efforts at understanding: "You are inattentive / and expect reason to Follow / as some future chain gang does / a well worn road" (*Gunslinger* 16).

Dorn's pre-*Gunslinger* work offers a number of precedents both for using the language of genetics so prevalent in *Gunslinger* and for this opposition between mutation and history. He refers variously to "our exclusively gelding mentality," "our gelding culture" (*Poems* 161), our "totally onanized culture" (*Poems* 97). In "Oxford," England needs a visionary, one form of mutant consciousness: "A seer is what England needs / she has been in the hands of / her 'history' and her literate / men" (*Poems* 205). In "The Problem of the Poem for my Daughter, Left Unsolved," Dorn expresses the fear that "the end / of applied genetics will be / the elimination of freely disposed / intellection, via the rule / that a science is oriented toward / Use, some predictable / breed" (*Poems* 96). These lines anticipate the result of Robart's efforts in *Gunslinger* to "hustle the futchah," efforts reflected in his combining the language of sociology and the image of a sperm bank: "Each datum is caught I got em / And stored cold in a special future" (97).

Mutation appears in *Gunslinger* especially in verbal form, in puns, neologisms, hybrid dictions, typographical errors that Dorn preserves, multiple typefaces. In Book III, Dr. Jean Flamboyant's three Great Beenville Paradoxes (a jokey reference to the three paradoxes of Zeno, who was a student of Parmenides, one of the poem's presiding spirits) represent a mutation in logic, and recall Lil's earlier reminder that *"We're at the Very beginning of logic / around here"* (23)—as indeed, was Parmenides. If Dorn's fundamental subject is indeed "the country of our consciousness," these playful mutations represent the desired reversal in consciousness that I noted earlier from "The North Atlantic Turbine": "the simplicity is / to reverse the stream." As one particular form of mutation, images of reversal make up one central thread of this poem that aspires to step outside history and seek "configurations / that cannot arise in a game / because no preceding generation can form them" (*Gunslinger* 138). Reversal operates at every level of the poem, from word to line to combinations of lines to the theme of a whole section. "Balls," the organs of generation, are reversed to "Sllab," a talking monument that spouts clichés for a quarter and is "Hecho en Tejas / para El Hughes Tool Co." (164). In Book I, I's death involves a perfectly circular reversal "since I is the same [spelled] back as ahead." I is not a person but a function of language, a palindrome, and the line reminding us of that point is printed backward for emphasis: ".daeha sa kcab emas eht si I ecnis" (56).

In "The Cycle," the poem's most obscure section, trade is imaged, as it was in *The North Atlantic Turbine,* as a circular mechanism to be reversed, "The Cycle of Robart's Wallet." In an epic invocation beginning "The Cycle," Slinger invites the poet to reverse this "Cycle of Acquisition" and deliver his audience:

> O Singer, we are assembled here
> beneath the rafters of the tanner's shed
> Turn the Great Cycle of the Enchanted Wallet
> of Robart the Valfather of this race
> turn the Cycle of Acquisition
> inside the Cobalt Heads of these
> otherwise lumpish listeners and make
> their azured senses warm *M*ake your norm
> their own   deliver them
> from their *V*icious *I*solation.   (89)

Similarly the theme of the night letter is reversal: "REVERSE SENSE" and skewed language, "ABSOLUTE LINGUALILT," the purpose of which is to "EFFECT RELATIVE DISLOCATION" (140–41). Conceivably, in the phrase "STRICTLY FRONT BRAIN DEXTROROTARY EQUATIONS" (140), Dorn could even be recalling the words about reversal that Charles Olson addressed to him in the 1955 letters later published as "A Bibliography on America for Ed Dorn": "The best definition of inversion I know is the chemical one—turning cane sugar by hydrolysis (another word for inversion) from the dextrorotatory it is to a levorotatory mixture of dextrose and levulose." And if, as Olson continues, "it is possible chemically to kill a person by inversion" (*Prose* 4), it is equally possible in *Gunslinger*'s upsidedown world to kill a person (I) and revive/invert him chemically with LSD.

The reversal of "I" is particularly important in understanding Dorn's approach to history in *Gunslinger.* For most recent poets, to talk about history has been to talk about the intersection of personal and social history, of biography and history. Not so with Dorn.

Appropriately, then, the first person to die in *Gunslinger* is just that—the first person, the "I," the perceiving subject or ego. I's problem is the conventional way in which he tries to prove events for meaning, to the point where Slinger says, "you seem / constructed of questions" (32). After a confrontation in a bar between Slinger and a stranger who insults his horse, we find this exchange:

> What does the foregoing mean?
> I asked. Mean?
> my Gunslinger laughed
> *Mean?*
> Questioner, you got some strange
> obsessions, you want to know
> what something *means* after you've
> seen it, after you've *been* there
> or were you *out* during
> That time? No.
> And you want some *reason*.   (28–29)

Trapped in fruitless teleological thinking, "I" is typical of "all the singulars of his race" (56)—"typical" in that he is quite literally a Type. When he asks the horse, who has just changed his name from Heidegger to Claude Levi-Strauss, what "the savage mind" is, this answer comes back:

> *That,* intoned Claude leaning on my shoulder
> is what you *have*
> in other words, you provide
> an instance
> you are purely animal
> sometimes purely plant
> but mostly you're just a
> classification.   (35)

I's death occasions some lively verbal play calculated to confuse the boundaries between first and third person and to foreground what Slinger calls "the metaphysics of the situation":

> *But it makes me sad*
> *to see I go, he was,*

I mean I *was so perplexed*
I's obsessions were almost real
me and I had an understanding
I dont like to see I die.

I dont wish to distract you
with the metaphysics of the situation Lil
yet be assured,
I aint dead.

I know that, Slinger.
It's possible you missed it
the Slinger allowed,
I speak of *I*
Him? Lil pointed.
Is that not I? Stilled
inside whoever he is.   (56–57)

"The metaphysics of the situation," briefly, are that the self is too fundamental a part of human consciousness, and of our thinking about history, to be killed so easily. I may be reversed or transformed, but not killed: "I is / part of the thing / and can never leave it" (58); "I is a reference to the past / and cannot be So dropped" (59).

I is preserved and resurrected, ten pages after his death, by having Kool Everything's five-gallon batch of liquid LSD poured into him, a batch strong enough, in the poet's words, to "turn one into an allegory." The subsequent lines, like so many in this poem that continually responds to its own language, do indeed become allegory:

if we make I
a receptable of what
Everything has,
our gain will be twofold,
we will have the thing
we wish to keep
as the container of the solution
we wish to hold.   (60)

This view of the relationship between self and group goes back as far as Dorn's 1960 essay "What I See In *The Maximus Poems*": "only

the individual . . . has the carrying power of the soul and its re-
sponsibilities of the community, also those historical" (*Views* 38). I
is reborn not as the "single" or "poor individual" (*Gunslinger* 56)
who left himself outside the group, an "untaught alien" (20), by his
insistent questioning, but as a member of "the cultural collective,"
not as a self but as the Self:

> we stand before an original moment
> in ontological history, the self, with one grab
> has acquired a capital S, mark the date
> the Gunslinger instructed,
> we'll send a telegram to Parmenides.   (67)[2]

Why the telegram to Parmenides? As the first philosopher to
consider the nature of being, he too stood "before an original moment / in ontological history" and, as a monist, allowed for no distinction between subject and object. Slinger is a Parmenidean
philosopher—"Difference I have no sense of," he says (31)—and a
Parmenidean gunfighter:

> You make the air dark
> with the beauty of your speed,
> Gunslinger, the air
> separates and reunites as if lightning
> had cut past
> leaving behind a simple experience.   (30)

And just as the subject is not to be separated from object in the
poem's ontology, self is not to be separated from the group. I
becomes a *changed* character, but still not the primary one. He
re-enters the poem uttering the puns and epigrams typical of the
other characters, but continues to drop in and out, and his voice
frequently cannot be distinguished from that of the Poet, Kool
Everything, or even the Slinger. Dorn considers the use of distinct,
individualized voices (for his characters or himself) to be a rhetorical convention that cannot capture the multiplicity of experience.
Asked in a 1974 interview why he did not write "a poem with the
'I' up front and the ego dominating the poem," he replied:

> Well, after all I wanted to write a poem about the penetra-
> tion of the only space anybody has ever run into, and that's

multiple. I mean, I don't believe the lone traveler, except for
short distances. But even in the mind of a lone traveler
there's a multitude of dialogue. So, by its very nature it's
true.   (*Interviews* 61–62)

Dorn uses I as simply another voice in a collectivity of voices, ex-
plaining the principle thus: "the characters are really a constellation
of one body" (*Interviews* 48). They are personae for "the aspects
of anybody's mind," of "the shared mind," and as such are barely
differentiated parts of a whole, what Dorn calls "the collective
voice" (28).

In *Gunslinger*, then, the culture's condition is represented by a
group, called variously "our company" (46), "the cultural collective" (148), "this group in which our brain / is contained" (116). It
is *not* to be symbolized by the fate of a representative sensitive individual—a radically different assumption from that underlying the
historical poems of a Lowell, a Ginsberg, a Pound, an Eliot. In a
poem from *Yellow Lola*, "The Word (20 January 1977)," Dorn
questions whether Henry Kissinger, someone who might occupy a
place alongside Howard Hughes in Dorn's personal iconography,
would use the word "moved" that an interviewer attributes to him:

Moved was a bit too classy
to be used to note an emotion
and I doubt that it occurred to him.
And who knows, it might
have seemed too Lowell-like
if it had crossed his mind

Sentimental, to be sure, cheap,
imported and ordinary   (71)

For Dorn, unlike for some of his contemporaries, how one "feels"
about history is beside the point. Personal witness is simply unin-
structive, another symptom of the times' "flat sedimentary inter-
nalism" (*Gunslinger* 121):

I think now the ego is pretty obviously dead. One of
the most obvious facts of present life is people talking about
themselves or referring to themselves or being preoccupied with themselves. That's about the most boring thing
around. It's a habit that really has seen its day. It's not

that it doesn't persist, but it turns out that everybody's everybody else. All our stories are so interchangeable. If they're significant they seem to be more interchangeable.   (*Interviews* 49)

Along with the death and resurrection of I, another of Dorn's strategies for destabilizing the "I" as a privileged center of speech and experience lies in the hybrid style that results from his shifting rapidly among the voices of his different characters. *Gunslinger*'s multiple dictions—pieced together from the languages of computers, English poets, geneticists, astronomers, rock singers, cartoon heroes, and geologists—become detached in this act of combination from any recognizable human users. In other words, the poem's style resists any attempt by the reader to tie it to an individual poetic sensibility somewhere "behind" or "in" the poem. To be accurate, one should speak of *Gunslinger*'s style*s*; certainly Dorn admits that "my interest in the extreme heterogeneous vocabularies of English is fanatical" ("Strumming" 86). Michael Davidson has pointed out that much of the poem consists of set pieces ("The Cycle," the Nightletter, the Beenville Paradoxes), each of which is set off by its distinctive style, or code, so that no stylistic continuity binds the sections together ("Archeologist" 175). Dorn himself describes the poem's manner as "highly artificial" (*Interviews* 61). This is no poem of personal witness organized around a central consistent voice; this is not Ginsberg's "I saw the best minds of my generation destroyed by madness, starving hysterical naked" (*Howl* 9). Adherence to such a unified voice presumes an ability to organize the world's multiplicities that Dorn wants to deny. The *Gunslinger* manner resists such illusions.

In *Gunslinger* language itself becomes almost a live entity, capable of spawning its own connections without human intervention. As Dorn says in the 1977 talk "Strumming Language": "it's important for the language to be allowed to generate its own definitions, deliberately and spontaneously"; "the instrumentation of language itself is an active audience, with its own ideas and its own content and its own need to make its expression" (85, 91). Indeed to allow language to take over the poem opens up the possibility for the kind of mutant meanings Dorn seeks: meanings that an organizing sensibility might suppress in the name of the coherence or unity that Dorn calls a "psycho-philosophical pressure [that] has nothing to do with a poem" (91).

It is hardly surprising that a poet like Dorn, an insistent generalizer interested in global forces and unconventional ways of understanding them, would question conventional notions of the "I"—to put it another way, that he would question the claim that we can understand history through the biography of a representative individual psyche. In a 1972 interview he describes the poetic use of the "I" as involving more limitations than possibilities: "I didn't want to have any truck with that first person singular excuse which I find one of the most effective brakes on current verse practice" (*Interviews* 30). In reviewing Robert Creeley's *Pieces,* he writes of the "incapacitating ratio of subject to object" that cripples much contemporary poetry (*Views* 119). It is appropriate that Heidegger, that great destabilizer of transcendent notions of personhood, philosopher of what the Slinger calls "the constructive process / of ruin" (16), and, not incidentally, a great user of puns and neologisms, should preside over *Gunslinger* along with Parmenides. We should remember, however, that Dorn seeks to revise rather than destroy notions of personhood or the subject. He wants not to refute the idea of presence entirely but to counter that "false presence" that, as he says in his novel *By the Sound,* is "one of the most prevalent of modern diseases" (177): the false presence represented by Hughes that is in turn "an echo of the psychological condition of the United States of America" (*Interviews* 31).

At the same time, Dorn knows that talk about the self can easily lapse into preciosity, as I comes to realize:

> I had one eye out
> for the prosecutors of Individuality
> and the other eye out for the advocates
> catching in that spectrum
> all the known species of Cant.   (*Gunslinger* 162)

In pursuing the ontological and historical concerns of *Gunslinger,* Dorn finally cares more for inventiveness than for intellectual rigor. In "Oxford," he walks the streets with two college students who claim that all historical discussion is dead:

> . . . at one point one of them said
> it's impossible to write of it
> every substantive fit
> to name and celebrate has been spoken

and named.

. . . .
                    But I said *everything?*
has been talked about
around Oxford. I was assured
it had been. I didn't *say* while walking
but I thought well then make up!
something!   (Poems 207–08)

Gunslinger is what Dorn, as he faces this apparent dead end, makes up.

DIANE KENDIG

Poetocracy: The Poetry Workshop Movement in Nicaragua

I remember attending a reading by Andrei Voznesensky at the Cleveland State University Poetry Center in the 1970s, my first reading by a poet who was not an American. I was flabbergasted to see the hundreds of people who showed up in mid-afternoon to hear the poet, including middle-aged and elderly Clevelanders with Russian roots, not the usual all-college crowd. I was also struck by Voznesensky's surprise at learning how few Americans knew of Robert Lowell—fewer, he felt sure, than the number of Russians who knew of him.

I saw similarly large, heterogeneous audiences for readings by Seamus Heaney and Czeslaw Milosz, and while I might come to other conclusions from these three examples, today I conclude what I have seen indicated elsewhere: that certain cultures grant a higher status to poetry than others do, its status in the U.S. being among the lowest. So I wouldn't be surprised if the following examination of the poetry workshop movement in Nicaragua, a country where poetry has always enjoyed a high status, and the popularity and quality I am claiming for the movement sound implausible to anyone familiar with poetry only in the United States.

Steve Cagan, who provided me with the term *poetocracy* to define the current status of poetry in Nicaragua, offers the following explanation:

> Of course, it [Nicaragua] is not to be understood as a country literally ruled by poets *qua* poets, and still less a country ruled by poetry itself. Rather it [poetocracy] refers to the sense one gets in Nicaragua that poetry is an activity that is natural, organic, appropriate; one feels that the great amount of poetry which is written, distributed, and

> published is not at all surprising, that the ethos of the San-
> dinista Revolution is one which rather obviously supports
> and is expressed through poetry.   (Kendig 3)

The current poetic force is nothing new. Rather, it is part of the country's historically strong poetic tradition dating back at least to Ruben Dario, the Nicaraguan poet whose work has influenced literature throughout the Spanish-speaking world. Steven White in his bilingual anthology of Nicaraguan poetry notes that the country, although quite tiny, "has produced literary riches that equal and even surpass those of larger and more developed countries" (viii). Except for the work of Dario and perhaps of Ernesto Cardenal, however, few Americans are familiar with Nicaraguan poetry for the simple reason that we are largely a monolingual nation and, as Grace Schulman notes in White's 1982 anthology, we are just beginning to translate Nicaraguan poetry into English (v).

My own work translating Nicaraguan poetry workshop poems has introduced me to the long tradition of Nicaraguan poetry—backwards, as it were—and to the equally long tradition of marrying politics and aesthetics. These translations are the ones I will examine here, but first I would like to describe briefly the Nicaraguan poetry workshop movement as a whole. It began in 1980 when Ernesto Cardenal asked Myra Jimenez to help teach the first government-sponsored poetry writing workshop in the town of Monimbo. Jimenez is a Costa Rican poet who had run poetry workshops for children in Costa Rica and Venezuela. The two men had previously conducted a grass-roots poetry workshop movement in the Solentiname community where Cardenal had worked and lived with a Christian utopian group. According to Cardenal, the two began by teaching contemporary Nicaraguan poetry to the Solentiname adults, then added the study of North American and Cuban poetry, and finally, Latin and Greek poetry. They decided to use the same method with the workshop in Monimbo (*Talleres* 9–10).

This workshop has grown to over 50 workshops currently (nearly one for every 1,000 square miles in this tiny country), not in universities but in work co-operatives, farm communities, civic centers, schools, hospitals, and army barracks. At least four national anthologies have been published from the movement: *Talleres de Poesia, Antologia,* a 320-page anthology compiled from all the workshops; *Fogata en la Oscurana,* an anthology of poems from literacy workshops; *Poesia de las Fuerzas Armadas,* from the armed forces' workshops; and *Poesia Campesina de Solentiname,* from the original Solentiname workshops.

The poetry workshop movement has received international attention by Cardenal's account, having been studied, published, and translated in England, Italy, Germany, and throughout Latin America (*Talleres* 11). He attributes to Uruguayan writer Eduardo Galeano the pronouncement that the poetry workshop movement is one of the only two recent additions to Latin American literature, the other being the *testimonio* genre (*Talleres* 12).

The popularity of the movement is less important to us, though, than its product, the poetry itself, especially as it weds ideology and aesthetics. Recently, John Beverly has noted that poetry is a "materially decisive ideological practice of the Central American revolutionary movements" in general and the Nicaraguan and Salvadoran revolutionary movements in particular (155). He further contends that "the issue is no longer *whether* ideology is happening in the space of the aesthetic . . . because the art work is precisely one of the places where ideology happens" (157). Where Beverly sees the issue as recently resolved, I would say that it was long ago resolved, at least in the field of poetry, where Nicaraguan politics have always "happened." An indication of the strong tradition of political Nicaraguan poetry has been traced in the anthology *Poesia Politica Nicaraguense.* In the prologue, Francisco De Asis Fernandez analyzes the relationship between the poetry and the history of Nicaragua from the Liberal Revolution of 1893 to the beginning of the 1977 insurrection. Generation by generation he describes the poets' involvement in each new conflict and the conflict's consequences for literature (7–25). His analysis is followed by nearly 300 pages of well-known Nicaraguan political poems by 58 well-known poets, including Dario's often-anthologized "Los Cisnes" (The Swans) and his less-often anthologized, more prophetic "A Roosevelt" (To Roosevelt), which addresses Theodore Roosevelt with: "Eres los Estados Unidos, / eres el futuro invasor. . . . " (28) (You are the United States, / you are the future invader). At the other end of literary history, the anthology contains ten poems by Ernesto Cardenal as well as the work of younger poets. In between is nearly every famous Nicaraguan poet who wrote between Dario and Cardenal—Cortes, Selva, Urtecho, and Cuadra—each with at least one famous political poem and usually with more. It is little wonder that many, though not all, of the poems in the poetry workshop movement continue in the tradition of political poetry. Many merge the political and poetical in revolutionary ways.

All of the poems presented here are translated by me; most appear in my bilingual collection titled *A Pencil to Write Your Name: Poems from the Nicaraguan Poetry Workshop Movement*. When I first read these poems in Spanish, I was moved by how cleanly the ideological and aesthetic properties meshed. Weaned as I was on contemporary United States poetry, including some of the protest poetry of the Vietnam era, I had not seen much politically interesting poetry, nor much, if any, aesthetically sound political poetry. I had not yet come to terms with the poetry of Ernesto Cardenal, and I was fascinated by Carolyn Forche's work, which was grappling with this same dialectic. The workshop poems, written not by established poets but by the common people of Nicaragua, sustained simultaneously the heretofore contradictory forces.

Not that all the poems maintained the balance. Some, like the following by Carlos Galan, tended to sheer ideology with little of the literary:

Commander Che

I see you in my white undershirt
with your fixed, serene stare.
Your ragged head of hair
and a quote of yours I wrote at your feet:
"He who works has the right to rest
but he cannot be a man of the vanguard."
I wrote that on my white undershirt
next to the poem
that I wrote for you, Commander.

(Talleres 208 [my translation])

This poem depends too much on the references to Che scattered throughout with little connection among the references. The writer seems to be watching the mirror more carefully than the photo as he writes. It is the kind of poem to which Cardenal refers in his *Talleres* essay when he says,

At the Ministry of Culture, and especially at my office, poems arrive from many people, from all regions, always with revolutionary themes (about Sandino, Carlos Fonseca, imperialist aggression, etc.), but they are always bad. . . . And certainly there is much bad poetry in all Latin America, often with revolutionary themes, poems to Che, for example, with good intentions but full of rhetoric.

(13 [my translation])

He distinguishes between such poems and poems that come out of the workshop, emphasizing the studied approach that the workshops take.

The following poems are all what Cardenal calls in contrast "good modern poetry" (10), written by common people working to create poetry rather than rhetoric. Among the hundreds I examined in the *Talleres de Poesía* anthology, four types of political poems became apparent, all grounded in Nicaraguan literary traditions. The first type, which will be called historical-political, consists of poems that take characters and occasions associated with political conflicts and transform them within the poem. The poem "I Had Heard of You" by Manuel Mena is a good example of the type and provides a good contrast to "Commander Che":

> I had heard of you
> but from a Cuban magazine got to know you better.
> You were an old man, almost bald
> and I knew you were a painter of life
> from beginning to end;
> and the gossip of Paris
> was that you worked in your underwear.
> As you loved women
> you loved your country.
> When Somoza bombarded Leon, Masaya, and Esteli
> with Yankee planes and bombs
> Franco had already bombed Guernica
> with Hitler's planes and bombs.
> This poem I dedicate to you,
> an old man named Picasso.   (Kendig 17)

This poem is excessive in details about Picasso, perhaps, but the details reveal more than a stereotyped knowledge of the subject of the poem. The subject is also less clichéd: Picasso rather than Che, an artist rather than a soldier. The political thrust of the poem comes from the focus on Picasso's artistic political statement, *Guernica* (1937). The poem makes an analogy between the Spanish Civil War and a Nicaraguan conflict that went on in the same epoch. (Ironically, Somoza took office the same year Guernica was bombed.) It is difficult to discuss formal qualities in a translation, but I will point out that this poem uses parallelism and rhythm in addition to repetition. Even the list of cities, in either Spanish or English, is rhythmically balanced: "Leon, Masaya, and Esteli."

In another poem of this type, "To the U.S.," Justo Fernando Valledos takes one of the often-overused heroes whom Cardenal mentions, Carlos Fonseca, and rises to aesthetic heights by letting the image and metaphor carry the meaning:

> I visited the tomb of Carlos Fonseca
> and saw its lighted torch
> and the flame that rose from that torch.
> They will never be able to put it out, the winds from
> the North,
> will never be able to put it out.
>
> (*Talleres* 33 [my translation])

Three of the five lines in this tiny poem recreate the image of the flame: it rises above a torch at Fonseca's tomb. The last two lines calmly assert that winds will not put out the torch, and the repetition of the assertion suggests that the winds represent the United States, which will not be able to put out the spirit of the revolution that the flame represents.

While the historical-political poems place primary emphasis on the larger event and the larger point of view, the second type, the testimonial, emphasizes the personal point of view and recent events. *Testimonial* is not my term but one which has been used recently to describe a genre of Latin American literature that delivers an oral or written statement of truth or facts in a variety of forms, including nonfiction prose, novels, and poetry. Juan Ramon Duchesne traces the genre to the "non-fictional documentary literary tradition" of the Spanish Conquest chronicles. Today in Latin America, he says, the genre "continues to respond to a complex array of communicative social functions of documentary, political, educational, and aesthetic character." Two well-known testimonial poets are Roque Dalton (1933–1974), a martyred poet from El Salvador, and, more recently, the Chilean Aristoteles Espana (1955–),

whose poems describe his daily life in the Chilean concentration
camps from September 1973 to July 1974. Most testimonial poetry,
in addition to being a personal accounting of facts, is narrative and
tends to be longer than any of the other three types. The following
poem, "March 1975," by Carlos Rapacioli, is a good example of a
testimonial poem:

> The dark night.
> The silence interrupted only by the croak of frogs
> that at that hour left the ponds
> surrounding the house.
> The clock on the wall sounded two in the morning.
> Rolando and I did not sleep.
> I did not look at him
> only heard his uneasy broken breathing.
> Soon those knocks on the door
> and the cries:
> "Open, in the name of the Guard,
> we know you are there. We have you surrounded.
> Open up or we'll open fire."
> We sat up. My Aunt Margarita opened the door
> and rapid footsteps entered.
> One guard asked:
> "Where are those sons of whores, don't deny them"
> She did not answer.
> Only her sobs escaped.
> Soon a searchlight lit up the house.
> Then all was violence
> the blows followed one after another.
> They took us to the street where a drizzle
> began to fall, rustling and freezing.
> I saw how they hauled Rolando
> through the mud, barefoot and shirtless.
> I fell and they hauled me up,
> threw us in a cell and there we stayed, sprawled out
> aching.
> At that moment Rolando perhaps was thinking the same as I
> yes, the same as I
> about the triumph of the Revolution of Nicaragua.
>
> (Kendig 29)

The poem is testimonial in its length and narrative form and in other features as well. It is one person's account of his arrest along with the arrest of his friend, and like most testimonials, it emphasizes the first-person point of view. The speaker does not say, "They hauled Rolando . . . ," but "I *saw* how they hauled Rolando . . . " (1. 25 [my emphasis]). By the same token the poet tells us both that Rolando did not sleep (1. 6) and how he knows Rolando did not sleep: "his uneasy broken breathing" (1. 8). This piling on of details and facts in order to create a statement of truth is a hallmark of testimonial literature. Very seldom do conjecture, thoughts, or feelings come into such poems. When they do, they are clearly marked and usually occur at the very end of the poem, as in the last three lines; here the speaker marks the conjecture with "perhaps" and gives us his thoughts at the time.

The third type of poem I call the revolution's lyric. Like the testimonial, these poems deal with the recent situation, events immediately preceding 1979, the battle of 1979, and its aftermath. Unlike the testimonial poems, however, these poems tend to be short and more lyric. The narrative, if it is presented at all, is less important than images, emotions, and metaphor. There is also less emphasis on the point of view. An example of this type, "Ceferino, the Peasant," by 14-year-old Grethel Cruz, begins with a narration of an event, but not one that happened to her and not the main thrust of the poem:

> When the Pretorian Guard arrived
> you were planting
> and working the earth with your rough hands.
> The sun on your back,
> thirst in your throat,
> thinking during the day
> of things to tell by night.
> When the guard arrived
> and asked for your son
> you hugged the squash
> and thought of the dinner hung from the *jocote*
> as for a long trip.
> They made you lie down as though kissing the earth
> aiming a gun at you
> (the one invented by John G. Garand).
> You said nothing
> but the tremor of your knees that May

made the guards' tremble with fear in July
when what you planted was blossoming.   (Kendig 11)

The first fifteen lines relate a story about a farmer who is out planting when the guard comes by looking for his son. The account is
descriptive and imaginative, filled with sensual detail. The poet
imagines Ceferino's thoughts (or what she has been told they were)
first as he plants, then as the guards interrogate him. His thoughts
under interrogation are of an image: a dinner hung from a nearby
tree as if in preparation for a long trip. Also it is characteristic that
the dinner is hung not from any tree, but a *jocote,* a particularly
native tree, the tendency toward naming native variation being
something I will dicuss more under the fourth type. We know the
son has left for a long trip. The father does not tell the guard even
though they threaten to shoot him. There the narrative ends, and
we do not know specifically what happened to Ceferino except that
he is vindicated.

The vindication is conveyed in the last three lines that turn on
the metaphoric meaning of the last line, "when what you planted
was blossoming." Surely the vegetation that Ceferino was planting
when the guard arrived was blossoming then, but there is the sense
as well that the revolutionary movement he planted his son in was
"blossoming" or flourishing as well. His knees' tremor could not
literally make the guards' knees tremble, but his son's retribution
for his father's being made to tremble could.

Another poem, "Rosa Maria Hernandez Got Married," by
Guillermo Ramos (Kendig 31), uses a structure similar to "Ceferino, the Peasant," but with a different twist at the end. It begins
as a narrative that blossoms in the last four lines to compare the
personal experience to the national one:

> That night I went to sit down
> at the old well of the empty patio
> in front of your house.
> From there I listened to the songs,
> and your friends and relatives
> came and went.
> I saw you parade through the living room
> with Alvaro, your husband,
> with your white dress, well-made
> you looked beautiful.

The party had ended at ten
and in an orange-colored car
you left, for where I don't know.
The night remained quiet,
interrupted only by the crow
of the rooster
and the rumble of the trucks of the militia
that kept watch at that hour.
You were married,
the war had just passed.

What I find interesting about the ending of this poem is that whereas "Ceferino" uses the personal as a metaphor for the national (Ceferino's blossoming vegetables represent the flourishing revolutionary movement), this one uses the national to suggest the personal. While the national conflict had just passed, so had the narrator's warring feelings for Rosa Maria Hernandez just passed.

Not all of the lyric poems contain a strong narrative line. Some of the most touching poems in the volume are very short ones that convey emotion as much by what is not expressed as by what is.

Tomorrow

Anxious,
I will seek your face
in the multitude
and all will be useless.
    (Gerardo Gadea, in Kendig 51)

This poem could describe any loss of a loved one, but it is especially poignant in a country where such a large percentage of the population has been killed in combat.

The last type of political poetry to be noted here is the imagistic. As the term suggests, these poems turn on one or two strong pictures, and pictures strongly associated with the Nicaraguan culture and landscape, the folk traditions, or the poetry itself. Reclaiming the images has been a goal for the Nicaraguan poets. As Cardenal said in "Nicaraguan Canto" (1972),

How often have we Nicaraguans overseas said over drinks
"ours is a land of shit"? In cheap hotels

where exiles meet, but then
we'd start remembering *tamales,* and tripe soup with
   coriander and wild chili peppers, the songs
to the Purisima in December (with the scent of madrono
   trees in bloom). . . .   (*Zero Hour* 21)

The poem goes on for five more pages, listing and cataloguing the
people, places, sounds, and sensations that are Nicaraguan, and declares: "My poetry belongs here, / like the trumpeting *zanate,* or
the wine-producing palm" (28). Many specific bird names, vegetation, and place names come up again and again in the anthology,
along with folk figures and other particularly Nicaraguan sights
that the workshops promote.

    The following poem by Raquel Melendez, "In the Mornings,"
uses the image of the *ceiba* tree, a Nicaraguan tree, which recurs in
the poetry of Antonio Cuadra (White iv–v) and Ernesto Cardenal.
Here the tree is the image for the way the poet sees Nicaragua during and after the conflict:

In the mornings
I hear the song of the *zenzontles,*
zanates, guises, and sparrows;
the waters of the riverbed that pass near the *ceiba.*
There the birds rise
and then come down to drink.
And that *ceiba* in the war
remained without leaves, alone and without birds
and with its trunk pierced by bullets.   (Kendig 23)

This poem, like so many of the imagistic poems, uses the return of
nature to suggest the end of the war.

    Another poem, this one by Erwin Garcia, conveys a singular, un-
forgettable image of a character long gone from the U.S. cityscape
but still alive and well in Nicaragua, "The Iceman":

In the morning I watch him pass
in the cream-white truck of Tenderi Ice;
when he arrives
At Doña Daysi's general store
he waves to me with his frozen hands.
             (*Talleres* 168 [my translation])

Finally, "Summer" contains several natural images as well as a folk character. It was for me a lesson in translation as well. It is written by Rommel Novoa.

> The strong wind
> the clouds passing swiftly
> smell of cashew.
>
> Holy Week approaches
> brooks full of sardines
> and seafish drying up.
> Rumors of the wandering Jew
> and the funeral cart
> and the whistle of the bear-horse
> in the mountains.
>
> Peasants making bonfires
> to drive away mosquitoes and snakes
> peasants peeling papayas
> for making sugar syrup.   (Kendig 47)

This poem describes what I am told is a typical summer scene in Nicaragua. In the first stanza we have appeals to three of our senses in the wind which is blowing, moving the clouds, and spreading the smell of cashew trees, a tree that comes up often in these poems. The last stanza contains a typical native scene of peasants making sugar out of papaya, a stanza that appeals to both sight and taste, especially if the reader is familiar with the taste of papaya syrup. The images of the second stanza are much more foreign to me, but not, I would guess, to a Nicaraguan, especially given what I know about the "funeral cart," which in the original is the *carretera-nagua,* a term I did not know and could not find a translation for.

When my friend and cohort in the translation project was making his usual semi-annual trip to Nicaragua, I asked him to ask about the word. He returned, saying his hostess had told him it meant "sort of a funeral cart." Six months later, however, he returned, excited, and said, "I've seen the *carretera-nagua* in a child's drawing." Someone had brought him a drawing of a skeleton horse pulling a funeral cart, accompanied by a human skeleton. A check with the same hostess confirmed what he immediately had felt: this grim-reaper pair represented the *carretera-nagua.* "Why didn't you tell me this six months ago?" my friend asked his hostess. "I didn't think you'd understand," she replied. There are some things we have to see for ourselves.

This poem and the others of this fourth type are not political in the sense that they make political statements or connections as do the three types previously discussed. However, they are political in that they are a part of the revolutionary government's effort to celebrate Nicaragua's geography, culture, and traditions.

All four types of poems can tell us a great deal about the Nicaraguans and Nicaragua. In a way, they contradict William Carlos Williams's poem, "Asphodel," when it says,

> It is difficult
> to get the news from poems
>   yet men die miserably every day
>   for lack
> of what is found there.
>   Hear me out
>   for I too am concerned
> and every man
>   who wants to die at peace in his bed
>   besides.   (161–62)

I would like to think that Williams speaks for most of us in his desire to die at peace in bed. In any case, in Nicaragua it is possible, and not difficult, to get the news from poems. Those of us who read poetry would do well to hear them out.

JOHN GERY

The Sigh of Our Present:
Nuclear Annihilation and
Contemporary Poetry

In his massive study published in 1967, *Death in Life: Survivors of Hiroshima,* psychiatrist and psycho-historian Robert Jay Lifton quotes extensively from interviews he conducted with *hibakusha,* survivors of the atomic bomb explosion of August 6, 1945. Among those quoted is a man referred to only as a "history professor," who at one point explains how he believes the Japanese should memorialize the dropping of the bomb:

> We should figure out the exact hypocenter—and possibly put some small artistic monument on it—or better still, leave it devoid of anything at all . . . in order to symbolize nothingness at the hypocenter—because that is what there was. . . . Such a weapon has the power to make everything into nothing, and I think this should be symbolized. (*Death in Life* 278)

Later in the book Lifton takes up again this history professor's idea of nothingness as a way of life, when he quotes him about his sense of the future. The man says,

> The story of Noah's ark is more than a myth to me. Except for a few humans and animals, it is a story of everything becoming nothing. Maybe this will happen again—everything disappearing and becoming nothing except for a very few. . . . If we continue to make and use more powerful bombs, there may only be a few people left . . . chosen by chance. . . . As for myself, I go the way of nothingness. I don't have a strong desire to go about telling people about these things, or to talk in a loud voice about my A-bomb

experience. But if I am able to be useful, I like to do what I can.   (*Death in Life* 392)

Lifton interprets the history professor's going "the way of nothingness" as a combination of *akirame*, or "adaptive resignation," and an awareness of annihilation (*Death in Life* 393)—that is, to be able to carry on in life "psychologically 'taking in' an experience, however extreme, and simultaneously reasserting one's sense of connection with the vast human and natural forces which extend beyond that experience and outlast its annihilation" (*Death in Life* 186), as well as to live with the consciousness that all life and civilization is threatened with total extinction.

With the continuing proliferation of nuclear weapons, currently numbering over 50,000 worldwide, today all of us, not the least of whom are poets, face "going the way of nothingness" in the manner described by the history professor. Living under the constant threat of nuclear annihilation, we have been unconsciously learning to conduct our lives as though the continuum of the past through the present and into the future will proceed indefinitely, beyond our individual deaths, yet at the same time we have come to absorb the fact (almost subconsciously, despite a healthy urge to suppress such knowledge) that within the two or three hours it might take to complete a nuclear war everything we know and take for granted can be utterly and finally extinguished. Elsewhere, Lifton calls this "post-modern" condition "the absurdity of our double life" (*Weapons* 5). And in his book *The Fate of the Earth* Jonathan Schell describes the quandary such an absurdity presents to the contemporary artist:

> Art attempts both to reflect the period in which it was produced and to be timeless. But today, if it wishes to truthfully reflect the reality of its period, whose leading feature is the jeopardy of the human future, art will have to go out of existence, while if it insists on trying to be timeless it has to ignore this reality—which is nothing other than the jeopardy of human time—and so, in a sense, tell a lie.   (165)

For American poets, Schell's paradox is particularly apt. Not surprisingly, most contemporary poets seem generally to avoid the political, social, and technological realities of the nuclear age, as though to treat them were to endow them with a significance poets strive to transcend. Terrence Des Pres explains this argument for the implicitly political nature of much of contemporary lyric poetry (and the fallacy in the argument) this way:

> By celebrating modest moments of the human spectacle—little snaps of wonder, bliss or pain—poetry implicitly takes its stand against nuclear negation. To say Yes to life, this argument goes, automatically says No to the Bomb. And yes, a grain of truth sprouts here. I expect many among us read poetry that way in any case. The upshot, however, is that poets can go on producing their vignettes of self, pleased to be fighting the good fight without undue costs—except *the* cost, which is the enforced superficiality, the required avoidance of our deeper dismay.   ("Self" 449)

Indeed, such poetry, in its unwillingness or inability to confront the notion of annihilation as both an external threat and an internal psychic crisis, inadvertently becomes an expression of what Lifton defines as "psychic numbing" or "desensitization," that state of mind experienced by one in an extreme situation (such as Hiroshima after the bomb was dropped or Auschwitz under the Nazis) and "characterized by various degrees of inability to feel and by gaps between knowledge and feeling" (*Life of Self* 79).[1] For contemporary artists to fail to confront the real potential for the extinction of not only their art but of all art may be, on the one hand, a healthy attempt to suppress a concept that is cause for utter despair, but it is also an assured means of desensitizing themselves to "our deeper dismay" and of failing to provide an imaginative expression for that dismay. In short, it is to acquiesce to (and therefore silently to condone) the dangerous conditions under which we currently live. Yet if Lifton is right in saying that we live in "the age of numbing" (*Life of Self* 80), it is not surprising that such poetry is commonplace.

Beyond the large body of American poetry (itself, ironically, largely ignored by the broader populace) that discreetly ignores the extreme situation of its own time, there is a fairly distinct spectrum of poetry that *does* reflect exactly the terror, apathy, anger, hopelessness, and resolve many of us tend to feel in the face of our own extinction. Of course, literature about annihilation is nothing new to the post-Hiroshima era, and we can find useful comparisons between it and eschatological portraits of humankind since before the Greeks.[2] Also, during a period of national attention to nuclear-related events (such as the Soviet-American competition to develop bigger bombs during the 1950s or the popular movement in favor of the Atomic Test Ban Treaty during the Kennedy administration) not surprisingly a rash of poems is likely to appear.[3] And as Americans become increasingly comfortable with nuclear technology and more sophisticated about its manifestations in their lives, no doubt poets too will discover more than simply doom and gloom in their treatments of the nuclear age—a trend already evident in the 1980s.

To simplify, though, a look at recent American poetry reveals four categories of response to nuclear annihilation. Most obviously, there is "nuclear protest poetry," in special issues of literary journals as well as in the work of such "political" poets as Allen Ginsberg, Gary Snyder, and others. In less overtly public fashion, poets writing out of what might be called the "post-romantic" or "confessional" mode tend in their work to create images of apocalypse and devastation in order to imagine the *subjective* experience of nuclear annihilation, or conversely, they incorporate the imagery of annihilation (imagery which has permeated contemporary thought) into metaphors of personal experience, in much the same way that Sylvia Plath used the imagery of Nazi concentration camps in poems depicting her own psychic traumas. A third category includes those poets who adapt alternative forms to the short lyric mode in order to open themselves to the discussion of the historical, scientific, and cultural conditions imposed on our era by what Lifton calls "nuclearism" (*Weapons* ix); this group of poets might be labeled "psycho-historical." Finally, perhaps the most intriguing poems concerning nuclear annihilation are those which treat not the devastation of a nuclear holocaust, as we might imagine it, but the psychic condition of annihilation itself, that very "way of nothingness" we already experience in the present yet must learn to imagine and articulate if we wish to survive into some future.

"Protest" poetry (often erroneously referred to as "political" poetry as though any other kind of poem had no political relevance in the U.S.) gained particular notoriety during the Vietnam War, building on the polemical style of the Beat poets of the 1950s. Since the U.S. withdrawal from Vietnam, small literary magazines and presses throughout the country have frequently printed limited editions, special issues, and anthologies attacking the political establishment on behalf of a variety of causes, including the "anti-nuke movement," as it is often called to its own detriment. Despite the small audience it is liable to reach, such poetry nurtures solidarity among political activists, if nothing else. Here is an example by Margaret Key Biggs from one such publication:

Dirty Words

I was caught up
with a bunch of graffiti freaks
whose highs come from
the ubiquitous scrawling
on bathroom walls.
A clean wall was more disgraceful
than the draft, to them.
For the initiation
they found a virgin wall,
gave me a new can of spray paint,
and told me to write
the vilest, filthiest words
I could summon.
With great care I wrote:
WAR—NUKES—MELTDOWN.   (Shipley 8)

Veteran protest writers such as Snyder, Daniel Berrigan, and Robert Bly handle the issue of nuclear destruction with more aplomb than writers such as Biggs, but is the message in their work any less unambiguous? In Robert Creeley's "On Saul Bellow's Thesis, That We Think Our Era's Awful Because We'll Die In It" (Sklar 104), Creeley's cryptic style makes for characteristic understatement, but in this poem as in most protest poetry, after introducing the idea of extinction ("and there won't even be a you left / to contest this most meager provision / your life"), the final couplet subtly but unquestionably places a responsibility on "you," namely, "the one presumably who's living" this life, to begin to live it by "contesting" what meager provision there is in an age of impending holocaust.

In the same anthology in which Creeley's poem appears, Berrigan's "Biography" approaches the necessity of social responsibility through reverse logic. His poem opens by telling us that he was "born alive" on St. Gregory's Day in 1921 but "born dead" on "Hiroshima Day, 1945" (Sklar 180). Then through a series of contrasts, Berrigan calls himself a "casualty of Hiroshima" who is "marked now / by the stigma of those fires": "Presumably dead, I have nothing to lose to death. / Pre- / sumed living, I have nothing to refuse life. Or so I hope" (Sklar 181). He concludes, in other words, that we have nothing to lose in resisting nuclear proliferation, since fundamentally it has already overcome us.

In his famous protest poem "Plutonian Ode," Allen Ginsberg, one of the most highly regarded of these dissentient poets, addresses directly the element plutonium (used in a nuclear warhead) as a new kind of god "named for Death's planet through the sea beyond Uranus / whose chthonic ore fathers this magma-teared Lord of Hades" (11). This three-part ode, specifically written to oppose the Rockwell Corporation's Nuclear Facility and Plutonium factory in Rocky Flats, Colorado, invokes the god of the 24,000-year cycle of the Great Year of Antiquity and compares that cycle to the half-life of plutonium decay, in order to "embody" the very power of plutonium and to "enter with spirit out loud into your fuel rod drums underground on soundless thrones and beds of lead" (14). In his final strophe Ginsberg calls on the power of poetry itself to defeat, through the sheer art of declaration, the father of Death, "destroyer of lying Scientists," and murderer of all others:

> This ode to you O Poets and Orators to come, you father
>   Whitman as I join your side, you Congress and
>   American people,
> you present meditators, spiritual friends & teachers, you O
>   master of the Diamond Arts,
> Take this wheel of syllables in hand, these vowels and
>   consonants to breath's end
> take this inhalation of black poison to your heart, breathe
>   out this blessing from your breast on our creation
> forests cities oceans deserts rocky flats and mountains in
>   the Ten Directions pacify with this exhalation,
> enrich this Plutonian Ode to explode its empty thunder
>   through earthen thought-worlds
> Magnetize this howl with heartless compassion, destroy
>   this mountain of Plutonium with ordinary mind and
>   body speech,
> thus empower this Mind-guard spirit gone out, gone out,
>   gone beyond, gone beyond me, Wake space, so Ah!
>   (16–17)

Ginsberg's absolute faith in the power of poetry to resist the destructive power of plutonium is as fierce and inspiring as Whitman's faith in the hearts of the American people, and his poems undoubtedly reach a wider audience than most of the others I am discussing. But putting aside the fact that his work is surely as much or more disregarded by policymakers than has been that of his dissident counterparts in Poland and Czechoslovakia, I wonder to what extent a poem like "Plutonian Ode" actually alters anyone's political thinking, inside or outside the political establishment. Nuclear protest poetry may well get heard by more people than most other poetry, but is it listened to?

Those poets less actively hostile to the U.S. government than Berrigan and Ginsberg also voice their objection against the way things are in their poems, as Des Pres has pointed out, but the difference stylistically with them is the prominence of the private voice or their use of "I." These poets, in fact, seem less interested in saying No to the bomb than in creating for us images and metaphors for nuclear devastation. Films of Hiroshima, Nagasaki, and above-ground nuclear tests before they were banned in 1963 have imprinted an indelible image on our imaginations of what a nuclear war might look like and sound like. Groups such as the Physicians for Social Responsibility and the International Physicians for the Prevention of Nuclear War have provided detailed speculations on the physical, biological, medical, psychological, and even meteorological effects of nuclear war. But what of the spiritual, emotional, and domestic effects? Are they not the realm of the theologians and poets?

So assume poets such as Bill Hopkins, in "Radioactive Lover" (Shipley 18), where he describes fallout in terms of a living substance or "sperm" permeating the landscape much like the Blob from Outer Space or the black death. Hopkins's poem is one of hundreds of American poems that use familiar images to capture what is essentially an unfamiliar experience. Others include William Stafford's "At the Bomb Testing Site" (41), with its perspective of the "panting lizard" waiting for history to change in the desert, and Mark Strand's "When the Vacation Is Over for Good," where the poet ultimately admits to being "still unable, to know just what it was / That went so completely wrong, or why it is / We are dying" (5). Greg Pape's more recent poem "Drill" (39) recalls the "duck-and-cover" civil defense exercises in schools during the 1950s and 1960s. But in "The Cocked Finger," Stephen Dunn acknowledges the "terrible dullness" that has come to pervade our sense of the apocalypse:

> I've gotten used to the rapes,
> the murders. I eat dinner
> and watch them on Channel Six
> and nothing shocks me,
> not even kindness,
> not even, though I'm afraid,
> the bomb.
> The finger that might
> touch it off is cocked
> like an apostrophe
> on the wrong side of a possessive,
> an error so obvious
> almost everyone can see it.   (Dunn 460–61)

More recent variations of Stafford's now famous poem include Ted Kooser's "In the Kitchen, at Midnight" (*Sure Signs* 45), where he ponders the power of survival belonging to the cockroach; Kooser's "At Nightfall" (*One World* 37), which obversely considers "our madness" in bringing to an end the swallow's ability "to guide her flight home in the darkness" after the "hundred thousand years" it has taken her to learn it; and Sherod Santos's updated "Near the Desert Test Sites," which mocks the "pampered opulence" of the tacky 1985 landscape of Palm Desert (77). And not unlike Strand, Baron Wormser attempts to explain the idea of extinction by creating a kind of fairy tale with three different personifications of death in "I Try to Explain to My Children a Newspaper Article Which Says That According to a Computer a Nuclear War Is Likely to Occur in the Next Twenty Years" (54–55).

And what about the aesthetic effects of nuclear warfare, with its brilliant colors, deafening roar, and brutal physical power? Lifton describes one symptom of "nuclearism" as "nuclear fundamentalism" or bomb worship (*Weapons* 80–99). Poets are certainly not beyond the allure of magnificent mushroom clouds rising miles up into the sky, as in Sharon Olds's short poem "When":

> I wonder now only when it will happen,
> when the young mother will hear the
> noise like somebody's pressure cooker

down the block, going off. She'll go out in the yard,
holding her small daughter in her arms,
and there, above the end of the street, in the
air above the line of the trees,
she will see it rising, lifting up
over our horizon, the upper rim of the
gold ball, large as a giant
planet starting to lift up, over ours.
She will stand there in the yard holding her daughter,
looking at it rise and glow and blossom and rise,
and the child will open her arms to it,
it will look so beautiful.   (Olds 20)

This poem, in saying nothing whatsoever about the horror of what it imagines (the darkest image here being of a pressure cooker), attempts to engage us in its common viewpoint through its use of familiar diction, domestic imagery, and colloquial versification. Yet despite its artful use of abrupt line breaks that interrupt its syntax, thus imitating the sudden nuclear blast, most of its impact as a statement of quiet abhorrence relies not on the imagery within the poem so much as on our shared notions of what a blast would be like—a new and now exploited source of endless speculation, as in Jared Carter's "Electromagnetic Pulse" (12), Richard Cole's "The Last Days of Heaven," and Dana Gioia's "The End" (51–52).

But the task of imagining nuclear war in a way that captures its meaning as well as its potential occurrence is not so easy as we might think, because to have that experience is, de facto, to eliminate all other experiences; any poem that relies as heavily on the existence of the individual consciousness (or private "I"), as does Olds's poem, structurally creates the paradox of presenting an image no human being could possibly survive to tell about. As Jonathan Schell writes,

> When we try to picture extinction we come up against the fact that the human faculties with which someone might see, hear, feel, or understand this event are obliterated in it, and we are left facing a blankness, or emptiness. But even the words "blankness" and "emptiness" are too expressive—too laden with human response—because, inevitably,

they connote the *experience* of blankness and emptiness, whereas extinction is the end of human experience. (138)

In other words, poems such as Olds's and the others discussed here do not portray the experience of nuclear *annihilation* but the experience of nuclear *war* up to, but not a millisecond beyond, the actual moment of annihilation.

On the other side of poems that use the imagery of nuclear warfare are those that exploit that imagery not to portray extinction itself but to describe contemporary experience. Whether Michael Burkard's "Someone" is about a conflict between two lovers, the poet's bereft consciousness, or a nuclear holocaust is, for me at least, uncertain. But, there is no doubt that the imagery permeating this characteristic poem—the "washed away" moment, the tree bearing "a song of ashes," the landscape devoid of "a village, horses drawn up, and the water there," and "the black sky out a window" which "will drift by" but "will be still as well" (16)—derives from that wasteland we associate with external, not just internal, annihilation. The title of Adrienne Rich's "Trying to Talk with a Man" points us not to the landscape of holocaust, but to the intimacy of a marriage. Yet unlike Olds, Rich mixes the imagery of domestic life with the arid "condemned scenery" of a Nevada test site: the "underground river / forcing its way between deformed cliffs," the "dull green succulents," the "silence of the place," "laceration, thirst," and so on. Instead of using familiar images for extreme horror, Rich uses extreme images to inculcate us with the intensely deadening effects of a familiar but painful situation:

> Out here I feel more helpless
> with you than without you
> You mention the danger
> and list the equipment
> we talk of people caring for each other
> in emergencies—laceration, thirst—
> but you look at me like an emergency
>
> Your dry heat feels like power
> your eyes are stars of a different magnitude
> they reflect lights that spell out: EXIT
> when you get up and pace the floor

> talking of the danger
> as if it were not ourselves
> as if we were testing anything else.   (*Diving* 3–4)

In this poem, not only does our shared notion of a nuclear explosion (together with our expectation that all weapons tested will eventually be used in warfare) help to convey the despair and frustration the poet feels, but in a fashion more subtle than Hopkins's or Olds's, Rich has woven a distinctly personal yet broadly human experience into the fabric of our conception of nuclear war and our impotence in preventing it. The feeling of dread created by a failed relationship between a man and a woman becomes identical to the deep cultural dread associated with nuclear annihilation. (That two primary poems I have chosen to illustrate this second category are both by women is not altogether arbitrary, especially in the case of Rich's poem; the chief perpetrators of nuclear weapons and those most responsible for taking us to the verge of annihilation are, to a person, men.)

"Trying to Talk with a Man" is neither a poem just about male-female relations nor a poem about nuclear weapons; its thematic scope broadens in a way that the poetry of nuclear annihilation must do if it is to transcend the sort of categorization I am doing here and change "our modes of thinking," as Einstein would have it do. Other poems (again, notably, by women) that blend consciousness of everyday life with consciousness of annihilation include "Nature" and "Lot's Wife" in Celia Gilbert's *Bonfire;* Maxine Kumin's "Lines Written in the Library of Congress After the Cleanth Brooks Lecture"; Honor Moore's "Spuyten Duyvil"; and a host of works by Denise Levertov, from several early poems, including "Another Spring" and "The Novel" in *O Taste and See,* to "Watching *Dark Circle*" and "Gathered at the River" in *Oblique Prayers.*[4]

Perhaps no other major poet has been more closely linked to the antinuclear movement in recent years than Levertov, yet not all of Levertov's poems express a direct objection to the threat of nuclear annihilation. Rather, because her *life* is intricately wrapped up in her public efforts to reverse the arms race, her poems inevitably *embody* that experience in the same way that any private experience informs a poet's sensibility. Levertov herself explains this congruence of the public actions of the individual and the private nature of lyric poetry in her 1975 lecture, "On the Edge of Darkness: What Is Political Poetry?":

> A striking characteristic of contemporary political poetry is that, more than in the past, it is written by people who are active participants in the causes they write about, and not simply observers. . . .
>
> For many of us who are thus involved, it is possible that our sense of political urgency is at times an almost hectic stimulus. . . . [I]f one is led by a resulting commitment to the attempt to combat what threatens us, and thus to the experience of comradeship in actions involving some risk, such as civil disobedience, then one is living a stirring life which—if one is given to writing poetry—is almost bound to result in poems directly related to these experiences. (*Cave* 120–21)

For Levertov, the danger of nuclear annihilation breaks down the distinction between the personal and the public, finally, by threatening the removal of each arena of existence as a point of reference for the other and by coercing the poet into confronting the fundamental nature of the poetic endeavor (not to mention of living itself). As Jacques Derrida puts it, in his attempt to define "nuclear criticism,"

> The only "subject" of all possible literature, of all possible criticism, its only ultimate and a-symbolic referent, unsymbolizable, even unsignifiable . . . is, if not the nuclear age, if not the nuclear catastrophe, at least that toward which nuclear discourse and nuclear symbolic are *still beckoning:* the remainderless and a-symbolic destruction of literature. Literature and literary criticism cannot speak of anything else, they can have no other ultimate referent, they can only multiply their strategic maneuvers in order to assimilate that unassimilable wholly other.   ("Apocalypse" 28)

Among those poets who deliberately "multiply their strategic maneuvers" in order to broaden our means of assimilating the meaning of nuclear annihilation are Marc Kaminsky, Frederick Turner, and James Merrill. All three use history—the history of atomic weaponry as well as broader cultural history—which provides them with a context other than the primary subjective one of the lyric. Kaminsky uses the lyric sequence, but Turner and Merrill have written "epics," the one complete with knights and epic battles, the other employing conversations between this world and another by way of the Ouija board, from which the poet is to become educated to write "poems of science."

Through the dramatic monologue, the imagery of the aftermath at Hiroshima, and the loose adaptation to English of our Western notion of Japanese understated verse, Kaminsky's *The Road from Hiroshima* recreates the history of the bombing of Hiroshima, touching on the actual physical damage of the bombing itself, the residual physical and emotional effects on the *hibakusha,* and most poignantly, the sense of emptiness that has pervaded not only the victimized city but the rest of the world since August 6, 1945. As Kaminsky confesses in an afterword, his sequence relies heavily on extant literature about Hiroshima (John Hersey's *Hiroshima,* Masuji Ibuse's novel *Black Rain,* Michihiko Hachiya's *Hiroshima Diary,* Lifton's *Death in Life,* and other works by and about the A-bomb victims); so although he would have us understand his poems as (paraphrasing Marianne Moore) "imaginary journeys with real pushcarts in them" (111), most of those "pushcarts" are readily available to us elsewhere—not as poems, perhaps, but in imagery equally as striking, if not more vivid than Kaminsky's. For instance, there are these lines in "Congregation," spoken by the compassionate minister on trying to pull a victim out of a ditch:

> I grabbed his wrists
> but the skin of his hands came off
> in my hands
> I was left
> with a few glovelike pieces
> and the raw flesh
> clawed at the mud and the blue
> smoke over the ditch
> as he slipped back into the ditch.   (62)

Kaminsky captures not just the death and destruction of the bombing but the instinct to survive, too, as in "Dragonflies," whose speaker, Nakajima Hiroshi, in reaching the "outskirts of the ruined city" suddenly finds himself "greeted by / dragonflies / flitting this way and that" and remarks, "And I hated myself, realizing / that even on the day of horrors / I rejoiced!" (63).

The question remains, though, given the descriptive quality of his sources, as to what justifies Kaminsky's creative adaptation when the originals are themselves so powerful as literature. Both the first and last poems of the sequence ask this question; at first the poet accuses himself of being a "merchant of disaster" (15), and later he wonders about

> the difference between being
> a profiteer
> on the spiritual black market
>
> and a prophet
> who must tear everyone's heart
> to shreds.   (107)

Yet in each case such self-derision is followed by an avowed obligation (to whom? to the people of Hiroshima and Nagasaki? to all humankind?) to "work all the horror / into a play / of voices in which the living and the dead / live again" (15). Not to write this sequence, he concludes, is to betray "myself and all that / I love" (108), as though the book itself serves to purge the poet (and presumably his audience) of guilt, if not responsibility, for the bombing. In this way, I think, a historical sequence such as *The Road from Hiroshima* fits as much into the category of "protest" poetry as in any other—because of its wish to popularize the catastrophe, not for profit surely, but to fulfill the kind of missionary impulse common among anti-nuclear activists, reminding us of the human consequences of nuclear devastation.

Though Frederick Turner's *The New World* appears initially to display an even grander missionary zeal than Kaminsky's book, in fact this poet uses history in an entirely different manner to propose, as it were, *real* journeys with *imaginary* pushcarts in them, to suggest a *plausible* future alternative to nuclear annihilation, thereby diminishing its power over our imaginations. Like Ginsberg but unlike Kaminsky, Turner is shy neither about the implicit power of poetry nor about the explicit ambitions of his own epic, which, he boldly asserts in his "Introductory Note,"

> is to demonstrate that a viable future, a possible history, however imperfect, does lie beyond our present horizon of

apparent cultural exhaustion and nuclear holocaust. Art has
the world-saving function of imaginatively constructing
other futures that do not involve the Götterdämmerung of
mass suicide; because if there is no other imaginative future,
we will surely indeed *choose* destruction, being as we are
creatures of imagination.   (vii)

The epic form Turner embraces furnishes him with a broader
range in which to incorporate his discussion of history, economics,
technology, politics, and even genealogy than that of a poet like
Kaminsky (who basically uses the lyric premise). And Turner's
mythic landscape—from "the ruined city of Hattan" (Manhattan)
to the "blue hills" of Ahiah (24), which we traverse with the hero
James George Quincy, beginning in the year 2376—is resplendent
with details and a populace quite unlike our own, yet unquestionably rooted in the twentieth century, which this poem means to
comment on.

What strikes me as odd, though, given Turner's announced
intentions, is the manner in which he sidesteps the feasibility of
nuclear annihilation merely by assuming its historical insignificance. In Part II, he describes how the standoff of the twentieth-
century superpowers has come to result in "an empty travesty of
government [lingering] in Washington," its bureaucratic and military forces "frozen forever in the great electronic deadlock / of
2072" (39). Some pages later, we learn that in "the late twentieth
century / the heavy machines of battle began to become / so expen-
sive that wars collapsed for lack of munitions" and that

> the weapons of horror—gas, chemical, nuclear,
> biological—were practically useless, and beyond an
>   exchange
> or two, which proved to the advantage of all interested
> parties except the combatants, were never used.   (52)

The near future Turner imagines includes a limited nuclear war,
but not the global holocaust feared by writers like Schell and Carl
Sagan. Indeed, Turner explicitly resists "the image of war desired
by the dream of the twentieth / century," with its "towering mushroom cloud / according to [our] most beautiful theory of cause"
and its "explosion that effaces distinctions, / reduces all wholes to
their parts, and resolves the complexities / embroidered in matter

into a burst of radiant energy" (53). Such a notion, he explains, is "childish," the object of our "nightmare lust for cleanliness," and the result of our desire to "fall back on the comfort of despair," as he essentially dismisses our nuclear fears as untenable and, by doing so, assumes the continuity of humankind. The weight of these assertions, though, ultimately rests on "the new world" Turner portends: Does his epic charm us sufficiently to abandon our now-ingrained sense of annihilation? And what of the tacit acceptance of the concept of limited nuclear war here? For me, it is not the *condoning* of warfare in *The New World*—albeit a warfare of knights using swords as well as "cheap, homegrown microprocessor[s]" (52)—so much as it is the poet's overriding faith in the human ability (unlike other species) to beat extinction, a faith that permeates the very structure of the epic form Turner uses, that troubles the reading of this otherwise yeoman effort to combine Eastern and Western philosophies, American family sagas, science fiction, medieval *chansons de geste,* and Augustan tropology.

To understand James Merrill's attitude toward annihilation in his highly unorthodox epic trilogy *The Changing Light at Sandover*, the key term is "resistance." To be sure, this is not the place to attempt a full or even partial explication of this complexly spun allegory with its multifarious implications. But despite (if not because of) its idiosyncratic format of asserting the elaborate existence of the otherworldly—a Dantean world of spirits, angels, and others, accessible to us only by way of the Ouija board of the "Scribe" JM (Merrill) and his "Hand" DJ (David Jackson), seated together at the board like priests before an oracle—this poem invites us to join with its cast of characters in considering developments in atomic science as harbingers of annihilation. "THE ATOM," we learn from the spirit Ephraim in Book II, "IT IS ADAM & LIFE & THE UNIVERSE / LEAVE IT TO ITSELF & LET IT BREATHE" (118). The subsequent struggle between the otherworld's desire for all matter on earth to "hold" and the human embodiment of the "EVIL WE RELEASED . . . / CALL IT THE VOID CALL IT IN MAN A WILL TO NOTHINGNESS" (120) persists and becomes more and more prominent as the poem progresses.

In Book I, *The Book of Ephraim,* the benevolent spirit Ephraim early on indicates his deep-seated fear of the power of a nuclear-initiated metamorphosis, when he informs JM and DJ of how "THE AIR / ABOVE LOS ALAMOS IS LIKE A BREATH / SUCKED IN HORROR TOD MORT MUERTE DEATH" (33).

"NO SOULS CAME FROM HIROSHIMA U KNOW," he adds later, because "EARTH WORE A STRANGE NEW ZONE OF ENERGY" caused by "SMASHED ATOMS OF THE DEAD" (55). Then in Book II, *Mirabell's Books of Number,* speaking from "WITHIN THE ATOM" (113), the spirits instruct the mortals in the ways of the universe by drawing a dichotomy between the power of the atom, which is likened to the mystical power of the pyramid (126) and is capable of being "A SPEARHEAD / OF UN-LIFE" (146), and the worldly power of "THE LIFE RAFT LAN-GUAGE" (119). As Ginsberg and Turner also believe, the latter power belongs to poets, who can "STIR THE THINKERS & DE-TER THE REST" (118), thus enabling us to spare "THE GREEN-HOUSE" (earth) from annihilation. But for both spirits and mortals, "THE SINGLE CONTEST IS THE ATOM": "PUT SIMPLY THE ATOM IS L SIDED / ITS POSITIVE SIDE GOOD ITS NEGATIVE SIDE AH WHAT TO SAY / A DISAP-PEARANCE AN ABSOLUTE VOID" (119).

As the poem explores this "contest" of the atom, it delves not only into nuclear physics but into genetics, astronomy, and the history of science, as well as into music, literature, and philosophy, all glossed with Merrill's characteristic light touch. Eventually, in Book III, *Scripts for the Pageant,* the concept of annihilation gains center stage. "The Last Lessons: 3," for example, opens with Gabriel, the "Angel of Fire and Death," once again defining nothingness:

> OUR POET ASKED: THIS BLACK BEYOND BLACK,
>   IS IT A STOP TO DREAM?
> POET, NO, FOR IT IS A DREAM.
> IS IT THE HOURGLASS DRAINED OF TIME?
> NO, FOR IT IS THE HOURGLASS IN WHICH
>   S A N D   R U N S   U P !   (448)

The negative power of the atom, JM and DJ soon learn, is intricately woven into "TIME'S REVERSIBILITY, / THAT IDEA OF DESTRUCTION WHICH RESIDES / BOTH IN MAN & IN THE ACTINIDES" (453). Such power "TO SUCK THE EARTH / EGG TO AN O" has always been present in the universe, but what has kept this power in check is matter, or the earth "GREEN-HOUSE" itself, whose "BIRTH" is "RESISTANCE," the ability to hold together. When JM finally realizes that "The Greenhouse from the start had been / An act of resistance," the spirit of George Cotzias congratulates him for understanding:

> JIMMY YES   A PLUS!
> OR DISOBEDIENCE   GOD AS PROMETHEUS?
> NOW THAT MAN TAPS THIS 2ND POWER, ONE
>   WELL
> TOO MANY & PUFF! Puff? THE WHOLE FRAIL
>   EGGSHELL
> SIMPLY IMPLODING AS THE MONITOR'S
> BLACK FILLS THE VACUUM MOTHER N[ature]
>   ABHORS.   (453)

Although JM and DJ seem to want guidance from the spirits they consult, *The Changing Light at Sandover* prefers instead to investigate the relationships between ideas, people, language, and symbols, rather than simply to protest the human misuse of the atom or to indulge in extremist predictions about our nuclear future. But just how seriously are we to take Merrill's concept of "resistance"? Critics so far seem deadlocked between those who consider the trilogy "a poem less of authority than of companionship" (von Hallberg, *American Poetry* 114) and those who admire its "grand heterocosm—a world elsewhere, a rival plenitude designed both to imitate and preserve the totality of our world, now threatened by extinction" (Berger 285). Toward the end of *Scripts for a Pageant,* the Scribe JM finally asks, in simple terms, "Resistance— Nature's gift to man— / What form will it assume in Paradise?" (511), to which Nature herself (e.g., Psyche or Chaos) replies that Paradise

> . . . WILL HOLD A CREATURE MUCH LIKE
>   DARLING MAN, YET PHYSICALLY MORE
>   ADAPTABLE.
> HIS IMMORTALITY WILL CONSIST OF
>   PROLONGATION, IN THE BEGINNING PHASE,
>   UNTIL HIS IDEAL IS REACHED IN NUMBER.
> THEN TIME WILL STOP
> AND LONG FRUITFUL SPACES BE GIVEN HIM TO
>   LEARN THROUGH SONG AND POETRY
> OF HIS OLD HELPLESS FEELINGS & WEARY PAST.

THE RESISTANCE? NONE. HE WILL, YES, SWIM
    & GLIDE,
A SIMPLER, LESS WILFUL BEING.   (512)

This exit speech, not unlike Prospero's epilogue to *The Tempest*, imagines an ideal post-apocalyptic world at once alluring and disconcerting. Is it an image of annihilation we can accept, or is this merely the suave poet Merrill poking fun at his own language and its poetic conventions?

What, then, is this "image of annihilation," this "way of nothingness," the nuclear age requires us to live with? My last category turns away from the imagery of nuclear war itself to concentrate on yet another level of Lifton's idea of "the absurdity of our double life." Lifton writes:

> A third layer of absurdity has to do with the mind's relationship to the "thing." We simply cannot locate in our images anything like this "nuclear holocaust." Here is the special absurdity of the mind, our struggle with our limited capacity to (in [Martin] Buber's phrase) "imagine the real."   (*Weapons* 5)

What Lifton means here is not the *process* of a nuclear holocaust (which we *can* imagine, with its mushroom clouds, fireballs, scorched human skin, and so on) but *the condition of extinction,* a condition that has already invaded our consciousness:

> The image in question, really *imagery of extinction,* has never taken on sharp contours for me. Rather than experience the ready psychic flow associated with most lively images, I must struggle amorphously to encompass the *idea* of violently attained nothingness.   (*Weapons* 58)

This condition of extinction is something we know nothing about, yet it has come to interfere with our daily understanding of the present as well as of the future, and it is that interference and its impact on us as human beings that poets are best equipped to articulate for us, as they uncover whatever they can about living, in no matter what age.[5] Poems such as Thom Gunn's "The Annihilation of Nothing,"[6] Alan Dugan's "Winter: For an Untenable Situation," and John Ashbery's "Blue Sonata," among others, treat precisely this psychic condition Lifton has identified without having to concern themselves with nuclear war itself.

In Dugan's relatively straightforward, satiric poem, for example, he captures our sense of the uncertainty of the future by focusing first on its effects on "our" current behavior ("oh we will burn the house itself / for warmth"), then on how "we" would be likely to consider the present (which *does* exist) from the perspective of a future that may or may not exist, after "the last brick of the fireplace / has been cracked for its nut of warmth" (130). Using an extended metaphor the way Rich does in "Trying to Talk with a Man," Dugan employs mostly accessible images to develop his idea—"the white refrigerator car" of winter contrasted by images of "the burning house, the burning tree, / the burning you, the burning me, / the ashes, the brick-dust, the bitter iron." But his poem is ultimately as much an account of earth's annihilation as it is of the end of an affair or the depletion of fuel supplies, because however we interpret it, it succeeds in conveying the *idea* of extinction without having to imagine anything particularly concrete about what extinction entails, since all of the poem's images are part of the present. What matters to Dugan is not just the possibility of annihilation but understanding how the uncertainty of it, the unknown quality of it, influences our current behavior.

Uncertainty is also at the center of Ashbery's "Blue Sonata," as it is in much of his poetry—so much so that critics have both praised him for reaching "a new threshold for incoherence and randomness, leading to affirmations of freedom" (Shapiro 32), and attacked him for his "poetry of non-production" which "threatens to destroy the enterprise of art altogether" (Richman 68). (This particular combination sounds strangely like the prescription for contemporary artists provided by Schell, doesn't it?)

Composed in imitation of the sonata form, "Blue Sonata" specifically considers how we understand the present, how we try to understand it from other temporal viewpoints, and how in the end we live in it. It begins by looking at the present from the perspective of the past, in order that we might recall how we used to look at the future with its contingent uncertainties and with the understanding that "*that* now" (the present which was once the future) "is our destiny / No matter what else may happen to us" (*Houseboat* 66). In short, we are both the mere subjects of time's fancy and an integral part of the present, that "part of the day [which] comes every day." And as long as "we not give up that inch," that "breath /

Of becoming before becoming may be seen," we can believe ourselves to be both present and in the flux of time. But in the second
stanza, the poet explains how, in coming to know something we
did not know in the past (some new idea about ourselves), there
inevitably comes with it "a grain of curiosity . . . that unrolls / Its
question mark like a new wave on the shore," and "we have . . .
gained or been gained / By what was passing through"; that is, in
the same moment in which we look backwards to gain some new
understanding of the present we create for ourselves the uncertainty
of our future, and as a consequence, "We live in the sigh of our
present" (67).

For Ashbery, if all we needed to understand the future was to
study the past,

> we could re-imagine the other half, deducing it
> From the shape of what is seen, thus
> Being inserted into its idea of how we
> Ought to proceed.   (*Houseboat* 67)

But such a complete parallel would be "tragic," he says, "For
progress occurs through re-inventing / These words from a dim
recollection of them." To extrapolate here, according to my focus,
we must remember that the *true* uncertainty of our nuclear future
relies on the fact that, despite the seeming inevitability of annihilation, it may after all *not* occur, and it would be "tragic" for us to
assume such a future, "to fit / Into the space created by our not
having arrived yet." It is at least *partially* up to us to decide how to
"re-invent" a way of "violating" the "space" of the future "in such
a way as / To leave it intact." In other words, given this critical role
to play in "the sigh of our present,"

> we do after all
> Belong here, and have moved a considerable
> Distance; our passing is a facade.
> But our understanding of it is justified.   (67)

In addition to its intellectual affinity with the nuclear age, "Blue
Sonata" in its tone of acceptance and resolve, *akirame* and self-
consciousness, accurately embodies the predominant sense of uncertainty of "our present." Its elusive style seems to me not only
appropriate, but essential to the difficulty of its subject matter. The
risk of arbitrary meaning, of creating chaos among that which is

signified, in an Ashbery poem such as this one partakes of what Derrida calls "destinerrance," namely, "a wandering that is its own end." In the nuclear age, argues Derrida, "destinerrance" itself, however, "no longer gives us the assurance of a sending of being, of a recovery of the sending of being"; that is to say, the "randomness and incalculability," which are an "essential" element of "destinerrance," are not just factors of uncertainty that affect the "margin of indeterminacy" of a "calculable decision," but are rather factors that may "escape all control, all reassimilation or self-regulation of a system that they will have *precipitously* . . . but irreversibly destroyed" ("Apocalypse" 29). In the nuclear age, to risk disorder or chaos has come to be the equivalent of risking annihilation, in that a missile sent, a word spoken, or a head nodded can have irreversible consequences on the very source from which it originates—or so we have come to realize. Such a mode of thinking, what Derrida calls "the aleatory destinerrance of the *envoi*," "allows us to think . . . the age of nuclear war," allows us to create those conditions for potential annihilation we have during this century.[7] But "only in the nuclear age," he adds, has this "thought . . . been able to become a radical one" ("Apocalypse" 30), in that only now can we, must we, scrutinize its metaphysical underpinnings. The poems in this fourth category, I believe, express this "aleatory destinerrance" and, by risking meaninglessness, renew for us in poetry the same question Derrida ultimately returns to: "Why is there something instead of nothing?"

As Derrida concludes, "nuclear war—as a hypothesis, a phantasm, of total self-destruction—can only come about in the name of that which is worth more than life, that which, giving its value to life, has greater value than life" ("Apocalypse" 30). "But," he points out, "as it is in the name of something whose name, in this logic of total destruction, can no longer be borne, transmitted, inherited by anything living, that name in the name of which war would take place would be the name of nothing, it would be pure name" (30–31). As such, like the history professor from Hiroshima, we are faced with going "the way of nothingness," whether a nuclear apocalypse occurs or not. I, for one, have no expectation that the omnipresent threat of nuclear annihilation will diminish in my lifetime, but "we do after all / Belong here." Maybe with the help of poets like Ashbery, Ginsberg, Rich, Merrill, and others, who are re-inventing our language, heaving our sigh, and imaging the real, we will yet be able to change our ways of thinking and spare ourselves and our kind from a last catastrophe.

Self

KENITH L. SIMMONS

The Missing "I":
Poetry from *Kayak* in the 1980s

In discussing the traditional function of little magazines, T. S. Eliot wrote:

> For this immediate future, perhaps for a long way ahead, the continuity of culture may have to be maintained by a very small number of people indeed—and these not necessarily the best equipped with worldly advantages. It will not be the large organs of opinion or the old periodicals: it must be the small and obscure papers and reviews, those which hardly are read by anyone but their own contributors, that will keep critical thought alive and encourage authors of original talent.   (Pollack 298)

From its inception in 1964, George Hitchcock's little magazine *Kayak* certainly served these functions. With no outside funding— not even grants from the National Endowment for the Arts (*Kayak* #59)—Hitchcock produced a magazine of contemporary poetry, fiction, and some criticism that did all of what Eliot asked; it encouraged writers of original talent, many of whom enjoyed their first national publication in its pages, and it provided a forum for discussions of poetic issues by poets and committed readers. Throughout its history, *Kayak* earned a special kind of respect among aficionados of small press publications (Anderson and Kinzie; Peters 44; Pollack 298) for the consistently high quality of its contents. With issue #64 in May 1984, Hitchcock brought the 20-year existence of his excellent little magazine to an end. "Any more," he wrote, "and it would risk becoming an institution. After that, ossification and rigor mortis. So we think it's time to close up the shutters."

It seems appropriate at a Jubilation of Poets to acknowledge the contribution of the magazine; at the same time, as academic conferees, we can take this opportunity to ask what its contents can tell us about the current state of contemporary poetry. Since a complete history and analysis of *Kayak*'s and George Hitchcock's contribution to contemporary literature is a project more elaborate than time permits me here, I will take a smaller time period—the 1980s—and focus on a single problem that has occupied both reviewers and poets during that period in *Kayak*'s pages: the problem of contemporary poetry's ability and willingness to fulfill one of poetry's traditional functions, the expression of the self.

One would expect this to be a central concern of poetry in *Kayak*. Although the magazine has been identified with surrealism throughout its history, as Peter Martin has noted, this description is somewhat dubious, arising from a much more obvious tendency toward inwardness and the dislocated image (Anderson and Kinzie 707). Hitchcock himself has clarified his editorial intentions by noting that he wanted to publish poetry "showing . . . tendencies [which] can . . . be roughly defined as various branches of contemporary romanticism" (Anderson and Kinzie 442).

Appropriately, a substantial portion of both the journal's verse and its criticism during the 1980s takes part in a uniquely contemporary controversy, which goes to the heart of the romantic tradition, questioning as it does poetry's ability to express the emotional and perceptual core of the poet. A number of critics and poets published in *Kayak* in recent years have articulated the sense that while one of the central functions of both traditional and contemporary romantic poetry is self identification and self expression, many contemporary poets with romantic inclinations may be unable to write poems that fulfill that function.

In his critical article "Contemporary Mannerism: American Poetry Slips into Something Comfortable," which appeared in *Kayak*'s September 1980 issue (#54), Mark Jarman charges:

> A mannerist poetry is being written in America right now and, in fact, seems to be a predominant style, if not the latest craze. The poems are reactions against the contemporary emphasis on the self, with its traditional roots in Whitman and Dickinson; as poems they point only to their form, and the focus they lack or evade is any emotion orig-

inal to the poet. . . . Mannerism is both [an inevitable] reaction and an evasion. . . . Through overemphasis, the self
in American poetry has been reduced. It is something like a
black hole. It no longer produces poetry, it eats it up. These
three poets [Norman Dubie, Ai, and James Tate, whose recent books Jarman was reviewing in the article] and others,
have responded with a style of poetry that will not be
sucked into the "hungry self," as Norman Dubie has called
it.   (67, 71)

In *Kayak*'s last twelve issues, there are five major categories
of poems that avoid the expression of the poet's personal concerns
or emotions and that could be said to create forms that dead-end
in themselves: poems that focus on the sound and structure of
language; poems that focus on objects without the romantic metaphor linking them to the poet's condition; dramatic narratives;
"found poems"; and poems that respond to other works of art,
generally by describing them. Each of these more or less blocks the
reader's path, deflecting us from consideration of the poet's individual self.

Within these poems there are few or no clues to the reasons for
this apparent retreat from self expression. A substantial body of poetry that appeared in *Kayak* during its last years, however, does
shed light on the problem. Although these poems take the poet's
self for their subject in ways recognizably romantic, at the same
time they suggest that the whole notion of a romantic transcendent
self has become problematic in the contemporary period. Rather
than *hiding* "the undesired self . . . with its secondhand senti-
ments," as Jarman charges James Tate with doing, the poets whose
work I will address last in this paper face the terrifying fact that
where we expect to find our unique being, we now find either a
splintered, unstable bundle of "selves" frequently at war, or else
nothing at all. The most radical contribution of post-structuralist
thought to contemporary intellectual life has been the notion that
the unique individual self, which was for romantic tradition the seat
and proper subject for poetry, is more than culturally conditioned,
it is culturally created—in short, an illusion of culture. The preoccupation with this concept by semiologists, novelists, filmmakers,
and literary critics is a defining characteristic of this period in our
cultural history. For a magazine that was created to express a

uniquely contemporary strain of romanticism, the question of how to deal with the loss of self, or at least the loss of certainty about its nature, would naturally be of immense concern.

First, let us turn to poetry that can legitimately be said to block the reader's access to the poet's emotions. In his *Black and Blue Guide to Current Literary Journals,* Robert Peters referred to Heather McHugh's offerings in *Kayak* #59 (June 1982) as "word riffs" (46), a useful term for poems that are essentially joyful but impersonal wordplay. McHugh's "I knew I'd Sing" begins:

> A few sashay, a few
> finagle. Some make
> whoopee, some
> make good. But most
>
> make diddly-squat.
> I tell you this
> is what I love
> about America—the words
>
> it puts in my mouth. . . .

Others who have contributed work in this vein to *Kayak* include Michael McFee (#54), Felix Pollack (#54), and Bob Heman (#58).

A related phenomenon is the poem about objects or abstractions, which in traditional romantic poetry would catalyze a meditation on the self. But these poems remain focused on the object or abstraction for its own sake. Sue Owen's poem on the birth and life of a "Zero" (#60) is a good example of this type of poem, as is Michael McFee's "possuma" (#62) on the American, literary, and natural history of the possum. As with the poems about language, these poems short-circuit access to the poet.

"Found poems" are a regular feature of *Kayak.* Unlike McFee's poem, which weaves fact into poetry, the found poem is generally a word-for-word transcription, although graphically rearranged into verse lines, of something that appeared elsewhere as prose, such as an advertisement or a list. For example Mark Doty's "Twentyfive Racehorses" (#64) is simply a list of horses' names:

> Summer June, Rusty Stars, Stormy Red,
> Prairie Star, Niagara Dancer,
> Deeper Than Deep,
> Oh Why Not.

In a journal that prints a great deal of verse with images on the order of "I have a clock of leaves a wrist of bells" (from a poem by Tom McKeown in #59), Doty's racehorse names do in fact present an interesting flow of mental images; but since the poems are always clearly identified as "found poems," we are always aware that they do not express any dream or hallucinatory experience of the poet who contributed them.

David Wagoner is particularly adept at the found poem. While most poems of this type and most of Wagoner's own found poems are humorous, his "In Distress" (#54), selected from *International Code of Signals* published by the U.S. Naval Oceanographic Office, is a harrowing account of the sinking of a ship after a serious nuclear accident and failed attempts to rescue its crew, told through radio communication between the ship's officer and the rescue team. Other contributors of found poems include Tom Hansen (#57), Robert Dana (#58), Jackson Wheeler (#60), and Tom Wayman (#62).

The third variety of poem found regularly in *Kayak* that masks the self is the dramatic narrative poem. Clearly, not all dramatic poems provide an opaque shield for the poet. While classic dramatic monologues like those contributed by Hayden Carruth and Lyn Lifshin to issue #63 (November 1983) provide personae that shield the poets, they do reveal basic values: Lifshin's social/political consciousness and Carruth's awareness of the power and limitations of art and the inspired moment.

Further divorced from the romantic lyric and more appropriate to our discussion are the dramatic poems of Frederick Morgan (editor of *The Hudson Review* and regular contributor to *Kayak*) and Pattiann Rogers (a *Kayak* regular during the 1980s). Morgan's "Captain Blaze" (#58) is a gothic tale told by a lawyer who received a summons from the mysterious and probably evil Captain Blaze, erstwhile tropical sailor, in the dead of night to consult about a will. When the lawyer arrives amid strange sounds and not-quite-seen intruders, Blaze is dead in his chair. The poem is entirely mystery and atmosphere; when the coroner finds that Blaze has been dead for 48 hours, the persona's final line is "I mentioned to no one I'd taken his call that same morning."

Pattiann Rogers has created a family of strange children named Albert, Sonia, Cecil, Gordon, and Felicia, who engage for fun in Borgesian speculation. In "Parlor game on a snowy winter night" (#56), the children begin with the proposition, offered by Albert, that "False china eggs in a chicken's nest stimulate / The hen to lay eggs that are real, / And they also occasionally fool weasels." After several stanzas of speculation on the different ethical judgment that chickens and weasels would bring to bear on this deception, the children turn to speculation about illusion and reality:

> "China eggs, whether warm or not," said Felicia,
> Mocking herself in the mirror, "at least consistently
>   maintain
> Their existence as false eggs."

> "Perhaps the true egg, unable to maintain its reality
> For long is actually a weak imitation
> Of the eternal nature of the glass egg," replied Albert
> Drawing his initials on the frosty windowpane.

> "Someone must investigate how the real image
> Of a false egg in the chicken's true eye causes the cells
> Of a potential egg to become an actuality," said Gordon
> laying his book on the table.

> "Can we agree then that the false china egg,
> A deception but actual instigator,
> is the first true beginning of the chicken yard?"
> Asked Sonia, filling in the last line of the gamesheet.

> Albert, rushing outdoors to discover
> What the dogs had cornered in the brush beside the barn
> Found a weasel in the snow
> With bloody yolk on its whiskers and a broken tooth.

In "the pursuit as solution" (#59), Albert wants to know what is on the other side of his mind. The poem is an infinite regression on what would happen if he could enter a bird's throat without hurting it, pulling the whole world in behind him and eventually pulling the bird into its own throat, turning Albert's mind inside out.

Mark Jarman has asserted that, "The most stimulating struggle in contemporary American poetry . . . [is] between narrative and non-narrative verse" (334). A wide range of narrative poetry representing a variety of degrees of opacity in regard to the poets' emotions comprises a substantial portion of the poetry Kayak has published since 1980. Jarman himself is among those who have contributed narrative poems to the journal (#61), as are Robin Skelton (#54), Sharon Olds (#58), Mekeel McBride (#58), and Carolyne Wright (#61).

A last category of impersonal poem frequently found in *Kayak* is the poem about other art forms. Virtuoso examples that have appeared during the 1980s include Robert Bly's "20 Poems in homage to max ernst" (#55). Five of the 20 are illustrated by graphics from Ernst's *A Week of Kindness,* a collage novel first published in 1934 and reprinted by Dover Books in 1981. These five allow us to understand that each of the 20 is a verse equivalent to the collage, supplying some narrative detail, but generally captioning the picture. Other poems of this type include Stephen Dobyns's "Three Poems after Paintings by Balthus" (#58) and Herbert Morris's "the music," on a painting by Felix von Ende (#61). *Kayak*'s own graphics have inspired poetry, as in Allan Cooper's "Three poems on covers from *Kayak*" (#64).

It is clear that these five types of poems deflect the reader from the poet's personal concerns and emotions. In speculating as to the *reason* for the surprisingly large number of poems of this sort in a journal dedicated to contemporary romanticism, let us turn again to Jarman on "Contemporary Mannerism." At the end of his piece he remarks that the evasion he detects in much of contemporary poetry might be the result of a dilemma—the absence of *feeling,* which leaves the poet nothing but form. "Without feeling, form is all we have. . . . The discomfort I feel in reading the poems by these poets is the emptiness of mannerism. And their apparent refusal to face it" (71).

That there might be a dilemma at the heart of the phenomenon is plausible, but I would like to suggest an alternative reading of its nature. There is evidence to suggest that the dilemma is in fact the perception on the part of many contemporary poets that the singular core identity itself—at least as we know it through traditional romanticism—is absent. While many of the poems cited above could be said to evade the romantic issue of self entirely, in *Kayak*'s pages we find a substantial body of poetry that *would* take a traditionally romantic self-expressive position if the poet were not limited by his or her belief that the traditional romantic *self* is illusory, or dissolved, or simply lost.

The first of these—the notion that the self as it is usually understood is illusory—is addressed repeatedly in poetry by Greek poet Tasos Livadhitis, translated for *Kayak* by Kimon Friar. His

"Painting by an Unknown Artist" (#58) states the problem in a highly provocative way:

> And I have always lived with myself, like two acrobats
>   consumed with deadly hate,
> who swear at each other all day long and intrigue and plot
>   each other's death,
> but when the time comes, and the lights go on, and the
>   theater overbrims with an enormous expectation,
> then behold how both of them stand erect on the limitless,
>   fatal rope
> and find themselves now beyond hatred and danger and
>   admiration
> and time—in brotherly concord suddenly
>   within the supreme worth of Art.

At first glance, this is the classic romantic poem, wherein the limitations of human existence, in this case the divided personality, are repaired within the confines of art. But the controlling metaphor of this poem and those of other Livadhitis poems published with it force us to modulate that reading substantially. While art and its attendant risks bring the factions together in brotherly concord, it would be hard to argue that this high-wire act is more significant, more authentic, than the time between acts when the two acrobats actually plot each other's death. Rather than an ode to Art—and the word is capitalized here—it would be more appropriate to read the poem as an ironic comment on the absurdity of bringing about the temporary but utterly ungenuine focused identity or voice generally deemed necessary for art. The risks of art, here performance on the high wire, pale beside the risks of living daily with someone who plots your death: your own warring, schizoid being! Livadhitis's "Small Existential Parenthesis" (#58) reiterates his notion of the violence that he sees at the human core:

> Who are you then behind this face which changes every day,
>   who are you behind all your daily acts, behind the
>   acts you meditate at night?
> Numberless persons within you, each one seeks to exist
>   by killing the other—which is the true one? Which is
>   that face no mirror can give you?

> Rapes, violence, terrors, crimes you have not committed
>   dominate your blood. Each of your gestures is heavy
>   with thousands of alien and unknown destinies.
>   When you say: I hate, the first murder in the world
>   occurs in you again,
> while from the depths of your self-sacrifice then unsleeping
>   calculating eyes
>   of your hairy ancestor gaze at you ironically.

In other works by Livadhitis, the self is a terrifying kaleidoscope held in the weakest semblance of stability by faceless authorities. In "Precautions," "one morning you wake up and find to your surprise that you've become another person." Panic stricken, the persona runs to the police who look at him indifferently as he begs for "at least . . . a new identity card." In "Able to Work," the persona is executed every morning at seven and then summoned to identify himself before he is given newspapers to deliver (#58).

In other poems that have appeared in *Kayak* in the 1980s, the center where a stable identity might be expected disappears under the pressure of, and in reaction to, specific (although not always explicitly identified) life experiences. For Judith Berke in poems contributed to issue #59, self effacement—even to the point of mental illness—is a protective mechanism. In "scenarios," she plays out various childhood scenes involving herself and her absent parents: a surrealistic scene in Venice, a sad and lonely one in New York where "the Child plays chess, speaking / in two voices." "If," the poem suggests,

> the woman sat opposite the child,
> dogs around her, the man called
> father might enter. He might embrace
> the woman . . .
> It's hard to say because I'm
> never there.

In "the house," although her friends recommend that she paint her walls white and do other repairs, the persona paints her rocking chair the strange color of the walls and rocks calmly until she is possessed by a shape that enters her sleep, wraps around her when she wakes, breathes through her mouth, and speaks through her. In "dance," a man and woman dance around a table never stumbling although a surrealistic cavalcade of images and objects swirls around them. "The idea is you don't look / at the table. / You dance." In Rohana McCormack's "the woman sawed in half" (#63), the persona has a dream in which, at the command of her mate, she becomes a bat, a woman, a mouse, a dove, his "Beatrice," and an image from Chagall. Although she wakes

> no worse for wear.
> While I dandle at your side bedazzled
> by your urbane patter, you distract all eyes
> from pulleys and wires.

Franz Douskey's "Incipient Flu, or the Day I Went Out of My Mind To Avoid the Draft" (#63) has its persona sand its fingerprints, don a pink wig, and get a job singing torch songs in a smoky Paris night club to avoid induction.

> That was years ago. The turns,
> the false identities, the pastel
> wigs, and the talcum pallor.
> Let them come after me now.
> They'll never find the real one.

For Dionisio Martinez, loss of identity is a function of transience. His "one drawer full of night" (#62) asserts: "That's how it is every time I leave, / everytime anyone leaves: / something always stays." While, for the romantic, poetry might once have been the route back through memory to what has been lost, Martinez claims to be a crippled romantic who has forgotten how to use both the power of imagination and language for this purpose.

> If we could retrace a few steps
> between the people we were and the ones
> we've become after the losses;
> if we knew the way back to one vacant
> room, one drawer full of night.
> But somewhere along the way we forgot
> the language and the purpose of the stars,
> somehow we became our own absence.

One of the most interesting poets working with the absent self is Herbert Morris, who has published in *Kayak* regularly since the 1960s. Morris's poems are lush, extended, generally narrative meditations, which bear an ironic resemblance to paradigmatic romantic poems like Coleridge's "Frost at Midnight" or Wordsworth's "Tintern Abbey." Like them, the poems begin with a visual image that inspires a self-conscious meditation. But where the personality of the romantic poet would be, Morris's poems circle around an absence. Two excellent examples of this are "lost" (#59) and "Some Details of Conditions on Arrival" (#63). In "lost," the persona receives an anonymous envelope containing photographs of the same group of young soldiers posing in new uniforms. Although he doesn't recognize the men or the location, he suspects that "these lives pertain to me." One photograph in particular

> holds me longer,
> slowly, and much more deeply, draws me in,
> binds me, rivets me, all at once locates me
> at the center of its white light, its weather.

The soldiers pose on the outside stairs of a building; the persona scrutinizes wood and stairs until

> it seems to become all of a piece, wood
> gains a smoothness beyond wood, wells like light
> for all its seamlessness, but dark, cold light,
> so dark that what you touch you know you touch
> in the name of the irretrievable.

Certain he will find himself among the soldiers, although he knows he isn't there, he

> implore[s his] wrists and ankles to remember
> what they may have forgotten of that pose.
> . . . .
> but of course, they remember nothing, nothing.
> One looks even for one's familiar squint
> under the brunt of it, against the glare,
> but none of the young men, it seems are squinting,
> none of their faces bear a mark or crease.

Like the location, like the wood, like the uniforms, the men's faces are unmarked by any singularity. All dissolve in the anonymous light that drenches the photograph. Where the traditional romantic poem would bore inward from the image, here, the poet yearns for self-awareness but remains dead-ended on the surface of the photograph.

"Some Details of Conditions on Arrival" works in a related way, but here it is as if the poet has entered the picture, which remains equally suggestive and equally uninformative. The poem begins with a small blonde girl and four dogs on a blue and yellow carpet. Other elements of the scene are the absence of windows or a view; distant, half-remembered music; light that is "less than spare"; and sounds the poet cannot accurately pinpoint. The poet-persona enters, but the girl seems not to notice. Of the dogs, only one notices at first, then all four approach the persona. Although he knows neither the girl nor the dogs (nor whether the dogs belong to the girl), he knows the dogs' names and how to touch and speak to them. He does not know whose house he is in nor why he knows the dogs' names. A history, which he suspects he knew, he has forgotten or "is the sum of what has not been decided, / the burden entered with, strapped to my back."

> I want to ask her what it is she waits for
> why the light where she waits is less than spare,
> or less than light, but I know it is fruitless,
> fruitless to ask what it is I would ask,
>
> fruitless to hold out hope of being answered.
> How does one shape the sound of what detains us?
> How does one give the look of it, the feel,
> the weight of afternoon on tattered carpets
>
> in a house through which old tunes drift like smoke,
> where a young girl sits quietly with dogs,
> four dogs, none or all of which may be hers,
> somewhere rain dripping slowly from the trees?
>
> I want to ask whose life these dogs have strayed from. I
>   want to
> know the man they think I am. I want to taste what they
>   taste
> when they lick me. I want to hear the salt pronounce its
>   name.

The *urge* to seek his own identity is there; the ability to follow through, to penetrate, is not.

Ironically, during the nineteenth century and in much contemporary literature the problem for the romantic is solipsism. For the poets discussed above, and for many more working in the same vein, the problem is a feeling of divorce from a unified self, of being locked out rather than locked in.

For 20 years *Kayak* has performed the important function of making a place for fresh and original voices in the contemporary romantic tradition. Whether romanticism can flourish in the post-structuralist era when the very existence of a transcendent self is in doubt remains to be seen. Another open question is *where* fresh expressions of contemporary romantic literature are most likely to be seen in the absence of George Hitchcock's fine journal.

PETER A. SIEDLECKI

Gerald Stern's Mediation
of the I and the I

When Walt Whitman celebrated and sang himself, he included his readers in his salute by having each of them assume his assumption, that of a particular self to be signified by the pronoun *I*—a new self, a fully involved and aware self able to understand experience as it has not been understood before. By having his reader assume his perspective, the poet can do what the eye does for the rest of the body, one of the announced intentions contained in the preface to the 1855 edition of *Leaves of Grass*. Employing the first person as he does, Whitman not only charges his poetry with the immediacy and energy that comes from eyewitness accounts; he also establishes a situation that allows him to watch himself watching. Poems like "Out of the Cradle Endlessly Rocking," "When Lilacs Last in the Dooryard Bloom'd" and "The Sleepers" derive much of their power from the mediation of the two I's.

Most contemporary American poetry written from the first-person perspective divides into two categories that correspond generally to Whitman's two I's: the egocentric and the proprioceptive. The former, a result, perhaps, of T. S. Eliot's "objective correlative," places the poet at the center of chaotic circumstance, which is working its effect on him. The attitude of such poetry is decidedly modernist in that the circumstances can have a detrimental effect through their contrast with the narrator's expectations. Since the gap between what *is* and what *should be* cannot be bridged, there is an acknowledgment in the egocentric poem, either asserted or implied, of the necessity of tragedy. This awareness of disjunction is the controlling idea in Delmore Schwartz, John Berryman, Sylvia Plath, and others of the so-called confessional school.

The proprioceptive position, as defined by Charles Olson, demands a "washing out of the ego"; the poet functions as receptor, a

vessel for the poem's occasion. The proprioceptive poet is a re-
porter of stimuli experienced through the massive complexity of
the human body as a compound sense organ. The unique self, with
its peculiar rhythms, its tensions and relaxations, through which
experience is mediated, is the sole agent precluding the absolute
objectivity of the poem's report. The proprioceptive attitude is
conspicuously postmodernist. Ronald Sukenick, for example, has
admitted to the influence of Olson's poetics on his concept of the
Bossa Nova novel—that of no plot, no character, no interpretation,
no meaning, nothing but *being,* as object in the world.[1]

For the egocentric poet, the difference between what *is* and what
should be is irremediably disjunctive; and the first-person narrator,
necessarily, sees himself as victim, no matter how blithely he may
state his situation. This victimization is totally out of place in the
proprioceptive poem; if its first-person narrator apprehends chaos,
he acknowledges it as that which *is* and not as a condition suggesting what *should be.* Comment and judgment are suspended, and the
circumstance is merely presented.

While the egocentric posture is weakened perhaps by a pervasive
subjectivity that permits a biased view of circumstances as spiritually arid or boring or abusive or generally not as they should be,
the proprioceptive stance might be seen as excessively objective,
satisfied with the poem's function as created object having no responsibility. The former posture might be conducive to a sort of
poetic blindness that neglects all but the images and events that cor-
roborate the poet's vision of what should be. The latter position, on
the other hand, could become so all-inclusive and indiscriminate as
to be incoherent. But the strengths of the respective positions are as
obvious as their limitations. The immediacy and intimacy of the
personal response excites the voyeuristic urge in the reader who desires knowledge of how this *I* felt an experience in a shared universe. The proprioceptive approach encourages a more intellectual
urge that involves the mind's potential for establishing connections
where no such connections seem to exist except within the consciousness of the *I* that issues its particular report of its experience.

Christopher Clausen's reductive, and ultimately regressive, study
The Place of Poetry comments on Schwartz's position that confes-
sionalism is an inevitable result of the poet's isolation. Clausen suggests that when the poet finds himself incapable of writing for or
about anything other than himself the decline of poetry as a cultural
force is complete. Clausen finds a similar anti-cultural bent in the

Williams-Olson tendency to test the possibilities of language as contributing to the process of discovering that which is unknown even to the poet. He believes such an approach is pertinent to too exclusive an audience and accuses proprioceptive writers of seeking refuge from chaos in a quasi-scientific objectivity that removes itself from the felt concerns of humanity (124–26). The critic Ihab Hassan, long an interested observer of contemporary developments in fiction, recently in the *New York Times Book Review* expressed similar misgivings about the directions assumed by the postmodernists.

While some of Clausen's objections to the two approaches may be valid, he is on problematic ground when he implies that poetry could be revitalized as a cultural force, that it could regain the kind of popularity poetry enjoyed in the nineteenth century, if the poet would respond to certain traditional demands. Significant among these demands would be the poet's demonstration of concern for the audience and its desire to make sense out of life. Aspects of poetry that are familiar and, therefore, comforting to the reader, such as rhyme and meter, suggests Clausen, might be one way to bring order into the disorderly condition of contemporary poetry and into the life of the reader (122–25). He cites the persistence of rhyme and meter in poems written for children as a "conspicuous survival," and he blames the prominence of pop-poets like Rod McKuen not on the readers, but on the poets who have refused to acknowledge readers' needs and have, thus, abandoned them to the likes of McKuen.

Obviously, if poets were to conform to Clausen's concept of "traditional demands," they would cease to participate in the poetic process. They would have to confer on themselves the undue authority to order a disorderly universe, and in assuming this role, rather than that of maker, they would become reproducers of the reader's predilections, makers of something that fits. Rather than contributing to the development of artistic criteria, they would be maintaining stagnant standards. They would not be artists, but artisans, creating an unhealthy product.

In fact, Christopher Clausen's observations notwithstanding, poetry today, however unpopular, remains healthy; and its vitality is secured through the ever-changing efforts of innovators and experimenters too numerous to list here. This implied identification between health and popularity is the essential flaw of Clausen's study. Unpopular artists throughout history have made the most significant contributions to the evolution of cultural standards. Stravinsky and Schoenberg assaulted traditionally tuned eardrums and altered the standards of serious music, but neither of them ever attained the audience that Johann Strauss and Michael Balfe enjoyed. Yet there is no question which of these composers contributed more meaningfully to the art of musical composition. If, in fact, poetry remains less popular than it was in some glorious past, this merely confirms the accompanying fact that the need for ideal readers and great audiences remains as strong as ever. Perhaps, however, if the continuing opposition between the egocentric poet and the proprioceptive poet were to be effectively mediated, a truly revitalized, yet uncompromised, poetry would be the result.

Such is the poetry of Gerald Stern, whose work seems to be a logical extension of what was first undertaken by Whitman. Frederick Garber's excellent study of Stern's poetry makes much of the poet's "fiercely binary" world (38). An aspect of Stern's fascination with the binary is what, in my opinion, brings his work closest to Whitman's mediation of the egocentric *I* and the proprioceptive *I*. The intensely personal *I* of Stern participates warmly in a pulsating reality that is ultimately offered up for scrutiny before a dispassionate and nearly scientific *I*. This poet's greatest gift is his ability to move uncritically and unabashedly into experience, tottering toward it like a drunken man, having come so close to the monster he is examining that he is devoured by it. Yet a second perspective observes the disaster and asserts the adventure of it:

> I saw myself
> moving from body to body. I saw my own
> existence taken from me. I lost the center.
> —It lasted for fifteen minutes, then I slept,
> with three or four others, scattered on that roof
> as if we each had little rooms, the brilliance
> of the night keeping us quiet, all our efforts—
> at least my own—going into lying still,
> going into some secret humming and adoring,
> I was so changed, I was so small and silent.
>
> ("Three Skies" in *Paradise* 74)

It is not unusual that an experience, even a rather trivial one, should render Stern small and silent, but it would never render him alienated or victimized. The concept of alienation is foreign to

Stern's perceptions, which involve him in an almost Emersonian manner in each facet of his experience. In response to Schwartz's contention that isolation is the natural condition of the poet, Stern suggests that the poet's feeling of isolation comes from being immersed in an art that, because it is continuously evolving, remains not inaccessible, but unwanted by the masses. The American poet, he admits, is not central to the concerns of his society:

> Let me bring up the obvious. The state (and its owners) are not friendly to poets. Neither are corporations, shopping centers, universities, arts councils, synagogues, churches, sports associations, service clubs, unions, libraries, gynecologists, footdoctors, undertakers, farmers, landlords, truck drivers, policemen, fruit peddlers, and lawyers. ("Notes" 20)

From such a statement one could infer an intimation of regret and victimization, but not so with Gerald Stern. He continues the statement with a "so-what-else-is-new" response and an accentuation of the positive realization that "poets get the windfall of a little Lockean democracy here." Even the fact that in America "nobody cares that much about poetry" is viewed positively in that poets are not persecuted or jailed for their ideas as they are in some other political systems.

> True, to the extent that the spirit is crushed, or ignored, in four thousand different ways, it is not only the business of the poet, but, inevitably, it is his own life that is at stake. He is there because he can't help it; he is there by definition. But he is not the only one there, and sometimes he is a little luckier because he can sing about it.   ("Notes" 20)

But all is not passive acceptance of circumstances in Stern's poetry. There is rage. There is confusion. There is the awkward concession to absurdity and also, as he says of all poets, "loneliness and lost chances and incredible loveliness in a language which the state, and the owners, have not yet destroyed" ("Notes" 20). For Gerald Stern poetry is privilege, the privilege to record experience, the privilege to record the feeble as well as the noble responses to experience in a chaotic universe, the privilege to attach partial mean-

ings to random events. In "The Red Coal" Stern begins casually
with a photograph of himself and Jack Gilbert walking down a
Paris street in 1950. He recalls how it was then, when the two of
them pursued their art, before the "red coal" entered their lives—
before the effects of that consuming thing that uses up vitality and
burns away youth had been felt—that he had tried to understand
Gilbert's "great fame" and his own obscurity. This poem provides a
key to the power of his more recent work and the function within
that work of the mediation of egocentricity and proprioception. He
is a poet aware of his age and aware of the follies of immaturity.
Conscious of the red coal as Whitman was of the "delicious word
Death," Stern can look back sardonically at adolescent whinings
about torment and lack of fulfillment. He now finds fulfillment in
the most apparently trivial of experiences:

> Lucky life is like this. Lucky there is an ocean to
>   come to.
> Lucky you can judge yourself in this water.
> Lucky the waves are cold enough to wash out the
>   meanness.
> Lucky you can be purified over and over again.
> Lucky there is some cleanliness for everyone.
>
> (*Lucky Life* 16)

In celebrating and singing himself and the body electric, Whitman had invited a society to confront its own fleshly reality, and
for doing so, he was labeled immoral by contemporary critics.
Continuing in the direction established by Whitman, but without
stirring any of the furor, Stern celebrates in "Lord, Forgive a
Spirit" not the body but its life, even as it decays and disfunctions,
accenting the disorder that accompanies its placement into circumstance:

> So what shall we do about this angel
> growing dizzy everytime he climbs a ladder,
> crying over his old poems.
> I walk out into the garden and there he is,
> watering the lilies and studying the digitalis.
> He is talking to his own invisible heart;
> he is leaking blood.
>   The sun shines on him all day long

as he wanders from bush to bush.
His eyes flash with fire, his eyelashes blaze and
his skin shines like brass
but he trips in the dirt just like any gardener or grieving
    poet.   (*Red Coal* 16)

Rather than a sense of contrast or disjunction, a sense of simultaneity is constant in Stern's poetry—the simultaneous acknowledgment of the immutable glory of the singer and the mutable intention, the awkwardness and imperfection of the man. There is convolution in the apparent simplicity of his lines—a man finding his meaning in the phenomena that comprise his setting and discovering the meaning of those phenomena in the meanings he has invented for himself, and for the selves of any others who permit themselves his assumptions. That group is not large yet, for even this accessible poet is generally ignored. But he stands up to ignorance maturely, taking pleasure from being able to sing about it. For Stern it is persistence that matters most, not the "gaggery and gilt" that attracts the spectators. This is the same persistence that causes the Dear Mole to methodically bleed as he scratches his way toward his dark destination and realizes the small victory of arrival, cause enough for celebration; but the celebration occurs not because of a blasé acquiescence in matters of violence, carnage, or useless death. Stern celebrates man's ability to endure while doing what must be done to satisfy one's own vision; and, at times, enduring necessitates fighting hopeless battles. In "Behaving Like a Jew," after focusing on the dead opossum in the road, he decrees that he will not be philosophical, that he will be unappeased at the opossum's death; and the analytical self imagines the emotional self acting:

I am not going to stand in a wet ditch
with the Toyotas and the Chevies passing over me
at sixty miles an hour
and praise the beauty and balance
and lose myself in the immortal lifestream
when my hands are still a little shaky
from his stiffness and his bulk
and my eyes are still weak and misty
from his round belly and his curved fingers

and his black whiskers and his little dancing feet.
(Lucky Life 55)

Stern's poetry contains many such examples of forcing the reader to look at waste and what it has taken, by recreating with vivid imagery that which has been lost. He asks the reader to examine how life is used up, be it the life of a man, a city, a flower, or an animal. Such broad sympathies allow further examination, from different angles, of the egocentric *I* by the proprioceptive *I*. Stern's rural poems that focus on the truth contained in the lives of flowers, birds, trees, and other natural phenomena—so typical of the romantic's return to nature—provide one avenue of examining how the ideal is constantly encroached upon by the realities of the natural process, the most final being death itself. His city poems examine similar intrusions of artificiality on what might have been or could be. Still another method Stern uses to delve personally into the constant paradox of human existence is the technique I will label "name-dropping." Galileo, Nietzsche, van Gogh, and other geniuses who had to cope with hazards of reality as they pursued ideals become metaphors, as does the composer Villa-Lobos:

Let there be

spaces between the chords to match
the spaces between the leaves. It took me
half a life to come here, one small house
on a battered hill, one small tree
to match the house, a man against the tree
with cello strings in his hand, a little dull gleaming
to match his own gleaming, a little sobbing
to match his own, a kind of painful sliding
from string to string to match the hill
or the house itself, or even the man himself,
his elbow out in space, his left eye shut,
his heart already bursting from the tender sounds.
(Paradise 57)

Here is an outstanding example of the aforementioned simultaneity that is so exemplary in Stern's poetry. The poet's situation is rendered more understandable through the composer he has chosen to be his metaphor; and, thus, the composer's music becomes the

means of defining the particulars of that situation as the poet becomes the composer.

Perhaps the most powerful of Stern's assertions of the self examining the self occur in his poems of formal pronouncement. These
generally begin with an attitude of taking an important new step
that will negate a practice of the past. The technique is employed
with any of the various aspects of life to which Stern's sympathies
extend. An example occurs in the first line of "Behaving Like a
Jew"; and in "Burying an Animal on the Way to New York," he
turns the pronouncement into an imperative for the reader to face
the process that accompanies the arrival of death:

> Don't flinch when you come across a dead animal lying in
>   the road.
> You are being shown the secret of life.
> Drive slowly over the brown flesh.
> You are helping to bury it.
> If you are the last mourner there will be no caress
> at all from the crushed limbs
> and you will have to slide over the dark spot imagining
> the first suffering all by yourself.   (*Lucky Life* 20)

These incidental animals along the road, like the flowers along
the river's footpath, the birds in the garden, or the artists and phi-
losophers whose lives provided information, become Stern's occasion to become the self of the universe and relate its feelings while
revealing his own feelings to himself. Identifying with a squirrel, he
discovers the essence of human consciousness in "I Remember
Galileo":

> I remember Galileo describing the mind
> as a piece of paper blown around by the wind
> and I loved the sight of it sticking to a tree
> or jumping into the back seat of a car.
> And for years I watched paper leap through my cities;
> but yesterday I saw the mind was a squirrel caught
>   crossing
> Route 80 between the wheels of a giant truck,
> dancing back and forth like a thin leaf
> or a frightened string, for only two seconds living

on the white concrete before he got away,
his life shortened by all that terror, his head
jerking, his yellow teeth ground down to dust.

(*Red Coal* 23)

As he becomes the self of the components of the universe and observes that self responding to stimuli, all of Gerald Stern's poetry is written both against egocentric isolation and against the cool acceptance of a perceived world. All of it is poetry against gnosticism, against the hatred of the flesh and all the vicious twists and turns we take to calm our frightened souls, as he says in "Your Animal." Living in the midst of rural nature, or in Pittsburgh or Philadelphia, in Easton or New York, in Alabama or Iowa, he is living in the condition of poetry and writing a tense but natural poetry whose process is that of nature itself. At times it forms like the web of one of those Pennsylvania spiders on the iron bridge going across to Riegelsville, New Jersey; at times it lets each impression, however false, produce a new impression ("It was my brain fooling me, / sending me false images, / turning crows into leaves / and corpses into bottles" ["Blue Skies, White Breasts, Green Trees," *Lucky Life* 27]); but always it allows a very general self to realize its place, a place where the ego attempts so unsuccessfully to maintain control and yet persists:

I am working like a dog here, testing my memory.
My mouth is slightly open, my eyes are closed,
my hand is lying under the satin pillow,
my subject is loss
          . . . Lament, lament for the underlayer
of wallpaper circa 1935.

("The Expulsion" in *Paradise* 81)

LYNN KELLER

"Free / of Blossom and Subterfuge": Louise Glück and the Language of Renunciation

It is a commonplace of American feminist criticism that, historically, linkage of the words *woman* and *poet* has yielded a powerful
contradiction in terms, inevitably confronted by women attempting
verse.[1] Because those aspiring to the male status of poet have been
caught in a conflict with their own female identity, as Gilbert and
Gubar observe, "at its most painful the history of women's poetry
is a story of struggle against . . . self-loathing" (xxiii). The poetry
of Louise Glück testifies that being a woman continues to some
contemporaries to seem an impediment to being a poet, and that
women writers today may still struggle against consequent self-
loathing. At the same time, Glück's achievement suggests that these
pressures may, by providing major themes, compel or even enable
women to write. Her often extremely negative sense of womanhood—as both a biologically and socially determined experience—
has been crucial in shaping the language, tone, and style, as well as
the thematic content of her poetry. Her four collections of poems
develop toward increasingly complex thought and flexible style, re-
flecting her changing responses to the dilemma of being at once
poet and woman.

The shock-value of the opening poem in Glück's first volume,
Firstborn (1968), asserts her desire to be different—perhaps especially her desire to stand apart from other women poets, just as
earlier women struggled not to be taken for stereotypical "female
songbirds."[2] Here is the complete poem, entitled "The Chicago
Train":

> Across from me the whole ride
> Hardly stirred: just Mister with his barren
> Skull across the arm-rest while the kid

Got his head between his mama's legs and slept. The poison
That replaces air took over.
And they sat—as though paralysis preceding death
Had nailed them there. The track bent south.
I saw her pulsing crotch . . . the lice rooted in that baby's hair.

(3)

To begin one's book with such flaunted offensiveness—both
in the speaker's implied politics (her attitudes toward the lower
classes) and in her ghastly perspective—is a gesture of defiant indi-
vidualism. Glück's mature work is neither so histrionic nor so tech-
nically awkward as this, but the poem provides a preview of her
obsessions. It is immediately clear that Glück feels revolted by her
bondage to the human body and the physical world. In her work,
physical being is always a *memento mori;* the child always desires to
press back toward the womb and prenatal weightless unconsciousness; and the woman's body, particularly the genitals that are the
locus of her sexual desire, is the horrifying center of the death-that-
infests-life. The pulsing of the crotch in this poem suggests sexual
arousal, as if the woman were stimulated—willingly or not—by
the pressure of the child's head. Here we have an indication of
Glück's early preoccupation with woman's horrifying lack of control over her sexual desires—something that her poetry attempts to
compensate for and counter.

That first poem is only one of many portraits and dramatic
monologues in *Firstborn* through which the young poet examines
the situations of women in her society, finding nearly all of them
revolting. "The Edge" typifies the volume's sensationalized view of
the wife's misery in marriage. The husband is bored, hardened, and
associated with predatory violence; the wife is angry, wounded, yet
subservient. Her role: bitterly to bear his children, tolerate his sexual demands, and sustain herself on his leavings: "Mornings, crippled with this house, / I see him toast his toast and test / His
coffee, hedgingly. The waste's my breakfast" (17).

A poet's vision, some early poems condescendingly assert, is far
superior to that of the ordinary woman who accepts the roles of
wife and mother—roles determined not only by society but by the
woman's biological urges. Thus the speaker sets herself above her
fertile, giggling relative in "My Cousin in April." The cousin, ab-
sorbed in playing with her first child and pregnant with her second,

is seen as having given into the "stir" "in her body" despite anger at her husband. The cost of such accommodation is insensitivity, obliviousness: "she passes what I paused / To catch, the early bud phases, on the springing grass" (8). In "The Wound" the paisley pattern of the speaker's bedroom walls is "like a plot / Of embryos," and "ripe things" are the walls of a prison. The association of woman with childbearing and physical life is for young Glück a deathly trap the female artist must struggle to avoid.

In view of Glück's aversion to the women's roles that conventionally accompany adult sexuality, it is not surprising that her work is filled with nostalgia for the pre-sexual innocence of childhood. In the emblematic piece, "Flowering Plum," from her second collection, *The House on Marshland* (1975), the adult woman looks with worldly cynicism and some longing at her neighbor's adolescent daughter who gives herself with wholehearted joy to spring and the thrush's "routine / message of survival." The innocent girl sits under the plum tree

> as the mild wind
> floods her immaculate lap with blossoms, greenish white
> and white, leaving no mark, unlike
> the fruit that will inscribe
> unraveling dark stains in heavier winds, in
> summer.   (12)

The poet who would inscribe meaning upon the world, if she is a woman, inevitably finds herself stained, battered, and written upon by the world. She remains the object rather than the writing subject, and that is the way of nature, not just patriarchy. Once again, the locus of vulnerability is her lap—the girl's not yet pulsing but vulnerable crotch.

Attempting to thwart this natural cycle of ripening and unraveling from childhood's spring to womanhood's summer, Glück's response in her personal history would seem to have been anorexia. Anorexia is both a retreat from adult sexuality to a childlike state safe from sexual drives, and an assertion of control—two desirable things for those who share Glück's sense of woman's powerlessness. The urges behind anorexia, and the relation between those urges and the drives behind poetic creation, are the subjects of "Dedication to Hunger," an important sequence from Glück's third volume *Descending Figure* (1980).

The early sections of the poem suggest that coming into womanly sexuality is a loss and a deprivation, that even in the most loving instances, a man's kiss, "might as well [be] a hand over [the woman's] mouth." Gendered roles and heterosexuality itself silence and suffocate, perhaps even impose starvation on a woman.[3] The fourth section depicts the anorexic's consciously chosen dedication to hunger as a way of defying death and renouncing female sexuality:

> because a woman's body
> *is* a grave; it will accept
> anything. I remember
> lying in bed at night
> touching the soft, digressive breasts,
> touching, at fifteen,
> the interfering flesh
> that I would sacrifice
> until the limbs were free
> of blossom and subterfuge   (32)

Eradicating one's blossom means sacrificing the body that invites male domination and silencing. Glück's rejection of female sexuality, then, does not simply reflect self-hatred. Paradoxically, it enacts positive self-assertion, since she believes that a woman may escape man's control only outside of the gendered roles of wife or lover. Only without her sexuality and the fleshy curves in which it is embodied can she be sure of having or creating an identity as subject rather than object. The anorexic's starvation, as clinicians put it, "is a statement about autonomy, not an attempt at self-destruction."[4] Glück in an interview confirms this point when she identifies "the anorexic nightmare" as "the being taken over by sensation, and obliterated by it, obscured by it, your individual outline . . . dissolved in some larger shape" (Douglas 123). For Glück, denial of her body does not entail suppression of her essential womanhood, for, as she explains in "Lamentations," God at the creation divided humankind not into two but into three: "the man, the woman, and the woman's body" (*Descending* 46). As she sees it, the woman's fulfillment may depend on her subduing the woman's body.

In starving away not just blossom but also "subterfuge," Glück attempts to purge herself of the deceptions and evasions patriarchy has long associated with women. Just as man and woman are, for Glück, opposed as "thrust and ache," men in her work have a rigidly phallic singleness, while women tend toward the bending, fluent, multiple or, in negative terms, the duplicitous. This duplicity is closely associated with the female body and also with female language. In "Tango" she addresses her younger sister: "Your bare feet / became a woman's feet, always / saying two things at once" (*Descending* 24). Rather than being a dancer like her sister, she has become a "watcher," as if by remaining on the sidelines she could keep from female double-talk. In "Portland, 1968," female subterfuge, contrasted with upright singularity, is again tied to language. A stiff figure, presumably male, is likened to fixed rock that is being eroded by the sea's "transparent waves of longing":

> everything fixed is marred.
> And the sea triumphs,
> like all that is false,
> all that is fluent and womanly.   (*Descending* 27)

Glück's words suggest her ambivalence toward what is womanly: the triumph of the womanly sea (and, implicitly, of the female speaker) is at once a tragic prevailing of the morally inferior ("false") and a valuable victory of what is live over what is static and death-like. One might expect a woman poet to value the association of women and fluency—linguistic fluency being the ability to control words effortlessly, smoothly—but it seems that for Glück fluency is too closely associated with stereotypically female gushing, with the absence of control over one's falsifying tongue.

The closing sections of "Dedication to Hunger" make it clear that the kind of poet who may be likened metaphorically to the anorexic does not aspire to write with fluency. Glück explains that as an adolescent dedicating herself to the sacrifice of her "soft, digressive" flesh,

> I felt
> what I feel now, aligning these words—
> it is the same need to perfect,
> of which death is the mere byproduct.   (*Descending* 32)

The anorexic distinguishing herself through self-denial becomes "like a god" in her "power" to expose her own frame and to reverse the natural progress of temporal development. The poet, too, wants to remove young life from the progress of time, making it invulnerable to decay:

> I saw
> the hard, active buds of the dogwood
> and wanted, as we say, to capture them,
> to make them eternal.   (*Descending* 33)

Since the natural world is infused with time, such a poetic achievement is as god-like, as supernatural, as the anorexic's.

In the fleshless rigor of her style, Glück establishes a language of almost super-human renunciation, the poetic equivalent of the anorexic's "expos[ure of] the underlying body." The driving principle is reduction. Her collections are of minimal length. She pares away at her lyrics to keep them short, restricts her lines to three or four stresses, and so concentrates on monosyllabic words that she often generates entirely monosyllabic lines. When not limiting herself to simple short declarations, Glück tends to chop sentences into small units, often rearranging them so the effect will not be fluid.

Glück's characteristic tone, which some reviewers (Greg Kuzma, for instance) have mistakenly heard as unfeeling, is one of enforced restraint. Pressured by nearly overwhelming fears and longings, the poet as metaphorical anorexic triumphs by controlling the urge to cry out, by forcing herself to speak calmly: "You see, they have no judgment. / So it is natural that they should drown" (*Descending* 3). Although employing conversational elements ("you see"), her manner avoids the relaxed talk or confessional outpouring common among contemporary women poets. Such apparent naturalness would be suspect; as she says in one poem, "nakedness in women is always a pose" (*Triumph* 24). Not surprisingly, some aspects of Glück's style involve adopting conventionally masculine modes such as a reasoned explanatory manner and frequently abstract diction. When not abstract, her diction tends to be simple, providing the reader with the bare minimum of contextual information. Glück's figures often employ jarring linkages. Near incompatibility of their contributing elements—their derivation from disparate realms or their contrasting connotations—forces recognition of their separateness, as if each were a separate bone exposed in the poem's skeleton. Even her frequent use of the definite article reinforces the distinct outlines of semantic and syntactic units. As Glück put it in an interview: "My poems are vertical poems. They aspire and they delve. They don't expand. They don't elaborate, or amplify" (Douglas 117).

In that interview, conducted while Glück was working on her 1985 collection, *The Triumph of Achilles*, she immediately added that she was presently trying to write poems that *would* elaborate and amplify, precisely because she had "so clearly seen the absence of this strategy" in her earlier work. Her efforts to put some flesh on the bones of her poetry have, I think, meant true aesthetic growth, evident in much of *Descending Figure*, as well as *The Triumph of Achilles*.

Ironically, the female "duplicity" that in some contexts so troubles her has been crucial to her poetic success. Her best works capitalize on the rich "subterfuge" of paradox, oxymoron, homophone, and pun, as well as the suggestive power available in even the most pared-down phrases. These strengths are particularly evident in her most recent collection, in which she imposes less rigorous divisions than before between language and life, between spoken language and body language, between man and woman, even between woman and her body. Rather than taking the fanatical either/or stance of the anorexic, she now tries, in her own words, to present something "in its full complication—the yes and no being said at the same time" (Douglas 121).

Formally, this means she allows herself greater syntactical flexibility and more variation in descriptive manner. She even provides luxurious lists of blossoms and fruits: "camellia, periwinkle, rosemary in crushing profusion" (*Triumph* 41); "Crates of eggs, papaya, sacks of yellow lemons" (*Triumph* 19). Where her early collections contained only one or two poems of more than one section, her recent works are often sequences of lyrics; in *The Triumph of Achilles*, nearly a third of the poems are sequences, some with as many as nine sections. This expansion permits greater emotional range and fuller consideration of a subject.

Thematically, Glück has not relinquished her yearnings for an unchanging absolute, but at least in parts of *The Triumph of Achilles* she now admits her need for others and her need to give in to need itself. Significantly, in this collection anorexia and hunger are no longer dominating images, though the problem of desire and the need to restrict its satisfaction remains. This volume's preoccupation is with a solitude necessary for the artist, one thwarted by the body's erotic fulfillment, just as the anorexic's urge to expose underlying structure would be countered by satisfying her hunger. But where *Descending Figure* stressed the god-like triumph of the anorexic perfector, *The Triumph of Achilles* regards human imperfection and yearning with more compassionate ambivalence. Thus, in a poem tellingly titled "Liberation," Glück's speaker relinquishes her (anorexic) need to be in the position of control. She lays down the phallic gun of the hunter to take up the role of fleeing rabbit. This reversal is prompted by her recognition that resistance to life's processes condemns one to a condition of death-in-life, while willing participation in life's motion-toward-death is at least a temporary freedom:

> Only victims have a destiny.
>
> And the hunter, who believed
> whatever struggles
> begs to be torn apart:
>
> that part is paralyzed."   (*Triumph* 20)

Like Achilles in the title poem, she lets the mortal part free of her god-like ambitions and is rewarded with love as well as loss.

In *The Triumph of Achilles,* the body, its hungers and attachments, the "part that loved / the part that was mortal," are more genuinely appreciated than before. In "The Embrace" Glück's lover enables her to relearn the "original need" to be touched, leading her back to "a kind of splendor / as all that is wild comes to the surface" (*Triumph* 23). The volume overflows with passion, and that passion is welcomed more often than before. Glück seems now to believe that while one cannot simultaneously be a poet and a lover, one can appreciate being each in sequence. She emphasizes the joy of sensually satisfied lovers, even when they have been changed "to a mute couple." Their desires for language and a permanent verbal record are incompatible with their desires for a transitory physical union that dissolves ego boundaries and transcends language, but the situation seems merely ironic, not desperate or threatening:

> Then why did we worship clarity,
> to speak, in the end, only each other's names,
> to speak, as now, not even whole words,
> only vowels?

Finally, this is what we craved,
this lying in the bright light without distinction—
we who would leave behind
exact records.   (*Triumph* 33)

"The Reproach" also presents this conflict humorously; the poet reproaches Eros because he has given her what every woman supposedly dreams of finding—her "true love." In so doing, he has nearly deprived her of her art:

What is a poet
without dreams?
I lie awake; I feel
actual flesh upon me,
meaning to silence me—   (*Triumph* 39)

Art depends on desire; the artist, Glück still insists, must remain dedicated to hunger.

Yet there has been a shift in emphasis. She no longer sees this renunciation as a distinctly female necessity or as something to counter particularly female weakness. Nor is her abstinence governed by the terror of growth and development, by the anorexic's fanatical devotion to starvation, or, for the most part, by the disturbing abhorrence of female sexuality that characterized her preceding volumes. Thus, in the poem "Summer," both she and her artist husband relinquish without regret the sating passions of summer for the creative isolation of autumn. As desiring, separate individuals, "We were artists again, my husband. / We could resume the journey" (*Triumph* 35).

A happy ending to one poet's "struggle against self-loathing"? No, nothing so reassuringly simple. Certainly from a feminist perspective, Glück's increasing acceptance of herself as a woman, and her higher valuation of female sexuality and of female linguistic powers mark definite progress. Yet any individual's ability to change is inevitably limited. Glück's poetics were founded on the anorexic's renunciative orientation, and though flexed and stretched somewhat, they remain largely unchanged. The attitudes expressed in her recent work also remain strongly linked to those in her earlier collections. That Glück's model in her latest volume is the male hero Achilles indicates the continuation of a male-centered perspective. Some of her recent poems still present her own sexual desire and orgasmic experience as imprisoning forces before which she is despicably and terrifyingly out of control. Glück has not passed beyond self-loathing, and this makes reading her work still a profoundly uncomfortable experience. Yet it would be false to suggest that in Glück's case the ongoing nature of her struggle has greatly restricted the power of her art; on the contrary, one could argue that this inner battle is precisely what electrifies her poetry. Nor should feminist readers and critics turn away from her and others like her, devoting attention solely to artists who themselves bring feminist analyses to bear upon their experience or whose more inspiring personal histories better point us toward positive change. Feminist scholarship will be enriched by remaining in touch with the varied perspectives of the many women writing today, including those like Louise Glück, whose poetry raises crucial, disturbing issues about women's complicity in their own oppression.

LIONEL BASNEY

Having Your Meaning at Hand: Work in Snyder and Berry

Someone has remarked that you could read the entire body of English fiction (up to, say, Hardy) without realizing that adults work for a living. The novel-reading bourgeois in nineteenth-century England was not expected or allowed to work. Though reservations come immediately to mind, for the most part work, particularly in its commercial and industrial forms, was what literature in the service of truth and good manners was supposed to transcend.

The issue is an important one for understanding our century's reaction against older literatures. One of the ingredients of the modernism of Pound, Eliot, and Williams is the recognition in poetry of the economic entanglements of actual adult life. In their writing, and also (and especially) in that of Frost, what you do with your resources of time and ability to work, and the consequences of having no work, too much work, or degrading work, are confronted as human causes and imaginative subjects. Prufrock, Aunt Helen, and Burbank have nothing to do; the typist and the "small house agent's clerk" in "The Fire Sermon" lack moral resources partly because their work gives them none; and in "Choruses from 'The Rock,'" the "imperial expansion / Accompanied by industrial development" is judged as a type of not building well the city of God (Eliot 3–7, 17, 23–24). Pound's tirades against *usura* are accompanied by Canto XII's sketch of low-level, "ordinary" business careers (53–57). The vision of Paterson includes a sense of the social uses of work and capital. But it is in the soliloquies of *North of Boston* that this engagement with the theme of work becomes most concrete and personal. Partly this is because Frost narrows his attention to the representative individual, and then allows the individual to speak for her- or himself in place of the variously authoritative voices of Eliot and *The Cantos*.

> I'm a collector.
> My ninety isn't mine—you won't think that.
> I pick it up a dollar at a time
> All round the country for the *Weekly News,*
> Published in Bow.   (65)

> . . . It's rest I want—there, I have said it out—
> From cooking meals for hungry hired men
> And washing dishes after them—from doing
> Things over and over that just won't stay done.   (83)

Frost has set aside the scope of Pound's encounter with economic systems by choosing his pastoral constraints. What he has gained is the direct feel of work: what demands it makes on the individual, mind and body, and what adjustments (and sacrifices) are necessary to survive its grinding routine. Frost, in particular, was freed to talk about work because his poetry ignites at the point where consciousness touches its ordinary objective environment, the socially guaranteed world where objects are made, remade, circulated, bought and sold, speculated on. A writer can come to this ignition point from either direction. To come to it from the problem of consciousness means to turn the poem, which germinated in consciousness, back on itself; this is the effect of poems in the line of Stevens. To come to the ignition point from the perspective of one's environment means to turn the poem face out to the world; this is closer to Frost's intentions. Philosophically, this is the simpler option—consciousness is, to some extent, consciousness of the world—but it is not in practice the easier project. Consciousness of the world means all the different awarenesses available to people in differing relations to the world; and these must be shown without losing the "check" of our (and the poet's) sense of the actual. Frost's dramatic monologues are so rich in the sense of reality because two perspectives are always present—the immediate contact with the individual's experience, through his or her own words; and the poet's governing sense of the conditions, and general meanings, of this experience.

Both of these projects—turning consciousness back on itself and turning it out to the world—are aftershocks of romanticism. If

Wordsworth chose the human mind as the main haunt and region of his song, he still had to go to the world's life for images of the life of the mind. The tension here between exploring the subjective "region" and needing to break out of it for images to make that exploration possible has never disappeared, though modernism, with its clearer devotion to social realities, attempted to relax it. The tension is present with many recent poets, too, though in a modified and narrowed form. The desire to engage the world at large has diminished. It has been replaced by an urgent need to bring the individual body to consciousness, to make its experience available in as direct and unmediated a way as possible. The body, it is felt (with some reason) does not exist in society's consciousness; we are still living in some version of Norman O. Brown's repressive cultural myth.

Many of the poems, however, that attempt to bring the body into consciousness seem frustrated in the attempt. Brilliant as they sometimes are, they do not escape the tension we have outlined; and in them this tension becomes an all-but-crippling obstacle. The problem is that the body the poet wishes to introduce into the poem has no socially guaranteed reality; and therefore the poet has nothing to turn to for images of the body but the experience of the body itself—the very thing which, by the terms of the project, is not available to consciousness. This is like Wordsworth's going to the world for images of a mind that cannot really grasp the world.

I have used the term "frustration" for the effect of these poems. In fact many seem to abandon the original project and take its failure as their theme. If you go through a recent anthology, such as William Heyen's *The Generation of 2000*, for instance, you encounter many poems which concern the effort to communicate the meanings of the body, and the frustrated sense that this effort is doomed. I choose one example from Heyen's selection, Ai's "Why Can't I Leave You?":

> I know we can't give each other any more
> or less than what we have.
> There is safety in that, so much
> that I can never get past the packing,
> the begging you to please, if I can't make you happy,
> come close between my thighs
> and let me laugh for you from my second mouth.   (4)

The experience of the body is strongly evoked as the form of a relationship. But this is failure as well as success. The body "can't give" what would be necessary for a fully articulated relationship. The reason is that it never reaches the light, is never understood, though used and obeyed; and the reason for this is that the experience of the body has no form, apart from the privacy of sex, through which it might be articulated. This is true despite Ai's evocation, here and in other poems, of a world of rural work. In "Why Can't I Leave You?" work is present only as frustration and "idleness." The body put to work in the sexual experience does make a medium of communication, in part, because the body has no other function, nothing else to do. As a consequence, however, the body itself remains unarticulated. The strong poetry of the body ends up in a poetry of isolation, of the self trapped in a body; and also in a poetry that is frustrated in its own work, the work of bringing the body (and the rest of the self) into full consciousness.

This suggests, at least, a contemporary use for a poetry of work. It would place the body in a social context and in this way make it an instrument for articulating relationships with the world and with other people. Of course, the poet must ask, What sort of work will best serve this purpose? For society's vision of work is as defective as its consciousness of the body. There is no sense in which the poet can simply import into his or her poem a finished, adequate definition of the body's proper work and productivity; no such definition exists. It is something the poet will have to help to create.

A poetry of work, consequently, must exist in dialogue—probably in conflict—with social definitions of work and the body. There is plenty of opportunity for polemic in the work of the two poets I wish to consider, Gary Snyder and Wendell Berry. Though neither is a preacher in his poetry, both sometimes sound as if they were. Although both image and picture and model, they still sound, at times, as if they were presenting slates of legislation. Their ambiguity of tone arises from their efforts to confront and transform social and economic assumptions. Both poets are physical, and sexual, writers; and if they have escaped some of the hazards of bringing the body to consciousness, it is perhaps because they do so in the context of work and its social forms and communities.

Snyder and Berry have complex reputations. Each has been celebrated as a cultural figure apart from his writing, as a representative figure for homesteaders, small-scale farmers, and people pursuing alternative lifeways and (in Snyder's case) Eastern religion and philosophy. Partly because of his standing as a cult figure, Snyder has received more extensive critical attention. Critics such as Robert Kern and Charles Altieri have discussed his work as a tributary of modernist and postmodern poetics. Their work shows one way in which Snyder deserves to be taken with full intellectual seriousness.

The approach, however, has definite critical limitations; and these become apparent when a critic like Altieri confronts the fact that Snyder is offering programs in his writing, and not just visions, that Snyder wishes to change social practice and sees the poem as a vehicle for such change. Altieri is too serious and careful a critic not to admit the difficulty when it approaches.

> [E]specially when the poet himself claims the authority of a wisdom tradition, one must ask whether readers can seriously entertain in their imagination the hypothetical relevance of his values and his dramatic situations for their own basic concerns. . . . [This] involves the very conditions for a really deep participation in and commitment to the poet's work.   (*Enlarging* 150)

Altieri forthrightly admits that he cannot entertain Snyder's vision and values deeply enough to go the last step in engaging Snyder's poetry. One reason for this admitted limitation, I think, is that the very critical intention of thinking about Snyder in aesthetic terms, though it encourages us, rightly, to take the poet seriously as a poet, scants the poetry's range of reference. Snyder's aesthetic, like Frost's or Williams's, includes a social application of the poet's thoughts and of his poem's images. Unless this social component is taken into full account, the poem will always seem fanciful, too simply ideal, a vision that a serious critic cannot, finally, take seriously.

One difficulty with what Altieri calls "immanentist poetics" is that, socially speaking, the poet caught up in vision (or, as a modernist critic would have said, in the image) is static. It is as if he were in a trance, even if the contents of his awareness in the trance are "real," and carefully, exactly rendered. From the trance, though the poet speaks to us, what he says may almost inevitably seem to lack "hypothetical relevance." To start to read *Riprap,* for instance,

from the perspective of the title poem seen as an extension of im-
agism is to take too narrow a purchase on Snyder's imaginative
project. From the perspective of "Riprap," the lesson of the book
would be how objects mean more than words, nature more than
culture, immediate engagement more than history; and how the
poem, and culture, result from the skilled rendering of poetic, and
cultural, images.

But there are other perspectives on nature and the world of objects in the collection. These anticipate, more fully than a poetics of
the image, what Snyder will eventually come to in his broader social vision. Physical labor, for instance, is used to afford an enor-
mously extended vista of human time. When the narrator of
"Above Pate Valley" "Picked up the cold-drill, / Pick, single-jack,
and sack / Of dynamite," the tools join with the obsidian flakes he
has discovered earlier to form a bridge for sympathy, or at least
contact, across the intervening ten thousand years. The poem is not
a celebration of the individual in contact with nature pure and simple, of a flattened ecological morality. What the poem notes, and
what animates the contact with nature, is that people have worked
here, and that they are working here now. The objects their work
implies, both tools and implied products, such as arrowheads, identify meaning with an immediate practical use, and thus suggest a
culture functioning in both pragmatic and spiritual terms. The human involved with nature is not involved through metaphysical assumption or through an epistemological unity represented by the
poetic image. He is involved because he works here and has a relationship with the setting which is both immediately physical and
historically significant.

From this perspective the key poem of the *Riprap* collection may
be "Hay for the Horses," in which the evocation of work is accom-
plished through the voice of the old guy who drives the truck:

> "I'm sixty-eight" he said,
> "I first bucked hay when I was seventeen.
> I thought, that day I started,
> I sure would hate to do this all my life.
> And dammit, that's just what
> I've gone and done."   (19)

The poem evokes the physical feel of labor itself; and it does so
in Snyder's typical ways, with mouth-filling consonants and

assonance. But this evocation is paired with an account of work that is even more direct than Snyder's imagery, as well as more complicated in its grasp of a life lived in the natural world. The old man reminds one of Frost's "Death of a Hired Man," except, of course, that Silas never gets to address us directly, but is spoken for. Silas is enclosed in a larger community of marriage and ownership, and the central problem of that poem is whether the community can make room for his solitary, narrow, irresponsible identity. Snyder's worker talks directly to us without further comment from the poet or any other character. But his account of his life is filled out by Snyder's evocation of the conditions of work; and this context gives reasons for the old man's mingled tone, and for our final respect for him. He regrets his life and he doesn't, ruefully confessing and asserting, boasting, laying his life down in retrospective inevitability. The poem gives us a complex sense of work, time, work-time, and life-time, through the voice of the working man himself.

Hay-baling will not, of course, represent completely what Snyder calls "the real work"—the work of establishing a satisfactory philosophical, religious, and biological relationship with the world. Though there may be a sense in which work is a condition of the growth of vision, it is more consistently treated in Snyder as the way in which vision is *worked out*. Work is the *way,* social, economic, and ethical, for which Snyder's religious and ecological vision provides the plan. In books like *Turtle Island,* however, where Snyder's main task seems to be establishing the vision itself, work poems show up less often than in other collections. The practice is set aside, or postponed, while the theory is set in place, as in "By Frazier Creek Falls":

> This living, flowing land
> is all there is, forever
>
> We *are* it
> it sings through us—
>
> We could live on this Earth
> without clothes or tools!   (41)

The moment must be read as a moment of ecstatic vision, and therefore simpler, more constricted in its occasion, than the work poems in *Riprap*. Here the subject confronts the natural setting, and receives a guarantee of the validity of human relationships with nature.

Even while his central concern is to establish a vision, however, Snyder occasionally returns to the evocation of labor, to the voices of laborers, to the theme that culture requires work and work a world in which people and objects interact. Part of Snyder's vision is what he calls "the common work of the tribe" (Molesworth 2). To evoke common work is to evoke the tribe, as he is always doing among the temporary communities of lumbermen and sailors. It is important to notice, for instance, that "Six Years," Snyder's poetic account of his period of Japanese study, does not end, as Altieri (*Enlarging* 139) implies, with a "far bell coming closer"—an image of a religious vision of cosmic harmony—but with the voice of Soogy the oil sump in the poem's "Envoy": "How long you say you been Japan? / six years eh you must like the place" (*Country* 63). The final situation is that of the ship as a social fact, as a work-place. The ship is almost a womb, delivering Snyder and his fellow-sailors back to alien New York. Here in the city, the hub of forces that exploit laborers like Soogy (though he survives, human, in Snyder's poem), you "pack your stuff and get paid" (105). This is the world in which vision must be established if it is to have social consequences.

In "The Real Work," from *Turtle Island,* a "long tanker riding light and high" is part of the scene the speaker views from a dis-tance. The poet is rowing, as the note tells us, past Alcatraz, but apparently for recreation only (32). The tanker that takes Snyder and Soogy back to New York is seen from inside. Similarly, after the volumes in which Snyder seems primarily concerned with his vision as a vision, actual labor and its somatic evocation become, again, a central part of his poetic work. In *Axe Handles,* Snyder includes poems entitled "Working on the '58 Willys Pickup," "Get-ting in the Wood," and (almost a parody) "Removing the Plate of the Pump on the Hydraulic System of the Backhoe." All kinds of work can be simply notated; they contain the vision that has been evolving in complicated intellectual ways since *Riprap*. "What have I learned," Snyder asks, "but / the proper use for several tools?" The list of tools here is more complete than in "Above Pate Valley":

> Wedge and sledge, peavey and maul,
>   little axe, canteen, piggyback can

> of saw-mix gas and oil for the chain,
> knapsack of files and goggles and rags,
>
> All to gather the dead and down.   (85)

The satisfaction the speaker takes in the work appears in the rhythm of these lines, verging on chant with the dactyls of the last two. The sense of wonder at recognizing a fellow worker across the distance of ten thousand years collapses here into the complexity of culture necessary to complete culture's task in the natural setting. Snyder is now the teacher, of his sons and other "young men . . . learning the pace / and the smell of tools from this delve / in the winter" (42). What he passes on is the achieved way that vision has prepared, a way of living by appropriate and satisfactory work. To do the "real work" is not to argue for the perspective from which it can be envisioned. To do it is, precisely, to do it: "To be shaping again, model / And tool, craft of culture, / How we go on" (6).

Farming: A Handbook seems to occupy roughly the same place in Wendell Berry's career that *Turtle Island* occupies in Snyder's. Both collections are crucial to the statement of a poetic vision. It is striking, therefore, that while work poems tend to disappear from Snyder's volume, while his vision is being most carefully articulated, Berry's book of statement is precisely a georgic "handbook" about agriculture. There are several reasons why Berry has not had to interrupt his account of work in order to establish a vision that would give that work its proper meanings. One reason is that Berry has accompanied his poems with a long series of prose essays, culminating in *The Unsettling of America,* in which his social and economic vision is stated and elaborated, taking the burden of discussion off the poetry. A second reason is that Berry's poems have been growing, consciously and explicitly, out of the work of his subsistence farm, his return to which, with his family, in the mid-sixties formed the animating moment of his verse ever since. Third, some of the difficulties of articulating a broad vision have been eased for Berry by his acceptance of a Christian sacramental view of work. This has not been an easy acceptance. Too many travesties of sacramentalism exist in modern Christian practice for Berry to simplify matters by importing a completed theory into his poetry. He has had to reargue the case from the beginning, setting it in terms available to secular discourse as well as to religious, in order to get from it again the kernel of worldliness and practicality it has always contained.

Finally, and perhaps most important, Berry's return to the subsistence farm was also a return to an established community of labor and labor-discipline. In his earlier books of verse, Snyder moved restlessly from community to community and from job to job. This itineracy gave him vivid images of the social marginality of labor in certain industries, and of the personal marginality of the rootless and the emotionally disjunct. But this restlessness also meant that the communities of work in Snyder's poems have always been, to some extent, virtual rather than actual—communities across time or temporary communities in workplaces. Even when Snyder came to rest, so to speak, in poems like those in *Axe Handles,* the community he can draw on, circles of friends and family members, is still narrower than the community Berry could feel certain of from the beginning.

For to return to the native hill is to return to a functioning community with a history of human relationships and a history of work. This is true even in instances where the human presence has done the natural setting harm, or has failed to fulfill that setting's promise of health.

> . . . Between
> history's death upon the place and the trees that would
>   have come,
> I claim, and act, and am mingled in the fate of the
>   world. (*Poems* 104–05)

The poet is joined to the world in its largest extent (in its "fate") by being joined to a particular place. The place has its own history; it bears the visible effects of other men's work and failure of work. To join the place is to join an established community and to take responsibility for the results of work one has not done.

There are dozens of poems like this in Berry's *Collected Poems,* enacting the assumption of these burdens and privileges. Berry keeps writing the same story, the story of the return to the native place. Some arc of this return appears again and again. When the arc shows him in the place itself, it shows him, more often than not, at work. I might have written, "under the sign of work," or "in the figure of work"—farming is an imaginative and emotional *form* for being at home as well as a practical means of sustaining biological life. But there is something wrong with saying it that way. Turning to responsible labor means, in one sense, leaving the figure behind and turning to the thing the figure stands for. Even more clearly than Snyder, Berry turns away from mere vision, or theory, to the application of theory as the actual means of his existence in the world.

Berry's emphasis on practical application might be rejected as a rhetorical device, the trope of sincerity; indeed, Berry, more than many recent poets, is a self-consciously eloquent writer. But what keeps this from being only a rhetorical device is the fact that the poet-farmer's work does not proceed from his imagination or understanding alone and therefore does not require validation either by his own experience or by his words. The "figure" of work has been provided for him by other imaginations—or by the social imagination of all the farmers, past and present, who have invented and perfected the work Berry learns to do and to write about. The poet-farmer comes into the landscape in the act of doing work; and this work has been defined, prescribed, for him by others whose experience in this place is longer and deeper than his. The poem, therefore, that the farmer writes has also been anticipated, and in a sense validated, by a social imagination larger than his private one.

The link between private imagination and public is the individual person, and therefore the body that does the necessary work. Some of the poems privately evoke the body's individual labor:

> Wake up,
> leave the bed, dress
> in the cold room, go under
> stars to the barn, come
> to the greetings of hunger,
> the breath a pale awning
> in the dark.   (184)

But far more typical is the evocation of labor with others, in the tradition of others, or even in the eyes and imagination of others:

> And in the corrective gaze
> of men now dead I learned

> to flesh my will in power
> great enough to kill me
> should I let it turn.   (225)

These "men now dead" show up in the poems as real life characters or dedicatees, or as fictional references: "By the fall of years I learn how it has been / With Jack Beechum, Mat Feltner, Elton Penn, / And their kind, men made for their fields" (187). These men come, of course, from Berry's novels; his fiction holds them, now, in its imagination of their work.

In *Clearing* (1977), Berry puts the actual names and places of the locale into his poems. The work of clearing scrubland focuses his sense of the complicated, half-lost victory of his place. Between the 1977 volume and the *Collected Poems* (1985), Berry revised some of this work by excising prose circumstances, names of historical people quoted from deeds, and names of specific locations. It is not hard to guess the purpose of these revisions; they make the poem more general, less a memorial record and more a meditation. But the excision is a loss as well. What work brings into focus is precisely the concrete, prosaic actuality of the place and its history. Work cannot be treated too metaphorically without ceasing to be work; and a place cannot be too figurative without ceasing to be the place itself. By the terms of Berry's own project the place cannot be *any* place, or every place, without losing its fundamental validity.

The poems of *Clearing,* even when revised, retain a good deal of specific detail. And in *The Wheel* (1982), the elegies for Owen Flood restore some of the sense of the real workman doing chores in a real place. Here again the bodily feel of work is evoked with unusual vividness:

> He went ahead, assuming
> that I would follow. I followed,
> dizzy, half blind, bitter
> with sweat in the hot light.   (*Poems* 241)

But in this volume, as in *A Part,* work is being joined with other social uses and rituals of the body, and transformed in this way into a direct source of art, a bridge between "low" or spontaneous culture in the farming community and the "high," self-conscious culture of the poet.

> He led me through long rows
> of misery, moving like a dancer
> ahead of me, so elated
> he was, and able.   (*Poems* 241)

Dance, specifically folk dance, becomes so comprehensive and spiritual a symbol in *The Wheel* that it is important to recall its uses as a figure for work itself, when it is done with ability and with "elation." In "Horses" this ritual form of work is unified with the somatic feel of stepping across rough dirt behind the team: "A dance is what this plodding is" (*Poems* 241). There is a parallel transformation of the farmer's work-language, "the other tongue / by which men spoke to beasts," into the actual form of poetry: "A song, whatever is said" (*Poems* 227). In this way the social imagination which had prepared the world for the poet-farmer to work in, and prepared the ways of work for him, also surrounds, supports, and gives life to the poem. And the poem in turn becomes a true language for the community's experience.

The disjunction Charles Altieri senses between what Snyder's work means to his popular, or broadly cultural audience, and what it can mean to the professional critic—quite apart from the specific critical judgments about the success or failure of Snyder's poems— is itself a symptom of the frustration of Snyder's project. Both Snyder and Berry intend their verse as the redaction of a cultural and ecological vision; neither intends to write "pure" poetry, poetry free of a practical reference, or even narrowly personal poetry. Both are moral poets; but the morality their work strives to embody has an inescapably social range. It is a morality for society to adopt, a morality only partially available to the individual without a community to help him bring it into practice. For such a poetry to succeed it must convince not only professional poetry-readers, but also "ordinary" readers, people of whatever professional sophistication who see poetry not as a specialty but as a guide and an exploration of their common life.

Both Snyder and Berry are rural poets. As their careers have developed each has turned more and more fully toward life in a specific natural setting, among a social circle defined first by the poet's immediate family and then by friends and fellow-workers. The advantage of this setting for a poetry of work is plain. Even in the context of corporate agribusiness and agricultural failure, farm work has a relatively clear social place and utility and is governed (at least in Berry's chosen practice, the practice whose persistent vitality he urges in his prose) by traditional disciplines and standards. This firm social definition makes a poetry of work at least conceivable by providing an imaginable social context in which the experience of the individual body can be brought into public consciousness.

Snyder and Berry, in other words, are duplicating the kind of pastoral and georgic constraints Frost chose for his early work. But Frost is not a direct model for either writer; the line is not a line of influence but of similar tactics in similar exigencies. Both the older poet and the younger poets are enabled to explore work by accepting the concrete if limited ground of rural life, with its direct natural pressures and its palpable if narrow communities.

But these constraints have changed their significance since *North of Boston*. In the crisis of our culture's relation to nature, the constraints do not detach the poet's project from economic and political issues, but ensure that it will represent them. John Lynen suggested some time ago that Frost's pastoral vision made his rural poems universal in their application (ch. 1). This would be too metaphoric a process to describe what Snyder and Berry hope to do. Their use of farm, garden, forest, and sea life represents other ways of living—other practical lifeways, philosophical in background but pragmatic and economic in application. Frost's farmers in "The Code," or "Death of a Hired Man," present the complexities of human relationships. Berry's Owen Flood, partly because he was an actual Kentucky farmer, presents us with a concrete way of life whose values Berry recommends to us. One point at which imitation is possible is the ideal and pattern of a certain way of work. To understand the poem, Berry seems to be saying, it is not enough to read it intelligently and sympathetically. To understand the poem you must be willing to pick up the reins yourself and join the work-dance.

THOMAS B. BYERS

Adrienne Rich:
Vision as Rewriting

I am thinking how we can use what we have
    to invent what we need.
                                    —Adrienne Rich

In her touchstone essay "When We Dead Awaken: Writing as Re-
Vision" (1971), Adrienne Rich defines the revisionary process and
tells what is at stake in it: "Re-vision—the act of looking back, of
seeing with fresh eyes, of entering an old text from a new critical
direction—is for women more than a chapter in cultural history: it
is an act of survival" (*Lies* 35). This act has been central to recent
feminist recoveries of women's history and identity, and Rich's criticism, both of others and of her own early work, has contributed
much to these recoveries. But criticism is not her only locus for this
activity. In a more recent essay, Rich offers a model of the art she
values most highly as "part of a long conversation with the elders
and with the future" (*Blood* 187). Her own art has taken this dialogical form in a very specific way. Key changes in her vision are
disclosed by the return to and rewriting of tropes from her earlier
poems. Thus she becomes her own precursor, and in the process she
also recognizes and overcomes other precursors within her earlier
self. This essay focuses on two pairs of her poems, examining how
in the more recent of each pair the poet has had to invent what she
needs—how she revises the meaning of an early trope and thereby
signals a shift in her concept of what a work of art is or should do.
Taken together, the two pairs should not only graph some of the
poet's changes, but also help to place these changes relative to
the shift from modernism to postmodernism in poetry, and from
the New Criticism to recent rhetorical theories of interpretation.[1]

The first pair of poems consists of "At a Bach Concert" (1951) (*Poems* 7) and "The Ninth Symphony of Beethoven Understood at Last as a Sexual Message" (1973) (*Poems* 205–06). In both cases, the musical composition serves in some sense as an exemplar of art in general, and the poems are essentially about what art works are and how they should be "read" and understood. "At a Bach Concert" is from Rich's first published volume, *A Change of World* (1951), which was selected by W. H. Auden for the Yale Series of Younger Poets. In an introduction (in Cooper 209–11) that epitomizes patriarchy in its genteel mode, Auden praises Rich for her "good manners" and "modesty," her avoidance of originality and willingness to follow in the tradition of her immediate modernist (male) precursors. He closes with a description of her poems in terms of attributes that paternalistic poets and teachers tend to value in their female students: "the poems a reader will encounter in this book are neatly and modestly dressed, speak quietly but do not mumble, respect their elders but are not cowed by them, and do not tell fibs." "At a Bach Concert" is a fine example of how the volume earned Auden's accolades:

> Coming by evening through the wintry city
> We said that art is out of love with life.
> Here we approach a love that is not pity.
>
> This antique discipline, tenderly severe,
> Renews belief in love yet masters feeling,
> Asking of us a grace in what we bear.
>
> Form is the ultimate gift that love can offer
> The vital union of necessity
> With all that we desire, all that we suffer.
>
> A too-compassionate art is half an art.
> Only such proud restraining purity
> Restores the else-betrayed, too-human heart.

Tonally, the poem is relatively distant and "objective." It places its highest value on a traditional artistic form that "masters feeling" in order to restrain "the else-betrayed, too-human heart." Its contrasts to the passion and compassion, the anger and commitment of the poet's later work are obvious.[2] It sees—and affirms—art as a defense mechanism. Its portrayal of the art work as above all a well-wrought urn, a container and restrainer of individual feelings, to be judged as an aesthetic object, places it as a characteristic late New Critical poem. There is an irony in this portrayal, however, since the poem itself is far more interesting for what it says and what it reveals of the poet than for its skilled but conventional formal properties, or for any sense of formal balance of tensions. Finally, the poem submits itself to the discipline of a male precursor, Bach, who is willingly accepted as master.

"At a Bach Concert" is thus an act of submission both to the dominant poetic theory of its time, and to the patriarchal and conservative interests served by that theory. Its implicitly spatial model for the work of art carries with it a disposition to erase historical process in general and art as historical phenomenon in particular. It exemplifies the very sort of attempt at assimilation that Rich has recently decried in an essay significantly titled "Resisting Amnesia: History and Personal Life" (*Blood* 136–55). In not only going along with the dominant ideology, but aesthetically justifying the repressions that such going-along requires, the poem raises the assimilationist's self-alienation and fear of naming (see *Blood* 142) to an artistic principle. It also assures the marginality of its author. For the pride and discompassionate self-restraint that it espouses are defined in its historical moment as "naturally" masculine, and the woman who adopts them suppresses her own identity, while aspiring to a role that she can never fulfill as well as those who are "born to it." This, indeed, is the double bind of assimilation; one can neither be who one is nor who, according to the culture, one ought to want to be. All in all, the poem is in many ways an answer to a question Rich has recently put to herself in print: "How is art curbed, how are we made to feel useless and helpless, in a system which so depends on our alienation?" (*Blood* 185).

The Beethoven poem presents a radically different case:

> A man in terror of impotence
> or infertility, not knowing the difference
> a man trying to tell something
> howling from the climacteric
> music of the entirely
> isolated soul
> yelling at Joy from the tunnel of the ego
> music without the ghost

of another person in it, music
trying to tell something the man
does not want out, would keep if he could
gagged and bound and flogged with chords of Joy
where everything is silence and the
beating of a bloody fist upon
a splintered table

Perhaps most strikingly, this poem asserts itself angrily against the male "master," rather than submitting to his example or striving for assimilation to his culture. Like the Bach poem, it takes the master's aspiration to form as defensive, but now the defenses are heard as desperate and deceitful, rather than beautiful. And the poem's response is to place more emphasis on art's presumed emotional content than on its formal restraint. What is conveyed by the music, against its creator's wishes, is the egocentricity and violence that underlie the formality of the patriarchal personality.

The poem implies that the New Critical model does not provide an adequate way of reading. Rich now takes the musical text to be more than a formal object and suggests various semiotic and reader-based anti-New-Critical theories of interpretation. Most obvious is the feminist-influenced psychoanalysis that reads the message as one of sexual desperation and aggression. To arrive at that reading, one has first to shift one's whole sense of what the work is. The word "message" in the title is essential here; it restores a sense of both a sender and a receiver, and suggests that the act of reading is a process of decoding. In short, it offers a rhetorical, rather than a New Critical, model for the understanding and appreciation of texts. In this case the individual understanding offered does not pretend to "objectivity" or "disinterestedness"; it is overtly metaphoric, and is clearly based on a reading performed from a particular reading frame—that of Rich's feminism in general, and her strong revolt against the male world at this stage of her career in particular. Hence the poem's interpretation of the symphony can also be seen as an example, and to some extent an implicit affirmation, of reader-response theory, with its emphasis on the reader's role in making meaning.

Terry Eagleton has convincingly criticized such theory in general as a "consumers' revolution," whose arguments for readers' power are essentially frivolous when compared to the proper goal of a radical criticism, which is "to take over the means of production"

("Revolt" 452). This particular instance, however, is not a question of a mere adjustment in consumer relations. Rather, Rich's "reading" of Beethoven is, as much as anything else, an assertion of her will as a radical writer, as oppressed producer rather than consumer, to seize (psychic) control of the means of production. For the means at stake here are not presses, ink, and paper, but the codes of interpretation and canonization that have equally assured the masters' power.

As to the content, certainly Rich's version is not the only way to hear Beethoven, nor does it say all that is to be said about the Ninth Symphony. On the other hand, it is hard to hear the symphony now without thinking of Rich's powerful revisionary images of it. But the issue, finally, is not whether one accepts Rich's version as an accurate reading. More significant is the fact of Rich's own *self*-assertion, as well as her redefinition of her relation to male mastery not only in a specific work of art, but in the system of which that work is a notable example. Here there is no submissive attention to a past master's achievement as in the Bach poem; rather, the focus is shifted from the master's authority to Rich's needs in her own moment.

Perhaps the most interesting aspect of the comparison of these poems is the intersection of notions of literary theory with political concerns. New Criticism is the theory of the specific male precursors against whom Rich rebels. Because it specifically advocates the formal containment of a work's material, rather than the decoding of the deep structure, it is also an ideal theory for the disguising of power struggles, of sexually-related violence, and so forth. For Rich, the shift to a strong feminist position as poet and reader requires the rejection of New Critical reading styles, values, and senses of what a text is. Historical and political engagement are clearly better served by a rhetorical model of literary discourse.

While the first pair of poems reveals a shift in critical theory, the second reveals one in poetics. The trope at issue is that of women's handwork; the two texts are "Aunt Jennifer's Tigers" (1951) and the more recent "Transcendental Etude" (1977). The former is one of the richest poems in *A Change of World:*

> Aunt Jennifer's tigers prance across a screen,
> Bright topaz denizens of a world of green.
> They do not fear the men beneath the tree;
> They pace in sleek chivalric certainty.

Aunt Jennifer's fingers fluttering through her wool
Find even the ivory needle hard to pull.
The massive weight of Uncle's wedding band
Sits heavily upon Aunt Jennifer's hand.

When Aunt is dead, her terrified hands will lie
Still ringed with ordeals she was mastered by.
The tigers in the panel that she made
Will go on prancing, proud and unafraid.   (*Poems* 4)

Rich's own remarks on this poem, in "When We Dead Awaken: Writing as Re-Vision" (1971), are an important starting place; she discusses how even in a formal and consciously distanced poem of her early period, she can discover clear (if latent) feminist concerns (*Lies* 40). Perhaps most interesting, however, is the fact that the needlework tigers, like Rich's poem itself, are ineffectual as rebellion, because the very means of their rebellion are inscribed in the oppressor's language, and thus reveal an unhealed split in the psyche of the oppressed.[3]

The tigers display in art the values that Aunt Jennifer must repress or displace in life: strength, assertion, fearlessness, fluidity of motion. And the poem's conclusion celebrates the animal images as a kind of triumph, transcending the limited conditions of their maker's life. Accepting the doctrine of "ars longa, vita brevis," Rich finds in her character's art both persistence and compensation; she sees the creations as immortalizing the hand that made them, despite the contrary force of the oppressive structure of Aunt Jennifer's conventional marriage, as signified by the ring that binds her to her husband. This doctrine is utterly consonant with what was, according to Rich, "a recurrent theme in much poetry I read [in those days] . . . the indestructibility of poetry, the poem as vehicle for personal immortality" (*Blood* 168). And this more or less explicit connection helps show how deeply implicated Rich herself was in Aunt Jennifer's situation and her achievement, despite the "asbestos gloves" of a distancing formalism that "allowed me to handle materials I couldn't pick up barehanded" (*Lies* 40–41).

The problem, however, is that the tigers are clearly masculine figures—and not only masculine, but heroic figures of one of the most role-bound of all the substructures of patriarchy: chivalry. Their "chivalric certainty" is a representation by Aunt Jennifer of her own envisioned power, but it is essentially a suturing image, at once stitching up and reasserting the rift between her actual social status and her vision.[4] Aunt's name, after all, echoes with the sound of Queen Guinevere's; her place in chivalry is clear. Her tigers are only Lancelots, attractive because illicit, but finally seducing her to another submission to the male. So long as power can be envisioned only in terms that are culturally determined as masculine, the revolutionary content of the vision, which was all confined to a highly mediated and symbolic plane in any case, will remain insufficient. Indeed, the fact that assertion against the patriarchy is here imagined only in terms set by the patriarchs may be seen as this poem's version of the tigers' "fearful symmetry." And the "immortal hand or eye" that framed their symmetry is not Aunt Jennifer's framing her needlework, but patriarchy's, framing Aunt Jennifer.[5]

In "Transcendental Etude," on the other hand, the context and meaning of the woman's work are quite different. The trope appears in the extended simile of the poem's last stanza, right after Rich's declaration of "a whole new poetry beginning here":

> Vision begins to happen in such a life
> as if a woman quietly walked away
> from the argument and jargon in a room
> and sitting down in the kitchen, began turning in her lap
> bits of yarn, calico and velvet scraps,
> laying them out absently on the scrubbed boards
> in the lamplight, with small rainbow-colored shells
> sent in cotton-wool from somewhere far away,
> and skeins of milkweed from the nearest meadow—
> original domestic silk, the finest findings—
> and the darkblue petal of the petunia,
> and the dry darkbrown lace of seaweed;
> not forgotten either, the shed silver
> whisker of the cat
> the spiral of paper-wasp-nest curling
> beside the finch's yellow feather.
> Such a composition has nothing to do with eternity,
> the striving for greatness, brilliance—
> only with the musing of a mind
> one with her body, experienced fingers quietly pushing
> dark against bright, silk against roughness,
> pulling the tenets of a life together
> with no mere will to mastery,

> only care for the many-lived, unending
> forms in which she finds herself,
> becoming now the sherd of broken glass
> slicing light in a corner, dangerous
> to flesh, now the plentiful, soft leaf
> that wrapped round the throbbing finger, soothes
>   the wound;
> and now the stone foundation, rockshelf further
> forming underneath everything that grows.
>   (*Dream* 76–77)

Rather than focusing on a response, displaced or overt, to her domination by men, this woman simply leaves them behind. She walks out on the "argument and jargon" that are a patriarchal style of conversation and turns toward the making, out of natural and found materials, of a work that is a communication of her "care for the many lived, unending / forms in which she finds herself." Form is more discovered than wrought, and it is also the scene of self-discovery. There is no reinscription in patriarchy here. Rather, there is an ethic of care, of the sort that has long been a role assigned to women, but is now also to be seen as a value higher than, rather than supplementary or inferior to, the values and activities of men.

This difference marks a progression in Rich's own life and work as well. She has moved from a feminism whose defining property is its adversary relationship to the patriarchs (hence a feminism still in a sense caught within patriarchy) toward a vision of power in community with other women, more nearly outside of and hence safer from the mastery of patriarchal discourse.[6] And it is also in this light that we must understand the different aspirations for the work of art in the two poems. In "Aunt Jennifer's Tigers" the work is to provide a compensatory mastery, a transcendental, even if symbolic, value. The real Aunt Jennifer will be immortalized in the work, even though her physical life will end. This notion of compensation, like the tigers themselves, is patriarchal. On the one hand it is the artist's particular assertion of a will to power that is part and parcel of the phallogocentrism of our male-defined civilization; on the other it is in this case also a panacea for the oppressed, a substitute for the heaven promised to the meek by religion. To the degree that Rich accepted this notion when "Aunt Jennifer's Tigers" was written, her own work was a re-capitulation;

like Aunt Jennifer's it revealed but could not heal the self-alienation of the oppressed.

These are the reasons why the somewhat ironically titled "Transcendental Etude" rejects such a notion of art, in favor of one that has "nothing to do with eternity / the striving for greatness" and "no mere will to mastery." The new notion celebrates the fearless asymmetry of the mortal woman's hand and eye. The movement from Rich's early, modernist poems to her more recent work is a move from the eternal and spatial to the temporal, from mastery to care, from an imagination that survives the physical self to "a mind / one with her body," from stasis to process. It is also a movement from the rigors of set forms to the *bricolage* of the woman's work in "Transcendental Etude." It is, finally, a move from hierarchy and symbolism to immanence, and hence from modernism to postmodernism in poetry.[7]

There is a certain irony in the structure of this essay, for it seems to place "Transcendental Etude," with its devotion to process, temporality, and immanence, as a kind of *telos* in Rich's dialogue with herself. It is truer to the poet, and to the integrity of her career, to recognize that this poem, like all of her writing, is "indicative of a continuing exploration, not of a destination" (*Blood* xxii). What does emerge from the discussion, however, is how Rich's changing worldview has required certain shifts in her poetics and her theory of interpretation, and how she has worked out these shifts by rewriting herself. "Every group that lives under the naming and image-making power of a dominant culture," Rich has said, "is at risk from . . . mental fragmentation and needs an art which can resist it" (*Blood* 175). The art that can do this is not that of a totalizing vision, but that of personal and historical engagement and process. It is, for instance, the art of Adrienne Rich.

Poem

LORRIE SMITH

Dialogue and the Political Imagination in Denise Levertov and Adrienne Rich

We are now postmodern enough to realize, as Thomas Edwards puts it, "that our own relation to 'politics' is essentially imaginative" (4). Not that what we call "politics" is imaginary, though we might wish apartheid and SDI were figments of our fancy or shadows in a cave. Rather, self and society are so intimately bound to each other that neither makes sense without the other; hence we must actively imagine our relation to others if we are to understand our lives in political terms. If we divest the imaginative of its Romantic associations with idealism and transcendence, we can begin to define the political imagination in literature as a dialogic mediation between the languages of the private self and the events and power structures in which the self is implicated.

For the past twenty years, Denise Levertov and Adrienne Rich have persistently tested and explored what it means to be a poet committed to political activism. Both resist the dangers that often beset committed writing: propagandizing, preaching to the converted, and subsuming authentic experience into abstract slogans and foregone conclusions. For both, dialogue provides the basis for formal and ethical solutions to these problems. Levertov, working within a liberal humanist tradition, and Rich, revising that tradition as a radical feminist, use dialogue as a vehicle for self-discovery and as the grounds for political engagement. Whether through an implied colloquy with the reader or in a fluid interplay of voices within the poem, dialogue invites a poetics of process and discovery that is particularly effective in revealing the complexities of "our own relation to politics."

Though active in different arenas, both Levertov and Rich contribute to a larger movement among women poets toward the merging of personal lyricism and political engagement. Women have been able to assume confidently an audience that will read their work and share their frames of reference—a condition that supports a mode of dialogic communication. In distinct opposition to an avant-garde poetics of hermetic indeterminacy, many women poets start from the politically loaded assumption that shared meaning and a common language are not only possible but are necessary and empowering to their audiences, that the enterprise of imagining our relation to politics can be a collective one. For many women, poetry is an active form of social communication, hence a potential agent of revolutionary change. Its utterance is not distinguished by qualities of "literariness" apart from and above the world of social contingency, but by its lucidity as plain speech.

These premises challenge two entrenched critical assumptions: that the poet's proper domain is the self in sublime or agonized (or, recently, *jouissant*) isolation and that didacticism, despite its honorable pre-Romantic heritage, is anathema to lyric expression and poetic craft. Most twentieth-century poets and critics have taken to heart Yeats's dictum that rhetoric is the quarrel with others, poetry the quarrel with the self. The exclusion of the reader, who is left in this model to overhear the poet's private quarrel, has greatly contributed to the popular notion that poetry is highbrow, elitist, and mystifying rather than a broadly accessible exchange between the poet and her public. In restoring the authority of collective values, much women's poetry mends the conventional division between the lyric self and others in the world; "I" and "we" often merge in this poetry, and the reader is often addressed directly. For both writer and audience, poetry provides access to power—not power *over* but power *with* others in a collaborative effort to imagine and realize alternative social orders. In fact, as Alicia Ostriker points out, poetry by women has been closely aligned with progressive social change: "At the grassroots level it is clear that a women's movement exists in poetry as in society at large, antedating and to some extent inspiring contemporary feminism in its more political branches, which in turn is being fueled by feminist thought and action and its creation of more conscious and courageous readers" (8). The most effective poems in this movement are those whose dialogues invite us to participate and provoke us to respond.

Dialogue has been tied to the political by twentieth-century critics who equate artistic with existential freedom and for whom literary evaluation rests on moral and ethical imperatives that allow us to judge how a poem *acts* in the world. For Sartre, literature functions as emancipatory discourse, creating a site where both writer and reader are free to collaborate in the discovery of meaning. This stance has been extended by feminist theorists like Hélène Cixous, for whom "writing is precisely the very possibility of change, the space that can serve as a springboard for subversive thought, the precursory movement of a transformation of social and cultural structures" (245). Mikhail Bakhtin provides a pragmatic link between these theories and current political poetry by women. For him, all language is inherently dialogic: every utterance takes place within a specific social matrix and in relation to others, and thus is invested with ideological and moral significance. The more monologic an expression, the more indefensible it becomes. Bakhtin distinguishes everyday from literary discourse, so that in poetry "the form is that of a concealed or overt dialogue with the reader" (Clark and Holquist 96).

Dialogue in poetry is not simply a formal structure or mode of address (as in Renaissance dialogues of Flesh and Spirit or Yeats's dialectical poems) but constitutes a more intrinsic epistemological and ethical stance toward experience. Poetic speech, even when it presents itself as lyrically subjective, is implicated in broader political and semiotic systems, and meaning is constantly generated, expanded, and refined in a dialectical process of social exchange and conflict. The aim of politically explicit poetry is not transcendence, epiphany, or confession, but a fuller imaginative grasp and elucidation of the relations between self and society. While Bakhtin's "heteroglossia" may be concealed or only implicit in some poetic utterance, the political poet consciously exploits the possibilities for communication and sense-making afforded by dialogue.

Dialogue represents an ideal paradigm of communication for political poets like Levertov and Rich, for whom poetry is a palpable, provisional, transformative force in the world of social relations. Rich, especially, conceives of her poems as conversations with her readers, whom she specifies as a community of women, as well as with the various voices of her self. Dialogue allows the political poet to dramatize and evaluate possible stances toward experience, to question what Rich calls "the assumptions in which we are drenched" (*Lies, Secrets, and Silence* 44), to listen and respond to other languages (either from within or outside the speaker's self), and to discover new imperatives for action and change. Dialogue implies continual process and hence provides a medium for the discursive, metonymic, open-field composition characteristic of much political poetry. Most important for the political poet, dialogue embodies a model of ontological freedom, ethical commitment, empathy, compassion, and honesty—values central to the vision of a regenerate society offered by many contemporary women poets.

Dialogical poetry, like oratory, assumes a participatory audience receptive to change. Whereas meditative lyric poems are spoken by a single voice (though the recent collaborative experiments by Olga Broumas and Jane Miller in *Black Holes, Black Stockings* call even this convention into question), a shifting and provisional dialogical stance breaks through the solipsistic "egotistical sublime" to project shared, social grounds of understanding, allowing the poet's private experience and utterance to attain the sphere of public discourse. While the lyric poet must first of all, as Levertov writes, "maintain dialogue with his heart, meet things with his mind" ("Origins of a Poem" 45), the political poet extends this impulse to a reciprocal and dynamic exchange with the reader. Invited to participate in the poet's inner colloquy rather than simply overhear the poet's private quarrel with herself, readers are provoked into their own inner dialogues as well as active collusion (or equally productive collision) with the poet. Thus, says Levertov, "The poet develops the basic human need for dialogue in concretions that are audible to others; in listening, others are stimulated into awareness of their own needs and capacities, stirred into taking up their own dialogues, which are so often neglected" ("Origins" 49). Though the dialogical poet sacrifices some control over the rhetoric and closure of the poem, the force of a dynamic interchange between provisional sites of meaning yields new discoveries, much as Pound's ideogrammic juxtapositions generate new perceptions or as an actual conversation opens new spaces of inquiry and fresh perspectives.

Denise Levertov's recurrent struggle as a humanist dedicated to pacifism has been to reconcile her simultaneous awareness of anguish and affirmation; the numinous wonder of the world and the evil of society are both mysteries she hopes to penetrate and elucidate through language. Her solution is a matter of individual ethics and, recently, Christian faith, both of which ultimately support her commitment to collective activism. Since the mid-1960s, she has cast this theodicy in explicitly political terms. Attempting first to account for the evil generated by the Vietnam War, the dualities of anguish and affirmation come together most forcefully in her poems on the threat of nuclear annihilation.

First posited in her love poems as a means of imagining and connecting with another's presence and in her nature poems as a means of attaining Whitman's "path between reality and the soul," dialogue becomes a central theme and imaginative stance in her political poems, allowing her to apprehend a distant war, empathize with others who suffer, and explore her own ethical and aesthetic dilemmas as an activist poet. Poems like "Conversation in Moscow" and "Dialogue," written during the Vietnam War, balance contrapuntal voices or posit multiple realities as she explores her own relation to good and evil. Levertov's most painful political poems, such as "A Cloak," "Modes of Being," and "Unresolved," lament the paralysis of speech and the inability to discover new knowledge through dialogue. In her last two volumes, dialogue takes on both social and religious dimensions and becomes a mode of ideal communication between humans as well as between the human and the divine. Dialogue allows Levertov to bridge imaginatively the gaps between her affirming vision and political anguish and to attain her ideal "osmosis of assertion and song." Her most successful political poems create a dialogic equilibrium, which sustains the discrete languages of anguish and affirmation and allows them to interact. In "Vocation" she adjures her readers to "Watch! Listen!" to the silenced voices of those disappeared in Central America; in "Making Peace," Levertov warns that we cannot simply imagine peace in the world but must actively "learn" the metaphors of peace "as we speak."

In Adrienne Rich's more revolutionary and collective vision, poetry plays a crucial role in changing the whole character of literary codes and social behavior. Throughout her work, Rich strives to realize an ideal language that is "common" in several senses: quotidian, plainly accessible, and communal. While Rich uses dialogue as an ideal form of communication, much as Levertov does, she goes further to specify its relations to a new woman-centered social order. Since this order must be created as she goes, the notion of learning by talking and listening (meditatively to her own conflicting voices, empathetically to others) is fundamental to the inseparable processes of personal growth and social change, self-disclosure and communal identity. Dialogue creates an open poetic field within which to test her own commitments and beliefs, to imagine different positions, to extend her sympathy to women in history, lovers, friends, and the patriarchal "oppressors" she must understand, and to connect intimately with her readers. As early as 1961,

Rich began dating her poems to call attention to their provisional, historically specific contexts. In the preface to *The Fact of a Door-frame,* Rich describes the growing importance of dialogue in her work; her terms parallel Levertov's notion of learning by speaking:

> In writing poetry, I have known both keen happiness and the worst fear—that the walls cannot be broken down, that these words will fail to enter another soul. Over the years it has seemed to me just that—the desire to be heard, to resound in another's soul—that is the impulse behind writing poems, for me. Increasingly, this has meant hearing and listening to others, taking into myself the language of experience different from my own—whether in written words, or in the rush and ebb of broken but stubborn conversations. I have been changed, my poems have changed, through this process, and it continues.   (xv–xvi)

In addition to serving these moral and epistemological imperatives, dialogue is particularly suited to Rich's political ends, for she views reciprocal communication as integral to women's history and a feminist future: "Today women are talking to each other, recovering an oral culture, telling our life-stories, reading aloud to one another the books that moved and healed us, analyzing the language that has lied about us, reading our own words aloud to each other" (13); such active, vocal understanding, for Rich, is a radical corrective to the "passive-voiced dominant culture." Truthful, empathic dialogue fosters a vital, progressive, and nurturing sense of community, which lies at the heart of Rich's visionary and re-visionary project.

Some of Rich's poems, such as "Dialogue" and "For L. G., Unseen for Twenty Years," alternate two voices in an actual conversation. Many others intimately address a specific "you" or speak on behalf of a community as "we." In poems such as "Trying to Talk with a Man," "For Julia in Nebraska," "Education of a Novelist," and "A Vision" (addressed to Simone Weil), Rich takes in different languages in order to understand her own relations and responses to others in the world and in history. "Culture and Anarchy" constructs polyphonic webs of meaning by alternating fragments from historical documents and letters with her own responses to these voices. As in Levertov's "Modes of Being," the voices enlarge and extend each other. For both Rich and Levertov, political impasses

are ultimately rooted in a breakdown of dialogue—conceived either
as the self locked into subjectivity or as a failure to imagine and
empathize with others; for both, silence is a significant theme as
well as an expressive *part* of dialogue (an idea worked out most
fully in Rich's "Cartographies of Silence").

In her 1986 volume, *Your Native Land, Your Life,* Rich uses two
primary dialogic modes. The first, an extension of her juxtaposi-
tional technique in "Culture and Anarchy," gives fragments of conversation. In "When/Then," two voices, one italicized, move back
and forth:

> *Tell us*
> > *how we'll be together*
> > > *in that time*
> > patch of sun on a gritty floor; an old newspaper, torn
> > for toilet paper and coughed-up scum Don't talk, she
> > said
> > *when we still love but are no longer young*   (47)

The majority of poems in the volume, however, address a specific
"you." We do not simply overhear these conversations, but participate in their fluid interplay of voices. Most effective are Rich's
poems addressed to the reader. In the twenty-ninth and final poem
of her sequence "Contradictions: Tracking Poems," Rich insists that
we connect the personal and the political:

> You who think I find words for everything
> this is enough for now
> cut it short   cut loose from my words
>
> You for whom I write this
> in the night hours when the wrecked cartilage
> sifts round the mystical jointure of the bones
> when the insect of detritus crawls
> from shoulder to elbow to wristbone
> remember: the body's pain and the pain on the streets
> are not the same   but you can learn
> from the edges that blur   O you who love clear edges
> more than anything   watch the edges that blur   (111)

Both Levertov and Rich experiment with a variety of dialogical
forms to enlarge both their own and their readers' capacities for

empathy and change: juxtaposing two or more voices, responding to excerpts from other writers or speakers, directly addressing the reader or an interlocutor. A dialogical imagination is central to their conceptions of a politically effective poetry, and dialogue embodies moral, ethical, and linguistic ideals that support a regenerative vision of society. Their work is exemplary for the ways it extends, critiques, and renews an exhausted lyric tradition, counters post-modernist hermeticism, and helps revitalize the strained relations between poetry and polity in America. Above all, they are writing poems in which people actively listen and talk to one another, thereby radically revising a tradition that upholds the central position and authority of the solitary—usually male—lyric voice. Their dialogical political poetry has far-ranging implications for the future vitality of American poetry.

MARY LEWIS SHAW

Concrete and Abstract Poetry: The World as Text and the Text as World

Since the mid-nineteenth century there has been a significant reciprocity of influence between American and French poets. Charles Baudelaire and Stéphane Mallarmé proclaimed Edgar Allan Poe as chief among their mentors; T. S. Eliot, Ezra Pound, William Carlos Williams, and Wallace Stevens considered themselves heirs to the French Symbolists (Baudelaire, Mallarmé, Arthur Rimbaud, and Jules Laforgue) and to twentieth-century French poets such as Guillaume Apollinaire, Blaise Cendrars, and Saint-John Perse. In tracing the development and interrelations of two major currents in contemporary French poetry, the following essay may help to elucidate the comparable directions that recent American poetry takes.

Characteristically anti-representational and self-referential, contemporary French poetry creates an effect of self-sufficiency, of autonomy from the world outside the text. While these attributes constitute the common ground of a vast corpus, they are not necessarily produced through homogeneous means.

In concrete poetry,[1] textual signs (words, letters, and sometimes other elements functioning as such) refer to their own material substance as the object of the signifying process. The text's arrangement rivets the reader's attention upon its presence as a tangible surface, whereas in the conventional poem the physical text appears to function as an intermediary screen, a symbolic veil *through* which the reader enjoys an intangible poetic object: the message or signified. Concrete poetry can thus be described as a kind of thickening or reification of the poetic sign. Like other poetry it can convey subtle and complex messages, but its meaning cannot be abstracted from its material form—"the medium is the message."

In most contemporary poetry, the impression of self-sufficiency results from a contrary procedure. Rather than drawing the reader's attention to the text's material substance, circular semantic play denies the reader any sense of access to a referent per se. Because of their suspension or deferral of the image-forming aspect of representation, many poems can be labelled abstract.

Distinct though they may appear, concrete and abstract poetry have a profound and paradoxical relationship. In attempting to realize what has long been a linguistic and poetic ideal—the perfect unity of form and concept implied in the principle of the Logos (as Word embodying its referent)—each type of poem rejects the traditional treatment of language as medium of representation. While abstract poetry severs its ties to non-verbal phenomena in order to become a self-sufficient utterance, concrete poetry tends to self-destruct; to exploit, reduce, and finally delete its very foundation: the verbal text.

The majority of well-known contemporary French poets engage in abstract and circular semantic play, and their works form privileged objects of theoretical analysis, whether of the structuralist, semiotic, or deconstructive type. In contrast, concrete poetry is rarely discussed and its proponents are not widely recognized as poets or critics of major and enduring significance. The difference in degree of success of these two poetic practices is not altogether surprising, for while the former exploits the richness and versatility inherent in the linguistic sign, the latter seems to cut itself off from the particular efficacy of language, and therefore from literary interest. Though concrete texts may declare themselves poetic, they rarely appear so, and their classification as poetry strains our understanding of that genre, as well as some of our most basic ideas about language itself.

By looking at the development of concrete poetry within a cultural context loosely centered in France, we can gain insight into its relevancy to the predominant type of contemporary poem. We shall see that in France, despite its claims as an anti-establishment, "supranational" art form breaking through all language and cultural barriers, concrete poetry arises as the logical consequence of a strong literary tradition, which it has, in turn, begun to color and shape.

French poetry begins to move in the extreme antirepresentational directions of abstraction and concreteness in the late nineteenth century.[2] The symbolists threatened mimesis by their rejection of explicit allusion and exact description in favor of undefined symbols and vague suggestiveness. The aim of this aesthetic was to open the text to a wider range of interpretations. The symbolists were also generally obsessed with the possibility of articulating the "correspondances" between the arts, a preoccupation manifest in Baudelaire's and Rimbaud's poetic practice of synesthesia and in Verlaine's and René Ghil's identification of poetry with music.

It is in the works of Stéphane Mallarmé that these aesthetic principles converge in the most pronounced way and that the origins of contemporary abstraction and concretism can be found. His *Un Coup de dés jamais n'abolira le hasard (A Throw of the Dice Will Never Abolish Chance,* 1897) is unquestionably one of the most undecipherable and diversely interpreted nineteenth-century texts (Mallarmé 457–77). It is also often cited as the first concrete poem.

Setting the scene for a hypothetical event, a shipwreck of cosmic dimensions, *Un Coup de dés* suggests that the fact of this catastrophe and the nature of its circumstances are without meaning for humanity—as all is determined by Chance. To quote one of its seminal phrases, in this text, "RIEN N'AURA EU LIEU QUE LE LIEU" (nothing will have taken place but the place). Despite its verbal complexity and heavy metaphysical overtones, the poem thus conveys a singularly "concrete" message. As in its avant-garde theme and uniquely convoluted style (exemplified by the circularity of the title), this text is revolutionary in its typographical arrangement.

As illustrated in the sample page (fig. 1), the verse is spread over the fold dividing two pages and dispersed toward the top, middle, and bottom of the page. The white space normally delineating the broad margins of a poem is here assimilated within it. The text is also composed of several different sizes and styles of type.

As Mallarmé explains in his preface to the poem, these typographical innovations are meant to produce a number of effects: to offer a visual representation of the reading process by showing the natural fragmentation of thought; to serve as a logical and syntactic armature enabling the reader to understand what is of primary and secondary importance, and grasp multiple subordinated clauses; and finally, to provide the reader with the necessary directives for its oral performance. In this respect, the text is said to function as a musical score. In recitation, the pattern of the verse on the page guides the reader's intonation, while the size of print indicates the appropriate strength and dynamics of the voice. The arrangement of this poem has had an enormous impact around the world throughout the twentieth century; its influence is apparent in American poets as different as e. e. cummings and Charles Olson.

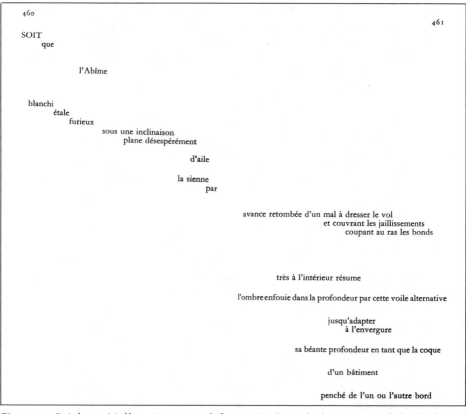

Figure 1. Stéphane Mallarmé, a spread from *Un Coup de dés jamais n'abolira le hazard* (1897), pp. 460–61 in *Oeuvres complètes,* Paris: Gallimard, 1945.

From Mallarmé's exploitation of typography and textual space, there results a powerful demonstration of the simultaneous autonomy and interdependence of aesthetic forms. Verbal, figurative, and musical symbolic systems converge within one and the same body of writing. It is important to underscore, however, that this accomplishment presents itself as only an effect of Chance—of the all-pervasive arbitrariness marring the unity of language and preventing the creation of the ideal poem. The poem-as-logos would have to overcome two dualities inherent in language: the sign's internal split between the signifier and the signified (as immaterial concept) and that which separates signs from their referents (the material objects to which they refer). It is the impossibility of achieving such a unity that explains the fundamental ambivalence of Mallarmé's approach to poetry. As is evident in many of his poems, Mallarmé sought to recreate through language nothingness and silence as well as the presence of the world. Like many of the later concretists, as much as by the beauty of poetry he was haunted by the beauty of its absence on the virginal white page.

In Mallarmé's paradoxical aesthetic lie the seeds of many modern efforts to purify the language of literature. The effort to write a poetry that speaks only of itself and thereby narrow the gap between the poem and its referent is characteristic of a "classical" line of twentieth-century French poets extending from Paul Valéry to Francis Ponge and Yves Bonnefoy. In America one may distinguish a parallel line including Wallace Stevens, Marianne Moore, Louis Zukofsky, John Ashbery, and the recent "Language" poets. Curiously, the same drive toward a pure, autonomous poetry motivates the experimentation of the concrete poets, though by virtue of their proximity to other art forms, their poems are often hardly recognizable as such. We find a striking synthesis of these seemingly contradictory tendencies (toward literary abstraction and concreteness) in the works of one of the Swiss founders of the concrete movement, Eugen Gomringer.

"Silencio" (fig. 2) is the liminary work of Gomringer's first collection of concrete poems called *Konstellationen* in honor of Mallarmé (Williams [127]). Like Mallarmé, Gomringer wished to restore to words their original, expressive power. To release their latent energy, he wrote in such a way as to free them from the flattening effect of syntax. In "Silencio," unfettered by any phrase, the word *Silencio* (silence) stands out and reverberates through textual space. Owing to the symmetrical, mirroring composition, the graphic image of *Silencio* appears to extend in all directions. In an oral performance this would obviously translate into a rhythmic composition of echoes.

Focused on the apparently critical nature of the concrete text's presentation, the reader inevitably wonders *how* it should be read: silently or aloud; top to bottom; left to right? In "Silencio," as in most concrete poems, the loosening of syntactic ties forces us to actively participate and choose how to complete the poem. The

silencio silencio silencio
silencio silencio silencio
silencio   silencio
silencio silencio silencio
silencio silencio silencio

Figure 2. Eugen Gomringer, "Silencio," 1954.

reader does not function as a passive receiver of the work. The concrete text is, in Gomringer's words, a "thought-object," which we
ourselves must determine how to use ("Poésie" 8).

The typographical arrangement of "Silencio" clearly solicits
something other than an ordinary reading—the intellectual deci-
phering of a verbal code. And the poem's semantic simplicity itself
invites a more profound sensory and psychological engagement.
This appeal to the subconscious does not however preclude the
communication of an idea. The word-cluster, though free of syntactic relations, is far from devoid of concepts. By its use of the word
silence to express its contrary—the absence of any word—the poem
makes a forceful statement about the nature of silence, about the
fact that silence, as the saying goes, is always heard. Moreover the
repetition of the word adds hyperbole to the truism suggesting that
silence can be deafening. As for the well-placed void at the center
of the poem, beyond its iconic value, it constitutes an opening, a
point of entry and reference for the all-important reader. "Silencio"
is thus, not despite of but because of its verbal minimalism, a complex, dense, and perhaps even a noisy poem.

Such intricate semantic play is not necessarily characteristic of all
concrete poetry. Indeed as the concrete value of a text becomes increasingly exploited its conceptual richness seems difficult to sustain. An eventual subordination of concept to form is suggested by
the cyclical evolution of concrete poetry in France.

One of the constant aims of concrete poets has been to detach their works from the analytical structure that language has traditionally imposed on thought. This desire was clearly expressed by the early twentieth-century poet Guillaume Apollinaire, whose *Calligrammes* (1918) are among the rare visual texts well known to French readers. In 1917 Apollinaire wrote: "Man is in search of a new language." "We must learn to understand synthetic-ideographically rather than analytico-discursively" (Salmon 144).

Led by Tristan Tzara, the poets of Dada put this theoretical rejection of the essence of modern European languages into practice. They set out to destroy European culture and values (which they themselves viewed as destructive) and, to this end, leveled a heavy attack on their most powerful instruments: European languages and literatures. Not surprisingly, several of the Dadaists—Hugo Ball, Christian Morgenstern, and others—engaged in the earliest known modern attempts to create poetry without words.

Although the Dadaists produced relatively few visual texts, their experimentation realized many of the ideals of the concrete movement. They closed the gap between the literary text and its referents—the infinite phenomena of the world—by stripping poetry down to its most rudimentary elements (letters or phonemes), and by placing the emphasis on the creative process, rather than on the finished and therefore necessarily imperfect work. And, in renouncing the very attempt at preserving either the forms of or ideology behind their work, the Dadaists cleared the path for other cycles of textual exploitation, reduction, and abandonment—a pattern clearly discernible in the history of the concrete aesthetic.

One such cycle begins with the work of Isadore Isou, who went to Paris during the 1940s to found the Lettrist movement. Like some of his predecessors in Dada, Isou argued for the reduction of the word as poetic unit to the letter. But he saw this reduction as a constructive, rather than destructive gesture. His positive attitude toward formal experimentation seems to have offered concrete poetry a fresh start. While the radical stance of Dada denied the possibility of a continuing tradition, the Lettrist movement expanded to incorporate many types of visual and sound poetry, and it continues to be practiced today. Isou himself, however, moved away from his initially stated doctrine, to advance more radical poetic theories most of which presume the impossibility of the verbal text as an embodiment of the poem. In the late 1950s, he argued, for example, the superiority of infinite and unperceivable art (Curtay).

Isou's trajectory away from the text is far from exceptional. Several concretists of the 1960s eventually vowed to abandon all attempts to create literature in favor of acting directly upon the world. In his preface to *The Last Novel in the World,* Henri Chopin affirms that after his book there will be no more "writing, concrete poems, lettrism or Chatter." Many of Jean-François Bory's pieces, such as "veux," "the world is dead," and the volume *Post-Scriptum,* show a gradual annihilation of the text. Though Julien Blaine's piece "Julien Blaine the i constructor" (fig. 3), makes its point by retaining an element of the letter, it is not so much a poem as a poetic operation on the world. It is the dot that draws our attention to the "I"—an extratextual sign that might otherwise have gone unseen—articulating the identity-in-difference of world and text.

Despite its impulse toward negation, concrete poetry, like abstract and representational poetry, continues to be written. While none of these appears in danger of extinction, remarkable in contemporary poetry is the increasing evidence that a fundamentally similar reduction of language's functions occurs in the two seemingly antithetical types. Each reduces the traditional complexity of the linguistic sign, as locus allying signifier, signified, and referent, in an attempt to eradicate the difference between the text and other things in the world.

Concrete poetry aspires to silence the otherness of the world by emphasizing primarily the material existence of the signifier. Thus, at its radical extreme, the concrete poetic perceives any image, object, or action in the world as a viable substitute for the verbal text. While this tends to limit the range of *what* poetry can express, it virtually explodes all constraints as to *how* it can express.

The seemingly more traditional, but in fact equally radical, abstract approach relies on a converse operation, which silences the otherness of the world by emphasizing the unlimited, reflexive play of meaning within the text. At its radical extreme this poetic treats the text as a viable substitute for the world. For obvious reasons this perspective suits the natural bias of poets, whose chosen activity is to write. Moreover, it has gained compelling extrinsic (i.e., other than aesthetic) justification in current philosophical theory, in particular, through Jacques Derrida's argument that presence itself is fundamentally structured as a writing (*Grammatology*).

Though the difference between these perspectives has generally produced antithetical works, the increasing importance of visual

Figure 3. Julien Blaine, from "Julien Blaine the i-constructor."

elements in highly complex and semantically circular texts suggests a movement toward reconciliation and the development of a heterogeneous type of poem.

A juxtaposition of texts simultaneously concrete and abstract yet highly disparate in their approaches to writing in-relation-to (as opposed to representing) their common object will illustrate this point: "Le soleil placé en abîme" (The Sun Placed in Abyss) by Francis Ponge and two visual "Soleil" texts by the concrete poets Pierre and Ilse Garnier.

The visual aspect of Ponge's poem is significant. There is clearly a concrete aspect to the arrangement of the passage cited below:

LE SOLEIL SE LEVANT SUR LA LITTÉRATURE

QUE LE SOLEIL À L'HORIZON DU TEXTE SE MONTRE ENFIN COMME ON LE VOIT ICI POUR LA PREMIÈRE FOIS EN LITTÉRATURE SOUS LES ESPÈCES DE SON NOM INCORPORÉ DANS LA PREMIÈRE LIGNE DE FAÇON QU'IL SEMBLE S'ÉLEVER PEU A PEU QUOIQUE À L'INTÉRIEUR TOUJOURS DE LA JUSTIFICATION POUR PARAÎTRE BRILLER BIENTÔT EN HAUT ET À GAUCHE DE LA PAGE DONT IL FAIT L'OBJET . . .   (164–65)

THE SUN RISING UPON LITERATURE

LET THE SUN ON THE HORIZON OF THE TEXT SHOW ITSELF AT LAST AS WE SEE IT HERE FOR THE FIRST TIME IN LITERATURE IN THE FORM OF ITS NAME INCORPORATED IN THE FIRST LINE SUCH THAT IT SEEMS TO RISE LITTLE BY LITTLE THOUGH STILL WITHIN THE JUSTIFICATION SO AS TO APPEAR TO SOON SHINE AT THE TOP AND TO THE LEFT OF THE PAGE WHOSE OBJECT IT IS. . . . (My translation)

The typographical placement of the subtitle "The sun rising upon literature" and the underlying comments upon its placement result in the creation of an iconic or, in a loose sense, performative poem. Because it refers not to the rising sun, but to its representation or counterpart within the text, the passage constitutes what it represents; it actually is what it describes. Semantic reflexivity is characteristic of Ponge's writing. Though many of his poems appear to treat concrete objects in the world, they do not. What they really treat are, to use Ponge's term *objeux* (objests), the reflections of objects in language.

The title of this poem, "Le soleil placé en abîme," is an allusion to the rhetorical figure that it applies, the *mise en abîme* (placement in abyss), which creates an infinite distancing of the represented ob-

ject through its own layers of representations. It is also a philosophical statement about the inaccessibility of the sun as origin of language and life.

Though they may engender the act of writing, sense-perceived
objects are necessarily extrinsic, for Ponge, from the literary text.
Indeed, as is articulated in the closing lines of this poem, their direct reflection within the text entails an eclipse and hardening of
the poetic vision and the subsequent death of the poem:

> *Le Soleil était entré dans le miroir. La*
> *vérité ne s'y vit plus. Aussitôt eblouie et*
> *bientôt cuite, coagulée comme un oeuf.*

> The sun had entered into the mirror.
> The truth was no longer seen there. Immediately
> blinded and soon cooked, coagulated like an egg.
> (My translation)

Pierre Garnier, founder of "spatialisme" and editor of several issues of *Les Lettres,* is one of the best-known French concrete poets.
He has produced much experimental poetry both visual and audi-
tory, and even semantic, in which, as Garnier describes it, the text
functions merely as a sign post on the road to the experience of the
poem. Thus, while Garnier carries the art of concrete poetry as far
as it can go, like the Dadaists, he is ever ready to abandon its particular forms. His simultaneous preoccupation with and disregard
for the specificity of linguistic material can be seen in two 1964
"sun" poems: "Extension 2," composed in collaboration with Ilse
Garnier, and "SOLEIL," a text "visualized" (rather than illustrated)
by the artist Theo Kerg.

As its title suggests, "Extension 2" (fig. 4) is not a literary representation of the sun (Williams [116]). Nor is it a verbal expansion
on the word *sun*'s connotations or semés. Rather it is an extension
of its letters, its graphic components. Unlike Ponge's poem, which
plays primarily on the "vertiginous thickness of meaning" associated with the signified "sun," Garnier shows how the signifier
"sun," like the referent "sun," proliferates verbal material, engen-
dering other signs. He explains this in the accompanying statement.
In *Once Again,* Jean-François Bory, who cites this poem as the "ultimate degree attained by visual poetry" comments on the func-
tional link between the text and the actual sun. *"Here,* by the

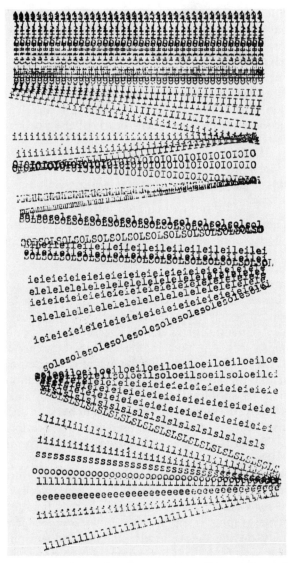

Figure 4. Ilse and Pierre Garnier, "Extension 2," 1964.

transformation of the word sun (soleil) into its concrete components, the word becomes, as it was in the first age, a living organism in space" (28–29). The function of this text (and according to

Garnier that of concrete poetry in general) is to reveal the word as an active presence in the universe—a presence of its own origin and end.

But for Garnier, as for a long and highly diverse line of poets and religious and philosophical thinkers, the presence of the word is curiously non-specific, or at least not specifically linguistic. This becomes clear in "SOLEIL" (fig. 5).

The title page reads "SOLEIL poem by Pierre Garnier visualized lithographically by theo kerg." One might be thus led to read the word *soleil* as the poem and the other components as commentary or exegesis and illustration. But a reading of the text shows that from Garnier's perspective the word *SOLEIL* is not the poem. The poem is also the lithograph, and whatever may become present to the senses of the reader:

SUN

word composed upon stone, revolving around its center of gravity o, vibrating tirelessly, intensely, in depth and on the surface, exploding in a thousand fragments SUN, ripping space, pushing back the crackling earthly crust, the fleeing shadows. space is abolished, time is abolished, replaced by a succession of intensities of the spatial word:

SUN

poetry is no longer in the dust of libraries. more than ever it is in the advertisement, the television, the film of our eyes, in the records and the radio of our ears, in our mouth, in our hands. it is no longer illustrated, no longer embalmed, it is rendered present, it takes possession of us, entirely, in a different way. . . .   (My translation)

The concrete poem is thus whatever the reader beholds—the reader whom Garnier has elsewhere called "this sun, at the ideal center of the poem.[3] Its poeticity is gained with its presence through the act of perception.

As the exchange between objects and perception is fundamental to writing and to reading, it is not surprising that re-presentations of this reflexive process have become equally central to concrete and abstract poetry. To this reader, the blinding solidification of Garnier's text in Theo Kerg's "visualisation" provides the perfect

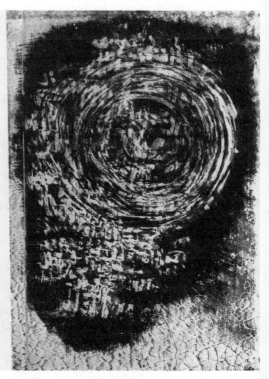

SOLEIL

mot composé sur la pierre, virant autour de son
centre de gravité O, vibrant inlassablement, intensé-
ment, en profondeur et en surface, éclatant en mille
fragments SOLEIL, déchirant l'espace, reculant la
craquelante couche terrestre, les fuyants ténèbres.
l'espace est aboli, le temps est aboli, remplacés par
une succession d'intensités du mot spatial :

SOLEIL

la poésie n'est plus dans la poussière des bibliothèques.
plus que jamais elle est dans la publicité, la télé, le film
de nos yeux, dans les disques et la radio de nos oreilles,
dans notre bouche, dans nos mains. on ne l'illustre plus,
on ne l'embaume plus, on la rend présente. elle prend
possession de nous, entièrement, autrement.

théo kerg crée actuellement, avec des textes de pierre garnier, un
livre de poèmes tactilistes, poèmes visibles, poèmes spatiaux, qu'il
présentera sous des formes inattendues, nouvelles, qui remontent
aux sources.

voici ➡

SOLEIL

hommage à pierre garnier, reproduction d'une litho en couleur de
théo kerg, format 72×53 cm, créée en 1964, exposée pour la première
fois à l'exposition annuelle du trait, au musée d'art moderne
de paris, du 16 avril au 10 mai.

Figure 5. Pierre Garnier, "SOLEIL," "visualized lithographically by Theo Kerg," 1964.

concrete closure for Ponge's abstract poem. Another sun has entered a mirror and coagulated like an egg.

The tendencies toward abstraction and concreteness discussed
here are clearly evident in the anti-representational, self-referential
visual works of such American poets as Emmett Williams, Jackson
Mac Low, Karl Kempton, Mary Ellen Solt, and others. Solt's geranium poem, for example (fig. 6), at first looks like a simple shaped
poem; but the words at the center—arranged not only visually but
also as a pair of acrostics—are mysterious, suggestive, and moti-
vated by complex semantic play. Whether concrete and abstract poetry may be merging in America to the extent that they have in
France remains an inviting topic for further research.

Figure 6. Mary Ellen Solt, "Geranium" from *Flowers in Concrete* (Fine Arts Department, Indiana University, 1964).

FRED E. MAUS

Ashbery and the
Condition of Music

It is commonplace to use music as a point of reference in articulating certain qualities of poetry. A poem might be called musical in order to convey that the sounds of its words go together in an attractive way, or a poem that combines rhetorical heightening with some sort of conspicuous rhythmic emphasis might seem close to music. Perhaps this is Roger Shattuck's idea when he claims that John Ashbery's poetry lacks some of the musicality traditionally valued in poetry (38–40).

These comparisons between poetry and music depend on strikingly superficial conceptions of music, especially in light of the complex, sophisticated discussions that have characterized music theory and musical aesthetics. It might be thought that superficiality is inevitable in comparisons of different art forms; someone might argue that a relatively precise description of music would direct attention only to its most parochial qualities, its points of divergence from other forms of expression or communication. But that is wrong. In fact, a more accurate, and perhaps more uncomfortable, conception of music can provide the basis for surprisingly deep analogies between music and other arts.

That is a large claim, not to be fully substantiated in a single paper. But the claim can be made plausible, at least, by careful reflection on brief passages of poetry and music. John Ashbery's poetry seems to offer a promising starting point: not only do Ashbery's poems frequently contain references to music, but in interviews and at readings he has often cited musical forms and musical experience as analogs for aspects of his poetry. Though Shattuck, for one, has found Ashbery's work to lack musicality, other critics have shared Ashbery's view that the poetry is importantly analogous to music. David Shapiro, for instance, writes that "Ashbery is an intellectual musician (3). Shapiro's wide-ranging book contains many pleasing allusions to Ashbery's interest in music.

The possibility of such conflict indicates that musical aspects of Ashbery's work might provide an especially challenging and rewarding object of study. Rather than investigating the details of Ashbery's comments about music and poetry, I shall take those comments as warranting a more independent investigation of common ground between Ashbery's style and aspects of Western instrumental music. A single example will serve to illustrate my claims; the brief poem "Whether It Exists" is suitable because many of its conspicuous features are shared with Ashbery's other work.

> All through the fifties and sixties the land tilted
> Toward the bowl of life. Now life
> Has moved in that direction. We taste the conviction
> Minus the rind, the pulp and the seeds. It
> Goes down smoothly.
>
> At a later date I added color
> And the field became a shed in ways I no longer remember.
> Familiarly, but without tenderness, the sunset pours its
> Dance music on the (again) slanting barrens.
> The problems we were speaking of move up toward them.
>
> (*Houseboat* 41)

For my purposes, what matters in the poem is the multiple indeterminacy that Ashbery sustains. I want to note four aspects of this characteristic indeterminacy. My observations will not surprise anyone who has been reading Ashbery, nor will they begin to constitute an interpretation of the poem. Their purpose is to focus the subsequent comparison with music.[1]

One, the sentences of the poem cannot be determinately assigned to one or more distinct speakers or subjects. The issue of such attribution arises most palpably at the opening of the second stanza: one does not know whether the singular first-person pronoun refers to the same person who said or thought "we" in the first stanza, or to whoever opened the poem with an impersonal journalistic generality. And the last two sentences of the poem leave the issue open, passing again through complete generality and the plural first person. The words of the poem could be the utterance of a single speaker or the thought of a single subject, but they could as well be a conjunction of speech or thought from several consciousnesses.

Two, some parts of the poem provide a context in which other parts of the poem might be regarded as quoting or mentioning sentences rather than using them. To see the point more vividly, one can imagine quotation marks around some sentences, indicating that they are quoted as the object of reflections that take place elsewhere in the poem, and such repunctuation seems to bring out implications that are already latent in the poem. For instance, the first two sentences could be set apart in that way: the third sentence, suddenly introducing self-reference and referring to a conviction, carries the suggestion that the opening records, or quotes, an expression of that conviction. Or one might set the first sentence of the second stanza apart with quotation marks, clarifying the suggestion that the singular first-person sentence is an illustration of generalizations offered in the rest of the poem. And there are other possibilities.

Three, the temporal references in the poem do not establish any determinate chronology. In particular, the opening of the second stanza indicates two times, one said to be later than the other, but it is obscure how those times are related to the "fifties and sixties" and the "now" of the first stanza. Also, the temporal references in the remainder of the second stanza are indeterminate with regard to the preceding parts of the poem. A different form of temporal indeterminacy comes from the indefinite relation between ordering in the poem and succession in a depicted situation. For instance, there is no evidence that the second stanza records speech or thought that occurs *later* in some depicted situation than speech or thought recorded in the first stanza.

Four, one does not know whether the words of the poem should be imagined as speech or as the content of unspoken thought. While this form of indeterminacy is hardly rare in poetry, Ashbery's shifts of tone focus the indeterminacy sharply: the poem alludes to public history or journalistic discourse and, perhaps, the public self-location of a generation ("We taste the conviction . . ."), but it also alludes to the privacy and, perhaps, inwardness of personal recollection ("At a later date I added color . . . "), and nothing in the poem definitely establishes its mode as speech or inner thought, either for the whole poem or for any part of it.

Ashbery's indeterminacies, in this poem and in many others, do not have the effect of rendering irrelevant certain questions about the individuation of subjects, temporal sequence, and so on; rather, the poems seem concerned to raise these questions and keep them before the reader. The feel of an Ashbery poem is neither vagueness nor purely non-representational word play, but it is tied up with the precise, unresolvable tension of Ashbery's indeterminacies.

The precision of Ashbery's uncertainties coexists with the precision of determinate relations within the poetry, relations that resist any simple mimetic interpretation. The delicate play of spatial language in "Whether It Exists" provides a fine example. The first stanza narrates a change between a time when "the land tilted / Toward the bowl of life" and a time when life "Has moved in that direction," that is, I suppose, from the bowl toward the land. To these reciprocal motions is added a third when "it," that is, "the conviction," a sort of fruit juice, "goes down smoothly." The banal idiom of a food "going down smoothly" carries a vivid sense of spatial movement in juxtaposition to the opening of the poem, though the poem does not imply any one space in which all three movements occur. In the second stanza the land tilts once more and another fluid goes down smoothly, as "the sunset pours its / Dance music on the (again) slanting barrens." And again the tilting is answered by a reciprocal motion: "The problems we were speaking of move up toward them." Indeed, one can trace a rather abstract narrative through the poem: the tension of the unrelated spatial references in the first stanza is resolved by the conjunction of corresponding references, now elaborating an account of a single space, in the last three lines of the poem. The schematic clarity of this narrative is unusual for Ashbery, but more generally "Whether It Exists" shares with much of Ashbery's work a sense of narrative order that cannot be specified in straightforward mimetic terms.[2]

In turning to musical examples I could easily argue my position with reference to recent compositions, works that are contemporary with Ashbery's poetry. However, I shall turn instead to passages from a piano sonata by Haydn. There are two reasons to choose a beautiful but in many ways ordinary piece from the standard repertory. For one thing, Ashbery has said that he finds music helpful in the actual process of writing, and he mentions composers from three centuries of the main tradition of Western instrumental music: Couperin, Brahms, and Carter ("Craft" 14–15). So on the

Example 1. Joseph Haydn, from Piano Sonata in G Minor.

face of it, there would be no biographical reason to prefer an analogy to recent music. And secondly, the musical properties that will concern me are shared quite generally by eighteenth- and nineteenth-century instrumental music as well as later music that continues that tradition. Accordingly, the opening of the second movement from Haydn's Sonata in G Minor will provide an appropriate example (ex. 1).

It is natural to hear this music as a succession of purposeful actions, but one cannot determinately individuate the agents of these actions.[3] The question is not whether there are actual determinate agents who are responsible for what a listener hears. Obviously there are: the composer and the performers. The question is how one *imagines* the dramatic action of the music. The Haydn passage, for all its simplicity, raises the issue sharply. One can trace three distinct lines of music through the passage, and that might suggest that there are three agents whose activity constitutes the passage. The model for such individuations would be speech or song, in which a single person can produce only one series of pitched sounds. But these three lines move with a notable coordination of purpose, producing a coherent succession of harmonies, and that might suggest a single agent performing a somewhat complexly articulated action. Or again, the upper line is set apart from the lower lines by its faster activity and greater melodic interest: perhaps the piece presents a solo agent and an accompanying agent. But to see, or rather to hear, the attractiveness of all these possibilities is also to recognize that the piece raises the question of individuation of agents without determinately resolving the issue.

There are further complications, particularly in connection with the middle line; its continuity as a single line becomes problematic when it moves by a large, dissonant leap in measure 2 or when it falls silent and suddenly reappears in alignment with the upper line

Example 2. Joseph Haydn, from Piano Sonata in G Minor.

in measures 5 to 6. But it will be more revealing to turn to the beginning of this same sonata, where questions of individuation are more obviously acute (ex. 2). Consider, for instance, the left-hand part at the opening. The large leap from the first pair of notes to the second might suggest a discrimination of two agents: one in a lowish register set against a faster-moving higher-register agent. Or perhaps there is one agent who changes register easily. Or, since there are two pitches for each sound, perhaps there are two agents here; or perhaps four, two in the lower register, two in the higher.

The use of register to individuate agents becomes more problematic in the second measure; in particular, the octave-related D's in the second half of the measure might imply a distinction of agents, as might the octave leaps at the opening, but now the higher D has been approached in a way that links it to what used to be the lower register. A more startling puzzle is raised by the convergence of two lines on the G at the beginning of the second measure: where the left hand had two notes at a time it now has only one.

Between measures 2 and 3 the left hand makes a larger leap than before, and the identity of the agent of that high G is utterly obscure. Even more remarkable is the sudden restoration of a three-line texture, effected by the entrance of a new highest line that corresponds in its general motion to the middle line at the opening. Has the agent of the middle line suddenly occupied a new register? Have the three old agents all shifted upward while retaining their respective positions? Is it plausible to regard what are now the outer parts as the activity of a single accompanying agent, with the focal, melody-producing agent now occupying the middle register?

Such enigmas of individuation are regularly associated with polyphony, that is, with musical textures in which several more-or-less independent lines are more-or-less coordinated with each other. Polyphony offers a close analog for the enigmas of individuation of speakers or subjects that rise in Ashbery's poetry. It is pleasing to recall the precision with which Ashbery himself has recognized this correspondence in a well-known comment on the ambiguity of his pronouns: "I guess I don't have a very strong sense of my own identity and I find it very easy to move from one person in the sense of a pronoun to another and this again helps to produce a kind of polyphony in my poetry" ("Craft" 25). In associating polyphony not just with the combining of distinct musical lines, but with the creation of a texture in which individuals cannot be determinately distinguished, Ashbery's comment reveals a subtle, sophisticated understanding of music.[4]

The same material from Haydn will permit me to illustrate analogs to other indeterminacies that I identified in Ashbery's poem. Music tends to depend much more on repetition of material than does poetry; one effect of this is to create an ambiguous impression that some passages are quotations of others rather than direct actions or utterances. To my ear this issue comes up quite strikingly around measure 5 of the opening of the Haydn sonata. It is easy to hear the music at measure 5 as beginning a sort of rumination on the earlier music, as though the first few measures had quoted material that will now be the basis for discursive exploration; but it is also easy to hear the passage as itself a recollection or quotation of the preceding material, especially when the passage is interrupted halfway through measure 6, becoming a fragment and thereby coming to seem more dependent on the more self-sufficient statements at the opening.[5]

Music does not possess the means of temporal reference that occur in language: there are no tenses or references to dates, no word *now*. But there is a succession of events in a composition about which one can raise the question whether succession in the composition should be imagined as temporal ordering in the series of actions that one follows. The passage in the Haydn sonata that begins halfway through measure 6 is sharply discontinuous from the preceding passage in many ways: texturally, harmonically, motivically, rhythmically. One especially bold discontinuity emerges only gradually, as the new passage continues to elaborate a single dissonant chord for six measures, establishing a drastically different rate of motion from that in the opening span. The discontinuities raise the possibility that the second span does not exactly succeed the first but is simply juxtaposed to it, as two scenes that are not temporally consecutive might be juxtaposed in a film. However, one can also imagine the passage as presenting a temporal succession or narrative within which drastic change occurs. Such a succession can serve as an analog for Ashbery's shifty temporality.[6]

The indeterminacy of music between being on one hand, a sort of picture of inner life and on the other hand, an imitation of purposeful behavior or eloquent utterance, is obvious and pervasive. Roughly, the indeterminacy arises from the impossibility of establishing whether the anthropomorphic qualities of a musical passage predominantly imply a first-person or a third-person perspective.[7] It is extraordinarily difficult to describe the conflicting emphases in specific examples; the problem is that the anthropomorphic affinities of a musical passage are typically subtle and manifold, and descriptions will consequently seem crude and incomplete. But consider, once more, the opening of the Haydn Allegretto (ex. 1). The melody rises successively to three high points. The increasing tension that a listener might sense at these three points comes in part from imagining a single voice that strains to reach increasingly high notes; perhaps this voice is imagined primarily as *heard*, though a listener may also identify with the imagined voice. In the first movement of the sonata (ex. 2), a similar increase in tension results from the succession of a high G and a higher B-flat. Here, however, there is no determinate quasi-vocal line that reaches these two high points; lacking the relatively straightforward allusion to a quasi-operatic vocal ascent, this passage may achieve greater intimacy and inwardness. But both passages are ultimately indeterminate with regard to a first-person or third-person orientation.

My earlier remarks about the feel of Ashbery's uncertainties seem apt with regard to the Haydn passages: the feel of the music comes from the precise, unresolvable tension of these indeterminacies. And further, the uncertainties I have described coexist with precise, determinate musical structures; at the opening of the Haydn, for example, the pairing of phrases in measures 1 through 4, with the second phrase closing off where the first phrase remained incomplete, constitutes a lucid—but non-mimetic—narrative succession.

If these suggestions are correct, then a properly complex and challenging view of music can lead to an illuminating comparison with Ashbery's poetry, clarifying the poet's sense that his work is analogous to music. A the same time, the nature of Ashbery's techniques, the extreme measures that he must take to move poetry so close to the condition of music, may help us to remember what an astonishing art music itself is.

STEPHEN MATTERSON

Contemporary and Found

In his anthology titled *An Introduction to Poetry,* Louis Simpson provides a useful definition of the found poem:

> A piece of writing that is read as poetry though it was not intended to be. Usually the poem is found in a passage of prose—it may be from a news item, advertisement, hand-book, travel book, or catalogue—which is then divided into lines of verse. Most found poems, though not all, are satiric, the unexpected attention catching the writer off guard. (422)

Appearing as it does in the glossary to an anthology, the definition is a sound, general one. But if found poetry were examined more closely, we can see that it raises certain ideas that challenge our assumptions about the relation it has to "conventional" poetry. On the face of it, the found poem *seems* to undermine the critical approaches we can make to conventional poetry. But, in a subtle way, it can also reinforce whatever validity those approaches have; that is, because the found poem is a distinct form, its relation to the conventional poem can be considered uncertain or ironic. But in practice, the found poem supports conventional forms.

The epistemological status of found poetry actually differs little, if at all, from that of conventional poetry. This may appear an odd statement, given that found poems almost always announce their status. By so doing, they are suggesting that an important difference exists between them and other poems. However, the experiments described by Jonathan Culler in *Structuralist Poetics* and by Stanley Fish in *Is There a Text in This Class?* do undermine some of the distinctions we usually make between poetry and other media.

Culler took a paragraph from a newspaper report and placed it in verse form. He then demonstrated how his constructed poem exhibited typical features of poetry—irony, tension, richness of texture—features that were not evident when the words existed only as a newspaper item. He concluded that poetry differs from prose because the reader brings to a poem (or to an apparent poem) certain generic expectations that are irrelevant to other media. Poetry differs from prose because of the "type of attention" given to it by the reader (161). Reading itself is, in Culler's words, a "structuring activity" (241). Stanley Fish came to a similar conclusion about the role the reader plays. After one class, he left on the blackboard a list of names and told the next class that the words on the board were a poem and their task was to explicate it. The group of students created a detailed exegesis of the list (322–37).

Both experiments, and the conclusions drawn from them, are important in an examination of found poetry. They affirm the reader's role in breaking down the distinctions usually drawn between media. They suggest that to read given words as a poem is, in effect, to create a poem, regardless of authorial intention. A difference, of course, is that found poems make explicit to the reader the fact that they are intruders from prose. It is conventional to have the term *found* somewhere in the title. Also, they are mediated by an agent; the poet or writer is offering them to the reader as appropriate models for the reader's structuring activity. It might at first seem that a poem with the title "Poem Found in a Dime-Store Diary" is making an explicit challenge to the reader's sense of what a poem is. But this does not happen. In fact, the reader is rather confirmed in his or her sense of what poetry is. This happens for two reasons. First, the use of the word *poem* in the title challenges the reader and stimulates his or her capacity to structure in an appropriate manner the words that follow. Second, the poem is, in a sense, ready made for the reader. A mediator has already selected the words on the basis of their supposed relevance to the structuring activity. They aren't selected at random; thus the structuring activity is not a challenge. The reader of a found poem doesn't usually have to resort to the ingenious cunning of Stanley Fish's students in order to structure meaning. Although the reader is breaking down media distinctions during the act of reading, he or she is doing so in response to a specific invitation.

There are, of course, other signals that invite the reader to read the words as a poem, and some of these are very simple. When we come across "Poem Found in a Dime-Store Diary," it is not only the title that indicates how it should be read. It might appear among a collection of other poems, either an anthology or a collection by the author. That signal might appear too obvious for serious consideration, but it is a sign directing the reader to provide the type of attention most appropriate to the language. Similarly, the very format of the words is an indication of how they should be approached. This particular poem has ten lines, each consisting of a single phrase; so something as simple as the appearance of the words on the page is a stimulus to our structuring activity. Saul Bellow once told John Berryman that he'd always wanted to write poetry. Berryman replied, "You do, you do!" "No, no," said Bellow, "I mean short lines." Perhaps our whole sense of the differences between prose and poetry depends on our readiness to accept the signals that features such as short lines provide.

While the found poem may appear to be an exclusively modern or contemporary idiom, it does have roots and analogies. Found poetry derives in part from modern poetry's relaxation of some of the formal restraints once considered characteristic of poetry as a discourse. The freer and more flexible verse forms resulting from that relaxation have allowed poetry to absorb prose forms without incongruity. But the roots of found poetry may be said to go back further. The irony Louis Simpson sees as the typical effect of the found poem could be achieved in the nineteenth century through the dramatic monologue. Browning, of course, exploits the ironic distance between the words of the monologue and the reader's perception of their deeper implications. Furthermore, such a technique had long been available to the novelist. The ironic commentator or the flawed point of view were well established in prose by the nineteenth century. The effects of such techniques are comparable to the effects achieved by the found poem.

Also, there are striking analogies between the found poem and the other arts. Andy Warhol and Jasper Johns took everyday items and made them the focus of their paintings. It is quite usual now to see an item such as a coffee pot in an art gallery. Its presence in that context invites the observer to focus on the object's aesthetic qualities rather than, as would happen in the kitchen, on its utilitarian qualities. In a similar way, found poems take a piece of language from its appropriate context. By placing it in an alternative context, the reader is invited to a reconsideration of its meaning.

Since I've been talking quite generally so far, I'd like to look at the "Poem Found in a Dime-Store Diary." Its "author"—I'll discuss the problems of authorship shortly—is Ian Young.

Place these slips inside your diary
    in the appropriate place
....
Tomorrow is my wife's birthday
....
Tomorrow is my husband's birthday
....
Tomorrow is my wedding anniversary
....
Tomorrow is my mother's birthday
....
Tomorrow is my father's birthday
....
Tomorrow my Holidays start
....
Tomorrow is
....
Tomorrow is
....
Tomorrow is

The poem appears to explore what society expects of the individual: having a wife or husband, appropriately commemorating birthdays and anniversaries. It also assumes employment, holidays, and being on speaking terms with your parents. The diary thus appears to reflect, or enact, the assumptions society makes of its responsible members. Being single, homosexual, unemployed, illegitimate, or orphaned are, it implies, simply deviant forms of behavior. Such kinds of behavior or states of being are placed outside of this text, or in its margins, as they are in the margins of "normal" social existence. The poem may in this respect be compared to Auden's "To an Unknown Citizen," in which the normative social statistical expectations are combined to make a composite figure. The differences between these poems, however, are interesting and may be said to derive directly from the differences between a "found" poem and a conventional poem. Auden's satire is accepted by us as satire; even while appreciating the poem, we recognize that Auden has made a careful—and creative—selection with the very intention of achieving a certain effect. Reading the found poem, however, we are of course considerably less certain about intention. I would say that because of this, "Poem Found in a Dime-

Store Diary" is more discomforting than Auden's poem. We feel
that we have helped create the found poem, just as we have somehow acquiesced in the social norms and expectations it presents.
That by being closely involved with the text, we too have margin-
alized certain experiences.

Like Auden's poem, this found poem suggests the empty, vacant
lives that statistics alone cannot convey. Its ending, that repetition
of the phrase "Tomorrow is," appears to echo Macbeth's "Tomorrow and tomorrow and tomorrow" speech. Actually this found
poem makes a trope of the word *tomorrow,* since nine of its lines
open with that word. That parallelism may suggest that humans
are trapped by time or committed to futile versions of the future. If
you were to consider the found poem as a deliberate echo of the
speech from *Macbeth,* you could argue that the word *tomorrow*
makes each of the activities following the word become meaning-
less, empty rituals signifying nothing, and that the whole diary
represents a "tale told by an idiot." Of course, we know that the
slips are not deliberate echoes of *Macbeth* or of anything but last
year's diary. However, pseudo-intertextuality becomes a pleasant
pastime when reading found poems, and it is perhaps most pleasur-
able because we know that we needn't act according to the respon-
sibilities conventional poems demand. It is another of the features
of the found poem: we are allowed to play freely with its signifiers,
partly because we are unconstrained by some of the limits that ideas
of intentionality, influence, scholarship, and dating usually impose.
In "Poem Found in a Dime-Store Diary" one is free to consider
intertextuality, the background of Auden and Shakespeare. And
what about that use of Empson's "Missing Dates," in turn echoing
Tennyson's "Tithonus"?

In criticizing other poems we are limited by certain factors as to
the influences and analogies we may suggest. With the found
poem, because we realize that intentionality cannot be invoked as a
factor, we are freed from those usual limitations. But this freedom
is itself limited by other factors. For one thing, the freer the interpretation of the found poem, the less likely it is to be serious, and
the more likely it is to attract the attentions of what has been called
the "Oh-come-off-it" school of criticism. We all know that the person who made out these slips didn't have any other writer in mind
when they were made. Only a tongue-in-cheek interpretation could
seriously propose the textual analogies of Shakespeare, Tennyson,
Auden, and Empson.

Well, found poems are not as simple as that, if only because one must start to classify them. Some poems are "found," some pretend to have been found, and others are, frankly, stolen. Even so, it seems that the principles we can apply to the found poem are appropriate also to the stolen. In 1965 a poem by Hugh MacDiarmid (C. M. Grieve) caused a controversy and actually raised questions not only of literary theory but also of legality, when someone pointed out that the words of the poem "Perfect" were taken from a short story by Glynn Jones. MacDiarmid said that the theft was "inadvertent." The matter was complicated by John Sparrow, who wrote to the *Times Literary Supplement* (TLS) to say that the words actually came from a writer called Kiedrych Rhys, and Rhys then wrote to confirm this. MacDiarmid was actually accused several times of such practice and was forced on the defensive on a number of occasions. In a private letter about "Perfect" (published in *The Letters of Hugh MacDiarmid*), he wrote that he wasn't worried about the legal position. This, he said, was because "it's the use we put things to that counts. If part of a loaf is torn out, beaten up into dough, and baked again as a biscuit, that is not any plagiarism of the loaf" (284).

MacDiarmid's use of other sources, however, made readers uneasy, and not only because of the legal implications. In the TLS debate, a feeling of insecurity surfaced among readers, which seemed to be a fear that the privileged discourse that poetry represented was losing its privilege. MacDiarmid's own intentions in the matter are not clear. Perhaps, in the light of his left-wing ideological commitment, the effacing of privileged discourse was in itself a desirable effect. Or perhaps there was an attack on the very concept of ownership.

So the problem of who "owns" found or stolen poems can lead to threats of legal action. But to whom do found poems belong? In his preface to the 1983 book *Syntax*, Robin Blaser writes "these poems do not belong to me." However straightforward that statement appears, it introduces several ideas that are at the heart of *Syntax* and that derive also from an understanding of found poetry. The author, or mediator, disowns the poems. Although he has found them, Blaser is unwilling to acknowledge any claim to ownership. To whom do the poems belong? To the people who speak the words Blaser mediates, or who appear in the found incidents? Scarcely; these people never intended to create poems at all and would probably be appalled at the interpretations the reader is willing to place on them. If they belong to anyone, it seems that the poems must belong to the readers. And yet each reader is free to "make meanings" of the poem; so each reader becomes the owner of the poem thereby made. We are back to Culler, in that reading is a "structuring activity." But it is as though Culler's concept is being taken a step further; perhaps the reader becomes the owner of the structure.

A great deal of *Syntax* is made up of the found; of what is over-heard, accidentally glimpsed, or experienced. The overall impression, however, is not that Blaser is a voyeur or an eavesdropper. He is, rather, somehow at the mercy of his poetic training or sensibility. To the poet, so much experience is raw material for poems that might never be made. In this sense, the book represents a structuring activity that is incomplete. The activity of the reader is required to take it a stage further, to complete the structuring activity through the act of reading. Here, for example, is a poem titled, as are about half the poems in *Syntax*, "The Truth is Laughter."

> on the bus, the small boy, newly
> into letters, spelled out the letters
> scratched in the glass F U
> C K loud-voiced, "Mom,
> what does that say?" "That's
> not a word," she said,
> looking straight at me "It
> doesn't spell anything."

The poem here, of course, is "found" in a different sense than I've been talking about in that it is a found "incident" rather than a found poem. But, like the found poem, the words of the mother are left without comment from the writer; Blaser doesn't fully mediate them. That is, as in the found poem, the reader has a certain freedom in structuring and interpreting the event. The mother here is in a position similar to that of the author of the words that make up a found poem. That is, her words and actions have meanings for the reader that she would not acknowledge or endorse. One of the poem's interesting features, then, is Blaser's refusal to give direction to the reader in the act of interpretation. In the whole of *Syntax*, this represents a willingness to involve the reader in the creative act. Each reader is left the freedom to explore the possibilities offered by the experience.

Of course, this feature is by no means exclusive to the found poem. But it is common in found poetry and in poems that masquerade as found. William Carlos Williams's celebrated poem "This is just to say," is a useful example. The poem, cast in the form of a note left on the refrigerator, sounds found. As with the found poem, the lack of a mediating voice leaves the reader with a wide range of potential meanings. Oddly, although this much-anthologized poem is firmly in the canon of twentieth-century poetry, there is no general agreement as to its theme. Any thematic interpretation is made self-consciously and somewhat uncertainly. As with the found poem, Williams's poem allows the reader a wide range of possibilities. He or she is free to decide whether it is "about" temptation, a re-enactment of the fall, or the triumph of the physical over the spiritual. Each reader is left free to construct a poem and, as Blaser's preface implied, the reader becomes the owner of the resulting poem.

For example, I might suggest three possible readings. The poem could be concerned with the uselessness or self-entrapment of sexual desire, comparable to "Th'expense of spirit in a waste of shame." There's the potential Oedipal reading, with the boy thwarted in an attempt to comprehend his origin; to learn of it from his mother. Or there's the reading that would suggest self-referentiality; it is the poem itself that "means nothing."

Syntax is an exciting and challenging book. But it is also frustrating. In a poem like this Blaser frustrates the reader's desire for poems that can be "consumed" or readily understood to give unequivocal meaning. But the book is also frustrating in a larger sense. That is, the book could be infinitely expanded, as though, once you start examining—"reading"—experience and all language as though it were poetry, then there need be no selection process. If poems are, as Culler suggested, made through a structuring activity, then anything can, with the appropriate (or inappropriate) attention become poetry. One of the works included in *Syntax*, "The Mystic East," is a list of place names taken from a map of historic Newfoundland. With such a poem, the concept of found poetry seems to have been taken as far as it will go without actually inviting us to see everything *we find* as a poem. When we read "The Mystic East," we make meanings of the poem as we impose an order on it. The words are mediated for us, however barely, in the kind of arrangement that Blaser presents, and, of course, the signals directing us to read it as a poem are all there.

I began with Louis Simpson's definition of the found poem, in which he states that its effect was usually ironic. Irony is certainly a feature of Blaser's work, but his found poems are by no means dependent on it. Perhaps *Syntax* is the farthest found poetry can go without becoming an entirely arbitrary choice of language.

THOMAS E. BENEDIKTSSON

Montana Eclogue:
The Pastoral Art of
William Stafford

Many critics of contemporary poetry have noted what they call
the new pastoralism of the neo-romantic poetry of the 1960s and
1970s. Jonathan Holden's remark is typical: "Even today, when
most Americans live in cities, the best American poetry in the Romantic tradition—the work of poets such as Robert Bly, James
Dickey, Galway Kinnell, Theodore Roethke, William Stafford and
James Wright—is apt to be pastoral" (*Rhetoric* 73). So, for that matter, is Louis Simpson's rather irritable reaction: "To read some
American poets, you would think that they lived far away from
roads and supermarkets, that they never had thoughts of the people
you meet, that they looked with the eyes of the crow and listened
with the ears of the beaver. That their habitation was darkness and
their house made of earth and stones. That they were pure in
thought and deed" (quoted by Holden, *Rhetoric* 73).

But is it accurate to use the term *pastoral* in this way? A strict
constructionist would say pastoral as a literary form is tied to certain specific conventions that died sometime before the advent of
the romantic movement. Yet most critics allow some latitude beyond the conventional genre of idealized shepherds and shepherd-
esses derived from classical models and find instances of pastoral
into the nineteenth century and beyond. As W. W. Gregg pointed
out in 1906, the constant element in all the varied forms of pastoral
is the "recognition of a contrast, implied or expressed, between
pastoral life and some more complex types of civilization" (4). This
recognition gives rise to the pastoral reaction against the sophistication of the court or the city in favor of the simpler life of the country. Heavily imbued with sentiment and nostalgia, pastoral is based
on a desire to retreat from the pressures of the present moment into
an idealized simplicity—in classical literature an Arcadian or Golden

Age; in romantic literature a cult of childhood, an ideal of the noble savage, a myth of an organic society, or an idyll of unspoiled nature. Written by the sophisticated in praise of the unsophisticated, pastoral is a literature of escapism and wish-fulfillment.

Since the pastoral impulse itself arises from the appeal of an illusion, recent writers have shown an interest in exploring the aesthetic and dramatic possibilities of the genre's self-contradictions. Modern theories accordingly stress reflexive or dialectical design in the structure of pastoral works. For William Empson, for example, pastoral design is a way of embodying the complex in the simple—an aesthetic of metonymy. For Leo Marx, pastoral design is metaphoric, an attempt to resolve within the text opposing "kingdoms of force," natural and technological, which are utterly incompatible in the real landscape. For Raymond Williams, the pastoral illusion contrasts with the "counter-pastoral" political reality of exploited peasants, and for J. R. Ebbotson, it must confront the Darwinian antipastoral of violence and natural aggression. Thus, though modern pastorals appeal to the universal desire for simplicity and escape, they also employ a rhetorical strategy that attempts to deal with the contradictions between the "real world" and the world of pastoral fantasy.

It is only in these terms that the neo-romantic American poetry of the 1960s and 1970s can properly be termed pastoral. As Gary Snyder puts it in a famous formulation:

> Class-structured civilized society is a kind of mass ego. To transcend the ego is to go beyond society as well. "Beyond" there lies inwardly, the unconscious. Outwardly, the equivalent of the unconscious is the wilderness: both of these terms meet, one step even further on, as *one*.
>
> (*Earth* 118, 122)

The poetry that establishes this unity springs from a pastoral impulse, but it must employ a conscious and artful rhetoric to convey a sense of primal unconsciousness. In the process it must continually struggle with the traditional aesthetic problems of pastoralism: how through a sophisticated literary form to express the value and wonder of the unsophisticated and unworldly, and how to deal with the sentimentalism associated with the effort, when the awareness sought for is so clearly antisentimental.

Partly because of the strong pull of the pastoral impulse in his work, partly because of his use of highly but subtly rhetorical pastoral design, William Stafford might be the most representative poet in this movement. In Stafford's work we find nearly every element of sentimental pastoral: a poignant nostalgia for his Midwestern childhood; a reverence for American Indians as "noble savages," whose tie with the land was elemental and spiritual and who lived in a kind of Arcadia before the encroachment of white people; a panegyric to unspoiled nature, imaged particularly in idealized versions of the Pacific Northwest. But Stafford modifies the sentimentalism inherent in these stereotypes with a rhetoric that quietly incorporates the surreal and demonic into the pastoral landscape; in fact, one of the special qualities of his poetry rests in its dialectic of the sentimental and the demonic, a dialectic achieved through the use of surrealist metaphor.

The Surrealist Mode: Sentimental Demonic

Surrealist technique, an important rhetorical element in Stafford's poetry, is a way of opening up possibilities of irrational, potentially mystical significance within what might be otherwise rational or merely sentimental. To give a simple example, we might examine the mild surrealism of "Universe is One Place" (81), in which a consciously sentimental, even trite pastoral subject—a farm girl bringing water to tired field hands—is opened to larger significance by dislocations in syntax and imagery:

> Crisis they call it?—when
> when the gentle wheat leans at the combine and
> and when the farm girl brings cool jugs wrapped in burlap
> slapping at her legs?
>
> We think—drinking cold water
> water looking at the sky—
> *Sky is home, universe is one place.*
> Crisis? City folks make
>
> make such a stir.
> Farm girl away through the wheat.

Syntactic dislocations—the repetition of "when / when," "and / and," "water / water," "sky / sky," and "make / make,"—open the signification to possibilities of non-coherence. The didactic "universe is one place" may be the coherent center of the poem, but the dislocations of the syntax force the final image away from the merely literal, holding forth the potential of metaphor without exactly establishing what the terms of the metaphor might be.

In other poems, the terms of the controlling metaphor might seem clear, even conventional, but the surrealist movement of the poem strains against that clarity toward more mysterious possibilities. In "Letter from Oregon" (123) the poet, watching the salmon fight upstream to return to their home waters to spawn, imagines returning to his own birthplace. The metaphor for this imagined journey is an eastbound train moving through mountains:

> Mother, here there are shadowy salmon;
> ever their sides argue up the falls.
> Watching them plunge with fluttering gills,
> I thought back through Wyoming where I came from.
>
> The gleaming sides of my train glimmered
> up over passes and arrowed through shoals
> of aspen fluttering in a wind of yellow.

To the extent that it provides a conventional rhetorical link between tenor and vehicle, the controlling metaphor is coherent and rational. The train-as-salmon image, in fact, is an example of pastoral design in Leo Marx's sense of the term, in which an object of technology is placed in a harmonious relationship with nature through a metaphor that makes it seem a part of nature. Likewise, the speaker's journey away from home and his imagined return seem by metaphoric extension part of a natural process, as inevitable as the migrations of salmon. But in the middle section of the poem, Stafford casts the comparison literally and figuratively into doubt:

> Only the sky stayed true; I turned,
>
> justifying space through those miles of Wyoming
> till the wave of the land was quelled by the stars;
> then tunnels of shadow led me far
> through doubt, and I was home.
>
> Mother, even home was doubtful;
> many slip into the sea and are gone for years,

just as I boarded the six-fifteen there.
Over the bar I have leaped outward.

The salmon's journey into the sea and back has become a metaphor for a migration from another mode of being, a "home" far
different from the Midwestern home Stafford left behind. The primal imagery of "tunnels of shadow" and "the wave of the land was
quelled by the stars" prepare us for the metamorphosis of the
controlling figure in the final stanza, where mystery and doubt are
not resolved but are intensified in a surrealist version of the same
metaphor:

Somewhere in the ocean beyond Laramie
when that grass folded low in the dark
a lost fin waved, and I felt the beat
of the old neighborhood stop, on our street.

Reminiscent of the fish in the wheatfield in Chagall's backdrop for
Aleko, this surrealist image annihilates the rational frame for the
poem's controlling metaphor and casts into doubt its ostensibly
nostalgic motive, quietly reintroduced in the last line. In place of
sentimental nostalgia we are left with a sense of indeterminacy and
a suggestion of some primal, unconscious being from which we
have migrated and to which we wish to return.

Seen, then, as an element of pastoral design, Stafford's surrealism is a way of introducing a more mystical level, which interacts
with the simple surface pastoralism of his poem. In this context Albert Cook's semiotic definition of surrealist metaphor is useful:

On the one hand the surrealist poem envisions a dream by
erasing, or tending to erase, the distinction between tenor
and vehicle, floating both the signifier and signified far
away from an object single or composite. On the other
hand, by according a dream significance to every object and
slight event in the waking world, the erasure of distinction
operates in the service of a giant reference, a giant
referent.   (36)

This technique, Cook maintains, "induces a surrender to primal
metaphor." He goes on to distinguish between pastoral and primal:

the pastoral vocabulary of some surrealist poets is not really pastoral but "preliterary and ultraliterary." Though he makes this comment regarding the vocabulary of "Mediterranean" poets like W. S. Merwin, the same could be said of Stafford, who uses a pastoral vocabulary to convey his sense of the primal or demonic.

In "Bi-Focal" (48), for example, the pastoral realm is the proper landscape for love, but love is "of the earth only." This benign surface is what we often call "nature," but nature's essence, the demonic, is rooted in darkness; it "legends" itself up from subterranean depths, "deep as the mine / the thickest rocks won't tell." By contrast with the chthonic, mythic level of things, the sentimental pastoral is mere illusion:

> So, the world happens twice—
> once what we see it as;
> second, it legends itself
> deep, the way it is.

Poetry could be the "map" of the surface or it could be the "legend" of the depths; many of Stafford's poems are such legends, in which the natural landscape becomes a kind of extended metaphor for the unconscious mind. These poems work not through a contrast of pastoral and demonic, but through a metamorphosis of pastoral into demonic through surrealist metaphor. As Holden has shown in his book *The Mark to Turn,* Stafford employs an extensive and surprisingly consistent series of conventions in many of his poems. Darkness, for example, is the realm of the irrational or demonic self; hearing and touch, not sight, are linked to the power of the imagination to contact that realm. Light, even moonlight, is the enemy of the revitalizing imagination (24–27).

Any number of poems might serve as models of this rhetorical technique, but "In the Deep Channel" (31) is representative:

> Setting a trotline after sundown
> if we went far enough away in the night
> sometimes up out of deep water
> would come a secret-headed channel cat,
>
> Eyes that were still eyes in the rush of darkness,
> flowing feelers noncommittal and black,

and hidden in the fins those rasping bone daggers,
with one spiking upward on its back.

We would come at daylight and find the line sag,
the fishbelly gleam and the rush on the tether:
to feel the swerve and the deep current
which tugged at the tree roots below the river.

This poem owes its resonance to a careful choice of metaphors. The "secret-headed" catfish is the emblem of the irrational and demonic within nature and within the self. Its mode of sight ("eyes that were still eyes in the rush of darkness") is denied us; but pulling the line, we can feel "the swerve and the deep current" in which it has its secret life.

In terms of the dualism of "Bi-Focal," "In the Deep Channel" would have to be considered an antipastoral poem, moving from the idyllic imagination into the demonic. But in another sense, it is a version of pastoral, written out of the pressure to escape poetically from the banality and moral turpitude of everyday existence. For Stafford is very much a poet of suburban academic life, whose rejection of that familiar world is as characteristically a literary gesture as was the Renaissance courtly poet's pastoral rejection of the court. The "literariness" of the enterprise is evident through Stafford's frequent use of a set of "deep image" conventions as artificial in their way as the conventions of traditional pastoral were for the Renaissance poet. It would be an error, however, to see this use of artifice as an artistic flaw; it is part of a conscious pastoral design, an effort to achieve within the literary text a unity that is denied in ordinary life.

The Didactic Mode

In pastoral terms, separation from nature is the fall of "man," and romantic pastoral elegy both mourns that separation and tries to heal it. In Stafford's poetry, separation is often represented by antipastoral winter landscapes that suggest nature in its most hostile and inhuman aspect. In "Doubt on the Great Divide" (126), for example, when we discover that one of the lies we have been taught is the lie of transcendence, "that God grips boards by thought into Plato's table," we find ourselves isolated in a desolate landscape:

"Mountains that thundered promises now say something small—
/ wire in the wind, and snow beginning to fall." And in "Winter-
ward" (127), doubt has become terror, infecting all of life.
Stafford's campers who have "pitched this fact of a life in dust"
cannot bear the hazards of living without certainty. Even summer
was a "green alarm," and in autumn "threatenings flared." Now
they look to winter as a refuge from fear and a fulfillment of what
they most fear: "Oh winter, oh snowy interior, / rocks and hurt
birds, we come."

This theme is the subject of many poems like "Walking the Wilderness" (138), one of a number of elegies about Stafford's mother:

> My mother in a dream dreamed
> this place, where storms drown
> down or where God makes it arch to mountains,
> flood with winter, stare upward at His
> eye that freezes people, His zero breath
> their death.

Even though it is possible to see individual deaths as part of a hidden pattern—"snowflake designs lock; they clasp in the sky"—
there is no consolation in the thought. And yet, facing winter in the
right way can be ennobling, an occasion to move toward what is
most elemental and authentic in life, and a final test of courage and
solitude:

> Warm human representatives may vote and
> manage man; but at last the blizzard will dignify
> the walker, the storm hack trees to cyclone
> groves, he catch the snow, his brave eye
> become command, the whole night howl against
> his ear, till found by dawn he
> reach out to God no trembling hand.

By occurring to us, by the mere fact of our imagining them,
these winter landscapes have a power over us, demonic in their capacity to revitalize us. They stand for the death that seems to be
our ultimate separation from nature, but which is actually the
promise of our reunion. The fact that they are unvisited, only imagined, is crucial to their idealization; and it is the poet's task to help

us imagine them, thus serving as an intermediary between our dull warmth and their vital cold.

Stafford never moves far from this role. He sees himself as a teacher; and didacticism, rare in contemporary poetry, is fundamental to his aesthetics. Many poems could be cited to demonstrate this sense of vocation. In "Representing Far Places" (96), for example, Stafford establishes a radical contrast between the "canoe wilderness," where "fish in the lake leap arcs of realization," and "society where the talk turns witty." But standing in the room, listening to the talk, the wilderness "fans in your head / canyon by canyon." Stafford represents far places; as a poet he is important because he can imagine the weather we are all sheltered from.

The didactic mode in Stafford's pastoralism is presented quite directly in "Montana Eclogue" (166), a poem in three parts (longer than most of his lyrics, which tend to be less than 30 lines.) Here he presents a major role of the transforming literary imagination and explicitly links it with the pastoral tradition.

The opening section of the poem presents us with a sentimental, stereotyped Western landscape: a high cattle camp in a remote valley of the Montana Rockies. It is after the trail drive, and only one man—Logue—remains to close down the camp. The setting is a "remote, stone cathedral" with highly generalized names: "High Valley," "Stone Creek," "Clear Lake," "Winter Peak." As Logue goes about his chores, the approaching winter begins to flood the country; the aspens feel its current, and above them, "high miles of pine tops bend." A significance attaches to the aptly named Logue, who "by being there, suddenly / carries for us everything that we can load on him." We have "stepped indoors" and have forgotten "how storms come"; Logue faces winter for us.

The title of this poem and its echo in "Logue" remind us of the literary tradition of pastoral at the same time that we are asked to observe nature in its inhuman aspect, a perception contrary to the pastoral tradition. Our Arcadia is Montana in the grip of the approaching winter, and our Thyrsis is the cattleman Logue. But Logue's name reminds us that he is made only of words; he is a literary invention no more substantial than Thyrsis. Logue is a repository of poetic value, and the movement of the poem through his point of view does not point to a reality beyond language. We experience winter through words, by inventing Logue, whom we imagine living in what we avoided when we "stepped indoors."

It is through Logue that we catch a glimpse of "those ranches our trees hardly hear of." Stafford moves into a more didactic and visionary mode as he describes a landscape even Logue cannot see, "the clear-cut miles the marmots own" near the timberline, high above the aspen valley and pine ridges of Logue's camp. We "citizens" who are "gripped in a job" or "aimed steady at a page" need to imagine through Logue the coldness of these high places, because they remind us of death. Stafford's language grows apocalyptic as he describes an ultimate winter:

> We glimpse that last storm when the wolves
> get the mountains back, when our homes will flicker
> bright, then dull, then old; and the trees
> will advance, knuckling their roots or lying in
> windows to match the years. We glimpse
>
> a crack that begins to run down the wall,
> and like a blanket over the window at night
> that world is with us and those wolves are here.

Through the pastoral design of the poem, death has become part of the beauty of this unvisited landscape, and we can be revitalized by the thought of it. The grandeur of Montana has shed grandeur on death, and the discovery of our own insignificance is liberating: "things can come so great / that your part is too small to count, / if winter can come."

It should by now be evident that Stafford's art is pastoral in more than a superficial way; he directs the sentimental impulse toward pastoral simplicity into a more profound literary encounter with the demonic and with the necessity to use the imagination to gain the strength to face death. The pastoral setting, then, is the boundary of the human; the inhuman world can only be imagined, but in the act of imagining it, we can transform it into an unvisited pastoral landscape, as in "In Dear Detail, by Ideal Light" (105):

> There, for the rest of the years,
> by not going there, a person could believe
> some porch looking south,
> and steady in the shade—maybe you,
>
> Rescued by how the hills
> happened to arrive where they are,

> depending on that wire
> going to an imagined place
>
> Where finally the way the world feels
> really means how things are,
> in dear detail,
> by ideal light all around us.

By "not going there" we can be "rescued" by our belief in an imagined place, and the pastoral cycle will be complete: Prospero can return from his island, the Duke from the forest of Arden. And we can face the rest of our lives "deep in a story strongly told."

BURTON HATLEN

Robert Duncan's Marriage of Heaven and Hell: Kabbalah and Rime in *Roots and Branches*

Robert Duncan, more consciously and more articulately than any other writer since Yeats, consistently argued that poetry itself has become the true heir of the Judeo-Christian religious tradition. Since Darwin, religion has generally devolved into one or another variety of pseudo-science: thus we see on the one hand the liberal transformation of religion into a psychodrama, and on the other hand the claim of the fundamentalists to offer an objective body of knowledge about the world, no less scientific than the information offered by officially certified biologists et al. What both the demythologizers and the fundamentalists have left out is, simply, *magic;* and it is the magical dimension of religion that poetry has, partly by default, inherited. By magic I mean a recognition that the boundary between self and world is fluid, so that a change in one necessarily changes the others, and an active search for ways to initiate and control this process. A threatened religion retreats into dogma, and in our time dogma has become the enemy of magic. Dangerously, dogma has also increasingly allied itself with the state, so that in the U.S.S.R. a state-enforced scientific dogma has made war on the will of human beings to come together in communities that nurture self and mutual transformation, while in the West religious dogma has sought state authority to annul the powers of love and sensuality. Thus was born Moloch, the state armored in dogma. Thus too a magical poetry inevitably locates itself "outside," in more or less overt opposition to Moloch.

As Dante and Milton and Blake discovered, in the poem dogma turns into story; rather than demanding assent, the poem invites participation. Committed from early youth to the principle of philosophical anarchism, Duncan affiliated himself with a poetic tradition descending through these poets and sought to create a poetry that would dissolve the dogmas through which the modern state seeks to legitimate itself. In his quest for an anarchist poetics, Duncan's career was interwoven with those of two fellow anarchists, Kenneth Rexroth and Allen Ginsberg; and some of the differences between Duncan's work and that of these two poets may help to bring his magical strategies into focus.

Rexroth, the grand panjandrum both of the San Francisco anarchist movement and the San Francisco Renaissance, wrote a poetry that seeks to reproduce as precisely as possible the cadences of plain speech. At the center of Rexroth's poetics is a Buberesque sense of an I addressing a Thou, which is, however, usually not God but rather another human being. In such a dialogic relationship, Rexroth believes, the person comes into being, and personhood itself negates the power of Moloch. Ginsberg, for his part, sought to defeat Moloch by annointing himself a prophet: he would bring down Moloch through a direct rhetorical assault. Duncan, like Rexroth, sought to defend the "helpless little happiness of the human world" against the "marches of relentless power" (*Roots* 21); and like Ginsberg he wrote a few Jeremiads. But for the most part his poetry is much less personal than Rexroth's and much less overtly prophetic than Ginsberg's. Rather he sought, I shall here argue, a poetry that will, like those religious rituals that have come to seem meretricious, summon up supernatural forces powerful enough to shatter Moloch. And in this attempt to make the poem itself the scene of a magical invocation that will transform and renew the world, Duncan is, I submit, a significantly more ambitious poet (however one may evaluate the relative success of their work) than either Rexroth or Ginsberg, who are ultimately content simply to defend the self *against* the world.

Versed in the lore of Judaism and Christianity and Buddhism and Theosophy, Duncan never became a believer in any of these religions. Rather he cultivated *writing itself* as a magical act; and in this essay I want to explore some of the ways this conception of the poem as magical act and of the poet as magus has shaped one specific Duncan text, *Roots and Branches*. I shall begin by defining as precisely as I can what I mean by *magic,* and by elucidating some of the occult and (in particular) Kabbalistic sources upon which Duncan draws. I shall then explore some of the ways in which magic works in *Roots and Branches,* paying particular attention to how what Duncan calls *rime*—i.e., patterns of repetition—here works magically. Finally, in my conclusion I shall return to the broader implications of the poetry/magic relationship and shall show how Duncan's sense of poetry as magic constitutes a direct challenge to the power of Moloch.

I define *magic* as a systematic procedure for drawing together opposing forces, with the goal of healing and renewing both the self and the world. This definition assumes, first of all, that the world is in some way broken, fallen. Common to all religions is a conviction that the world *should be* other than what it is. The state of perfection may be located in time, "in the beginning." Such is the official doctrine of Judaism and Christianity. Or the state of perfection may be in some sense above or within this world. This belief is common to Buddhism and Neo-Platonism. But all these ways of thinking agree that the world as we know it has fallen away from its rightful state of perfection. What should be One has become Many. On the whole, the orthodox versions of these various religions (though Buddhism is an exception here) have assumed that salvation, the recovery of the lost state of perfection, can come only through an act of God: the most obvious example is the incarnation of God as Jesus and His subsequent sacrifice of Himself for the sins of the world. In some instances, the priesthood may claim a power to reenact this world-transforming moment in a ritual of some sort: I am thinking chiefly of the Eucharist, although in Judaism the Seder similarly draws together the community around reenactment of a moment of divine intervention. However, both Judaism and Christianity have also nurtured semi-heterodox magical variants within which adepts have sought direct control over the process of transformation, including the Kabbalah, hermeticism, and alchemy; and it is these magical variations on orthodox religion that will occupy my attention here.

All the various magical currents in the Judeo-Christian tradition have certain qualities in common. First, they tend to conceive of the world in terms of opposing powers: the male sulfur and the female mercury in alchemy, *Din* and *Hesed* in Lurianic Kabbalah. Further, all forms of magic seek to join these opposing powers: the union of these opposites will, magic assumes, give the adept access to the crucible of creation. Finally, these various forms of magic seek as their ultimate end a recovery of a lost state of perfection, envisioned as reentry into a golden world (thus their debunkers saw the alchemists as materialists obsessed with gold) or into the Garden of Eden. The forms of magic I have mentioned here have differed primarily in the *methods* by which they hoped to achieve a

union of opposites and a return to Eden. The hermeticists of the
Renaissance engaged in a magical manipulation of *images* (Yates esp.
45–83). The alchemists, on the other hand, sought to combine various physical substances, especially sulfur and mercury, to create the
philosopher's stone, which would "turn everything to gold"—i.e.,
return humankind to the Golden Age (cf. Jung for a richly symbolic
interpretation of the alchemical project). And the Kabbalists, both
Jewish and Christian, saw *language itself* as the means through
which the broken world could be healed and Eden regained (Scholem 332–86). On one level, this sense of the power of language
issued in the so-called "practical Kabbalah," which attempted to
unleash magical powers through manipulation of the tetragramma-
ton and other letter combinations, derived from the Torah. But as
Gershom Scholem notes, this kind of practical magic shades into
"the still more radical view that the Torah is not only made up of
the names of God but is as a whole the one great Name of God"
(39). This belief in turn roots itself in a traditional Jewish belief that
the Torah is "an instrument of creation, through which the world
came into existence" (40). Thus for the Kabbalists, "the Name contains power, but at the same time embraces the secret laws and harmonious order which pervade and govern all existence" (40). It was
therefore primarily by learning and speaking or writing certain
words that the Kabbalists sought to redeem the world.

I have emphasized Kabbalistic magic here because Duncan, as a
word man, naturally conceived his own magical enterprise largely
in Kabbalistic terms. Duncan's interest in the Kabbalah is directly
attested to by the second poem in *Roots and Branches*, "What Do I
Know of the Old Lore?" The poem begins with a disavowal of any
knowledge of the old lore: "What do I know of the left and the
right, of the Shekinah, of the Metatron?" (3). Yet the references to
the Shekinah and the Metatron suggest that in fact Duncan does
know something about the Kabbalah. Further, there are many other
Kabbalistic references in the poem, the most significant of which is
the reference to the "Lord of the Hour of Midnight." For midnight
is, the *Zohar* tells us, the moment when all the opposing forces in
the universe are in perfect balance (*Zohar* 45–87); and the invocation
of the Lord of Midnight supports my belief, which I shall argue at
length later in this essay, that in *Roots and Branches* Duncan wants to
bring all opposites into balance. The final lines of the poem also
introduce a pattern of tree-and-garden imagery, which will recur
throughout the book and which always has Kabbalistic overtones:

The Rabbis stop under the lemon tree
rejoicing in the cool of its leaves
which they say is the cool of the leaves of that Tree of
    Trees.

Look, Rabbi Eleazer says,
the Glory of the Shekinah shines from lettuces
in the Name of that Garden!   (5)

The Shekinah is, briefly, the divine presence as manifested in the created world, which the Kabbalah envisions as female. Note that the issue here is not simply the Garden, but the *Name* of the Garden. And note too that the "Glory of the Shekinah" shines not from above but from the lettuces themselves. All these considerations will become important as we proceed.

However, only occasionally is Duncan's poetry about Kabbalistic doctrines. Rather than presenting "ideas," these poems are themselves magical acts that seek to unite opposites and thereby redeem the world. In this respect, Duncan's poetry seeks to achieve the goals sought by all Kabbalistic ritual. Gershom Scholem sums up as follows the goals of such ritual:

> The attitude of the Kabbalah toward ritual is governed by certain fundamental conceptions which recur in innumerable variants. In its role of representation and excitation, ritual is expected, above all, to accomplish the following:
> 1. Harmony between the rigid powers of judgment and the flowing powers of mercy.
> 2. The sacred marriage, or *conjunctio* of the masculine and feminine.
> 3. Redemption of the *Shekhinah* from its entanglement in the "other side."
> 4. Defense against, or mastery over, the powers of the "other side."   (130)

Many individual poems in *Roots and Branches* as well as the book as a whole can most fruitfully be read, I believe, as moving toward one or more, sometimes all four, of these goals. In this essay I shall try to elucidate some of the ways in which these poems define the universe as an interplay between opposites (male and female, law and love) and seek to marry these opposites, in the hope of recovering the lost unity of being traditionally symbolized by the Garden.

The Kabbalah sees the two great opposing forces in the universe as *Hesed* and *Din,* love and justice, female and male powers respectively. So too, the opposites in *Roots and Branches* fall into these two categories, even though in the course of the book they assume many different forms. A passage from "Adam's Way" suggests some of these forms. The tree of knowledge, Samael says, divides

> sun from moon,
> within from without, man from woman,
> above from below, this side from that side,
> good from evil, nation from nation—
>
> much more.   (162)

These opposing forces may assume either mythological or cosmological forms. For example, in "Osiris and Set," Set is presented as the "dark mind that drives before the dawn rays." Set, we learn, "fought against Osiris / conspired, scatterd the first light" (68). The opposites of darkness and light, evening and morning, also surface in a purely cosmological form at various points in *Roots and Branches.* "Night Scenes," for example, begins in the evening, at "the moon's up-riding" (5) and moves toward an early morning in the produce market. Light and dark, day and night, also suggest the great opposites of the sun and the moon, which for Duncan carry a medieval or Renaissance resonance. The sun is the male power. In the first H. D. sequence, Duncan invokes the "Father in the sun, Father in the air" (12)—but note the puns here: sun/son, air/heir. The Sun Father stands over against the Moon Mother, who appears at least twice in the guise of the night nurse, most strikingly in the sequence "Four Songs the Night Nurse Sang."

A marriage of Light and Dark, Male and Female, Sun and Moon—this project has been the aim of a fair amount of Western art, from Shakespeare *(A Midsummer Night's Dream)* through Lawrence *(The Rainbow).* But Duncan's list of opposites includes another, more challenging pair: good and evil. In its treatment of good and evil, Duncan's poetic enterprise becomes radical in the same way that Blake's was radical. Both Blake and Duncan seek a reconciliation of good and evil, and this aspiration places them in opposition to all orthodox religion, which uniformly seeks the triumph of good *over* evil. (Even the Kabbalah, as my quotation from Scholem suggests, sought to "overcome" the "other side." Thus in seeking to include the other side within the unity of the poem, Duncan may be leaving behind even the Kabbalah itself, at least the orthodox and specifically Jewish side of the Kabbalah.) Further, it is Duncan's treatment of good and evil that makes his poetry a historically grounded project. A metaphysical reconciliation of Male and Female may be easy enough, but such efforts don't have much effect on a world in which the alien, the dark, the female has been categorized as evil and treated accordingly. To "work through" (and note that Duncan read Freud throughout his life) this concrete and social repudiation of the Other, it is necessary to go down into History, to experience the alien (and for Duncan this includes his own homosexuality) *as evil* and recuperate it as such. Thus the title of my essay, for Duncan, like Blake, seeks a marriage of heaven and hell, those opposing orders that our culture has conventionally labeled "good" and "evil."

In Duncan's mythology, the Father incarnates the law. In the H. D. sequence, Duncan invokes the "father who has hidden His law in my heart" (12). And in "The Law" it is clear that we are again dealing with a male power:

> The Judge
> must have justice as His left hand,
> mercy as His right, to hold them,
> if He be, Love to whom we pray is,
> Fisher of Men from the cold living waters . . .   (28)

In its negative form, the Father's law excludes everything that is law*less*. So "Robin Hood in the greenwood outside / Christendom faces peril as if it were a friend" (29). In this territory outside Christendom live also the gay lovers of "Night Scenes" who have "come in along these sexual avenues / seeking to release Eros from our mistrust," but whose "nerves respond to the police cars cruising, / a part of the old divine threat" (6). The police cars suggest a bureaucratization of the law, and Duncan, ever the anarchist, is suspicious of any codification of the Law within the "deceitful coils of institutions" (30). Indeed, he suggests that such codifications actually *create* Satan and everything else that we call evil:

> Justinian or Moses, whoever directs, must
> propose "unnatural" restrictions
> and say with a loud voice:
> "Cursed be he that
>   confirmeth not *all* the words of this law
>   to do them"—designing therein
> nets to please Satan.   (28)

Because the Law as codified in Christendom and in the state denies Eros, a "marriage of good and evil" demands first of all a renaming of the Father, whose repudiation of the nighttime/female/moon-governed half of existence as evil first caused (and still causes) the Fall. So in the first H. D. sequence, Duncan invokes a Father who is, not justice, but Love, a "Father whose Love brought forth the Lover," a Father who "grows in the plant" and "moves the animal," a Father who is "evolving" and "whose signature is in the chemical bond." This Father is, Duncan insists, distinctly not that hoary nay-sayer whom Blake called "old Nobodaddy," and Duncan entreats this benign Father to "stand against Jehovah who is jealous in thy place" (12). So too, in "The Law" Duncan seeks to redefine Law itself not as a force of exclusion but rather as an inner law, an equilibrium, which even the outlaw (perhaps he most of all) obeys:

> Foremost we admire the outlaw
> who has the strength of his own
> lawfulness. How we loved him
> in childhood and hoped to abide by his code
> that took life as its law!   (29)

This law we can never know rationally, "For great life itself uses us like wood / and has no laws in burning we understand, / gives no alternatives" (29). "There are no / final orders" (26), then. Yet there is what another age called faith, which urges us to call

> upon Love too, Who by Law's naild
> to a cross. "Hail,
> Christ, and make good
> our loss."   (29)

On a mythic level, too, "The Law" enacts a redefinition, even a redemption of what we conventionally call evil. The poem begins with references to the serpent, traditional symbol of evil within the Judeo-Christian tradition:

> the Law
> constantly destroys the law,
> erasing lightly or with turmoil
> coils of the snake
> evil is, . . .   (26)

The "Law" (capitalized, thus suggesting a divine origin) here destroys the lower case "law," presumably the law of the state. In the process, the Law also erases evil, which has become, for reasons I have already elucidated, entangled in this lower-case law. Thus far we are in reasonably familiar territories. But by the time "The Law" ends five pages later, Duncan has achieved a metamorphosis of the serpent itself:

> It's the sense of law itself demands
>   violation
> within the deceitful coils of institutions.
>
> *What is*
> hisses like a serpent
> and writhes
>
> to shed its skin.   (30)

The institutions that codify the (lower-case) law are now themselves serpentine, coiled like rattlesnakes. And the higher Law *demands* a violation of the laws of institutions. But there is another kind of serpent here: *"What is"* itself. I detect here an echo of god's famous self-definition: "I am Who Am." What the theologians call Being is itself, it seems, a serpent, hissing and writhing as it struggles to shed its skin. This second serpent may be more Jungian than Mosaic, an uroboric process of endless self-making. Yet in some fashion the serpent here seems to have *become* God—a marriage indeed of Heaven and Hell. (For a full discussion of the role of Law in Duncan's work, cf. Finkelstein.)

As the benign Father is disentangled from the oppressive Father, a recovery of the Mother becomes possible—and indeed such a recovery is one of major projects of *Roots and Branches*. The entire book is haunted by real mothers (as he explains in the first H. D.

sequence, Duncan had two mothers, the one who gave birth to him and the one who adopted him when he was a few months old) and surrogate mothers (especially H. D.). The mothers are all in some way distant. The letters the poet addresses to his adoptive mother "always went alone / to where / I never knew you reading" (76). And H. D. is withdrawing into silence—after a stroke she can only coo like a dove, "hurrrrrr / harrrrrr / hurrr" (88). Yet the poet remains confident that the body remembers "the mother-tides of the first magic" (7). The Mother too can manifest herself in negative form, as "a witch's figure kept by old hatreds," "the dark emerging from its stinking hole" (16). But by taking "hell too as a mother" (16), the poet escapes the opposites of light and dark, and learns to see the Great Mother as working in all things:

> She is at work in her sleep.
> She draws in food from the country around her.
>
> . . . .
>
> She makes a temple of produce, in her buying and selling,
>   a place of transport and litanies.
> She surrounds her priests and appears in their place at the
>   tips time has before falling.   (9)

The marriage of the "renamed" Father and Mother will, the last lines of "Osiris and Set" suggest, link heaven and hell, the heavenly "in-law" Father and the material, evil, "out-law" Mother:

> Hail! forgotten and witherd souls!
>
> Our Mother comes with us   to gather her children!
>
> Now it is time for Hell
> to nurse at the teats of Heaven.
>
> Dark sucks at the white milk.
> Stars flow out into the deserted souls.
>
> In our dreams we are drawn towards day once more. (69)

We turn toward life as dark and light, heaven and hell, death and life meet once again. As the next poem in the book, "Two Presentations," suggests, we enter the new world—in the words of Williams—naked and cold and uncertain:

> But I was cold, lying in the narrow bed,
> naked. When did I lie there so?
>   The first light of morning
> came in over me, a cold thin wave
> where nerves shrank back from the bruise.   (73)

Yet at this moment, the mid-point in *Roots and Branches,* a birth *has* occurred, and it is toward such a birth of the soul out of the great archetypes of Mother and Father that the entire book has been moving.

The goal of these various redefinitions and metamorphoses is, simply, "to release the first music somewhere again / for a moment / to touch the design of the first melody!" (6). Through a union of left and right side, *Din* and *Hesed,* the Kabbalah seeks to recover Adam Kadmon, original man, and thereby to recover, spiritually, the unfallen Garden. So too, Duncan prays to reenter the Garden:

> Lift me up. Give me a hand,
>   out of the hell that is still underground
>
> into the sunrise share, the new man.
> What Herbert in his Temple sought
> and Henry Vaughn
> upon the sunset-flooded lawn
>
> was suppliant for, O for Thy grace unfurld
> that love and judgment has in balance,
> all tones coming forth into one scale
> to govern and release the music of our dance.   (11)

The poetic heritage Duncan here claims for himself is Christian rather than Jewish, but the example of Vaughan suggests how the Christian Duncan can appropriate the Kabbalistic heritage. Christian hermeticism shares with the Jewish Kabbalah an aspiration to liberate the "new man"—who is at the same time the old man, Adam Kadmon. This new/old man lives in the "morning world," on the "sunset-flooded lawn"—in time, but also in the eternal light of glory. And Christian and Jew share a belief that grace issues out of a balance of love and justice, *Din* and *Hesed.* This balance releases a harmony that allows human life to become a dance, for Duncan, as for Yeats and Olson, a symbol of the perfect fusion of freedom and order.

The "you" of the prayer quoted above is at one level God. But the prayer comes from "A Sequence of Poems for H. D.'s Birthday," and more immediately it is H. D. herself that Duncan here asks to "lift me up. Give me a hand." Indeed, throughout *Roots and Branches* H. D. is Duncan's spiritual mother/muse, and that he should ask this woman poet to lead him "into the morning world" tells us something important about the role not only of the Mother but also of Art in Duncan's mystical *praxis*. The artist, like the woman and the homosexual (whose sexuality itself is criminal), lives outside the law, under the aegis of the moon. But the artist lives by an inner law; so true art by its nature always unites light and dark, male and female, good and evil, in the absolute freedom and perfect order of the dance. Perhaps Duncan's most explicit statement of his conception of art comes in "Nel Mezzo del Cammin di Nostra Vita," a tribute to Rodia, builder of the Watts Towers. The towers are outside the law (lower case): the city officials, we learn, have "initiated condemnation hearings" against Rodia's towers (21). Rodia's towers are also, in his words, "taller than the Church," and Duncan immediately comments that Art is "dedicated to itself," seeking to gather all "its children / under one roof of the imagination" (22). Charles Olson gets the central words in the poem: "The poet" he says, "cannot afford to traffic in any other sign than . . . his self," for "otherwise God does rush in"— and so poetry is overwhelmed by dogma. From the opposite perspective, Duncan quotes Burckhardt, who declares art "the most arrogant traitor of all / putting eyes and ears . . . in place of profounder worship" (23). The opposition seems clear: art *or* religion. And Duncan opts for art—although for him, as we have seen, art is itself a form of religious *praxis*.

Not only does Duncan opt for art, but he commits himself to a particular *kind* of art: the collage. Rodia built his towers out of bits and scraps from the city dump, and Duncan too will make his art out of such gatherings. Throughout his career, Duncan was fiercely loyal to a poetic lineage that passes through the major imagists: Pound, Williams, Lawrence, and H. D. (cf. *The H. D. Book*). Duncan's loyalty to the Imagists' tradition suggests that his interest in vision will take the form not of a search for some "mystical" realm beyond this world, but rather for the numinous *within* the concrete particulars of the world. Indeed, Duncan insists that all the major Imagist poets were in fact visionaries, *seers*. They all saw infinity in a grain of sand and eternity in a wild flower. Further, the poets from whom Duncan saw himself as deriving all sought to honor the numinous reality of concrete particulars by refusing to subordinate such particulars to general ideas, in the manner that Western thought has agreed to see as logical. Rather Duncan's masters—and here I would include not only the major Imagists but also such later Poundian poets as Olson and Zukofsky—allowed these particulars to illuminate one another through juxtaposition, thus creating a poetics of collage.

For Duncan, the word *rime* denotes the mutual echoes that develop among such particulars. From Pound he borrows the notion of "subject rhymes": images that echo previous images. But Duncan is also interested in the purely aural echoes of more traditional rhyme. For Duncan more explicitly than for Pound and Olson (but here Duncan may link up with Zukofsky), *sound itself* is a form of power. Duncan's sense of *rime* is, then, rich and various. And for him, rime unlocks the system of correspondences that hold the universe together, and thus it gives the poet a magical power no mere priest enjoys. In *Adam's Way,* Eve defines *rime* as follows:

> There's a way of speaking that's most like this
> where thought and feeling is not our own
> but belongs to a voice that would transmute
> into a music joy and grief, into one living tree
> in which beyond our selves we find release.
>
> "Rime" the demon calld it and made a wry face
> as if it were wrong
> where words are obedient to song's measure
>   beyond our will.
> But the daimon calld it "Melody"
> and spoke, again, of our Author's delight
>   in various Truth.   (158–59)

Rime, Duncan here suggests, allows power beyond our conscious intention to enter our words. True rime, he suggests, should always surprise us: thus his distrust of conventional rhyme, a preplanned pattern decreed by the will of the poet. Because true rime is always unplanned, there is something uncanny, terrifying about it. Suddenly we find ourselves in what Duncan calls a "joint" in time. In a reading at Orono, Maine, in 1971, Duncan read "From the *Mabinogion,*" which ends as follows:

> we saw the land behind us—
>
> our wastes, our age, our hearts' loss
> —and I do not know what we saw:
>
>> this man a wreckt car,
>> this man a Lover turn away
>> this man an empty glass upon the bar,
>> this man a parody of what he was,
> because of our Lord.
>
> That is what the tale says.
> That is our adventure.
>
> For I think we've been in
> this joint before.   (117–18)

Joint here means, of course, a bar. But it also means, Duncan said after reading the poem, a nexus or crossroads *in time,* or what Duncan calls only a few pages later in *Roots and Branches,* "a hinge in the ways" (121). At such moments, we may realize, Jungianly, that we are characters in an old story—and, also, that we must live out the adventure to the end. At such moments too, we realize that we are words spoken by something larger, Eve's "author," or the "Lord" of the Mabinogion poem.

Duncan's rimes may take the form of what Pound called subject rhymes. Thus certain recurrent motifs echo throughout *Roots and Branches.* For example, in the third poem of the book, "Night Scenes," Duncan quotes from *The Tempest,* and then develops this allusion into an image of erotic/spiritual ecstasy:

> *Where the Bee sucks, there,* the airy spirit sings, *suck I!*
> Where does the bee sip? harvest what honey
>   in what beehive?
> *In a Cowslips bell, I lie* —at the ledge
>
> youth spurts, at the lip the flower
> lifts lifewards, . . .
>
> . . . .
>
> as in a cowslip's bell that is a moment comes Ariel
>   to joy all round,
> but we see one lover take his lover in his mouth,
>   leaping. Swift flame of
> abiding sweetness is in this flesh.   (7–8)

This cluster of images will recur at least five times in *Roots and Branches*. In "Variations on Two Dicta of William Blake," for example, Duncan describes

> —the poet's voice, a whole beauty of the man Olson,
>   lifting us up into
>
> where the disturbance is, where the words
>   awaken
> sensory chains between being and being,
>   inner acknowledgements
> of the fiery masters—there
>   like stellar bees my senses swarmd.   (51–52)

The bees, of course, rime with the bees of the quote from *The Tempest*. But the sense of rising up into an ecstatic surrender to a higher power—here specifically poetic—also rimes with the "Night Scenes" passage. A similar conjunction of figures recurs fifteen pages later in "Structure of Rime XVI":

> *The bees have left the hives of my dream.*
> *The sun has not died, but in the rose of night and day*
> *the winged denizens of the light are gone,*
> *no longer to the seminal tip come,*
> *no longer to my naked bone.*   (65)

Here, the departure of the bees becomes a metaphor for death, and the passing of bees, sunlight, flower, and "seminal tip" issues in an elegaic regret.

After another 15 pages, this cluster of figures recurs once again in "After Reading H. D.'s Hermetic Definitions," a love poem written to Duncan's longtime companion Jess. Here the bees serve as a figure both for productive work and for the power to "go to the heart of things":

> I do not remember
> bees working over the garden on such a day.
> But in the full sunlight
> the warmth of its fire
>
> hums;
> and, coverd with pollens,

> the honey gatherers
> go to the heart of things,
>
> shaking and waking the flowery horns,
>
> taking the sweet of song
> to fill their dark combs.   (82)

Around this central image, Duncan builds the story of a domestic dispute: on an overcast day, the bees and the poet are both disoriented, and the poet complains that he "can't find the bee book." But then, reading H. D., the poet realizes that "We too write instinctively, like bees, / serve the Life of the Hive . . . " (83). This discovery in turn allows the poet to hear Jess telling him

> he wasnt angry about lunch.
> It was because
> I hid what I wanted
>
> from myself, made
> the ease of the thing impossible;
> teaching the mind
> *not* to find the sun's rimes . . .   (83–84)

If we try to live by the will, it seems, we can't hear the sun's rime. But this is a poem about grace: how the gifts we need come to us without our asking. So Jess, H. D., and finally

> the bees came in,
> came to mind, from *their* place or time
> into this place, misplaced,
>
> when I rememberd not where the book was
> but their song in the sun.   (84)

Still later in the book, in "Sonnet 1" (122) and in *Adam's Way* (129), the bees will return again. However, I will not discuss these passages in detail; the examples I have already offered should suffice to suggest how the recurrence of this cluster of images builds a system of echoes that reverberates through the book.

In addition to structuring his book around such large patterns of subject-rimes as the bee cluster, Duncan builds individual poems around smaller patterns of sound echoes. Consider, for example, the opening of "Night Scenes":

> The moon's up-riding makes a line
>   flowing out into lion's mane
> of traffic, of speeding lights.
> And in the nest of neon-glow and shadows
> the nets of the city's merchants and magickers
> restless move towards deserted streets where morning
>   breaks,
> holding back heaviness, emptiness, night,
>   with a hand of light fingers tapping,
> obscuring the drift of stars, waiting . . .   (5–6)

Duncan, I believe, hears rimes not only in the half-rime of "line" and "mane" but in all the interlocking patterns of sounds that I have underlined. The young Duncan wrote to Pound, asking for some basic poetic principles. And Pound replied, enigmatically, "follow the tone leading of the vowels." The music of the quoted lines results partly from patterns of vowel sounds, but also, as my markings imply, by an interplay of vowel and consonant patterns. For example, the terminal positions in the first two lines establish the "i" and "a" vowels as primary. Both vowels have appeared previously in the opening line, in "riding" and "makes," and "makes" also offers the same "ma" sound as "mane." Further, the "li" of "line" will be echoed by "lion" and "lights." Sometimes these patterns pass through a series of modulations; thus the "moo/ma/me/ma" sequence, which finally resolves itself with the return of the initial "moo" in "move." The link between "moon" and "move" also seems thematic: we're seeing a pattern of movement here that is controlled by the moon. So too, the "nest/nets/restless" sequence is thematic. Here the sound-play suggests two ways of looking at the city, as refuge ("nest") and trap ("nets"); and the tension between the two issues in a "restless" movement. So too, the buried (because, alas, all too obvious) "night/light" pairing echoes, in miniature, a pattern of day/night oppositions, which is, as I have previously noted, working throughout this book.

Despite this intricate interplay of sound patterns, I would guess that very few readers would hear this passage as "rhyming poetry." For the rimes come, not according to a predetermined pattern, but rather as the movement of the language dictates. These indeterminate rimes establish a play of harmonies without creating a closed system. This play of harmonies in turn affirms Duncan's sense of the world as a place where opposites can and should come together—but as rimes that acknowledge the integrity of each part, even as these parts freely come together in a larger whole, rather than as inert bits of matter controlled by the dictates of an immutable law.

I offer two more examples of the resonance that Duncan's rimes can take on. The first comes from "Two Presentations": "But, of that other Great Mother / or metre, of the matter . . . " (76). Note that the linkages Duncan creates here are not conceptual or even etymological. It may be possible that "mother," "meter," and "matter" all derive from a common Sanskrit root. Yet if so the three words had diverged by the time of classical Greece, and I can discover no evidence that the Romans saw an etymological link between *metrum* and *materia*. Rather it is the poet's ear for *sound,* not his intellect, that allows him to link these words and thereby to discover a new possibility of meaning: mother is to father as meter is to logic as matter is to spirit.

My second example is even more daring. In "A New Poem," Duncan sets out to name the shadowy figure who guides him across "the bewildering circling water way" (120), which we call Poetry. "It would not be easy calling him / the Master of Truth" (120), says Duncan; "name after name I give him":

> Ka, I call him. The shadow
> wavers and wears my own face.
>
> Kaka, I call him. The
> whole grey cerement replaces itself and shows
> a hooded hole.   (121)

"Ka" is, in Egyptian religion, the soul itself. And "kaka" is, of course, the child's name for shit. By riming the soul and shit, Duncan has, in one deft verbal maneuver, linked soul and body, the high and the low, even good and evil. Indeed, it might be suggested that this single rime sums up the entire action of *Roots and Branches*. The rational intellect may try to read what Duncan has done here as implying either a reduction of the soul to shit, or an elevation of shit to spiritual status. But in fact Duncan has done neither of these things. Instead he has simply *rimed* the soul and shit, thus telling us that the two, however opposite they may seem, are also eternally linked, like Set and Osiris, sailing together in their boat across the sea of life.

Duncan's rimes, I have proposed, are political acts, and the "Ka/ Kaka" rime offers a case in point. All hierarchies elevate one person, quality, or value by denigrating (although often only tacitly) other persons, etc. If we celebrate the soul, we inevitably denigrate the body. If we celebrate "masculine" qualities like reason and strength and order, we denigrate "feminine" (although not necessarily female) qualities like intuition and empathy. If "we" are humans, then "they," who are so different from us, must be super- or sub-humans, demigods or demons, or perhaps (this is the usual choice of current sci-fi) mindless robots. Robert Duncan has devoted his life to unmasking and unmaking such exclusionary hierarchies. When Kenneth Patchen demanded to know "whose side are you on," Duncan replied, "When you draw a line I'm on the *other* side, Kenneth" (Bernstein and Hatlen 120).

In his poetry, Duncan has sought what he sometimes calls *chiaroscuro,* a sense that objects cast shadows and thereby shade into one another, and sometimes calls *enjambment,* a sense of meaning as something "variously drawn out from line to line." These last words come from Milton's preface to *Paradise Lost,* which I quote because Milton too is one of Duncan's fathers. In the same 1971 lecture from which I have quoted previously, Duncan made clear his lineage: "I am a reincarnation of Blake who was a reincarnation of Milton who was a reincarnation of Dante." These were three ostentatiously religious poets and three fiercely committed *political* poets, but also three writers whose poetry transcends dogma. In *Paradise Lost,* but *not* in *De Doctrina Christiana,* Milton was free if not to align himself with the "devil's party," at least to let Satan have his say. Indeed, Milton's Satan has more to say, and says it more eloquently, than God Himself, and it is precisely because *Paradise Lost* allows such scope to the voice of the Other that we still read the poem. So too, Duncan wants to allow the voice of the Other to speak. And like his august predecessors, he recognizes that *only* in the poem (in the broadest sense of that term, for a multiplicity of voices is also, as Bakhtin has argued, audible in the "dialogic" novel) can we hear this voice, simply because the monologic voice of expository discourse maintains a rational decorum that silences the Other.

In Milton's time, the Other was the Devil and the Papist; but in *Paradise Lost,* Eve and even Adam (at those moments when he is something more than God's puppet) also speak in the voice of the Other: everything that God's perfect reason would deny is Other, and ultimately that includes the whole human world. In our time, the counters in this game have changed in some ways: Milton's sense of the Papist as Other now seems ludicrous, and the Holocaust has effectively deprived Western society of its most time-honored Other, the Jew. Yet there are among us still many who hunger after righteousness; forbidden by the rules of polite discourse from satisfying this hunger by raging at Papist or Jew, many of this breed have chosen the homosexual as the new scapegoat. Behind the new homophobia there lurks, of course, the ancient male fear and hatred of the woman. For what is so dreadful about the homosexual, if not his refusal to be a "manly" man, his rejection of the privileges of the male, his implicit declaration that he'd rather be a woman? (And note too that it is the *male* homosexual, far more than the lesbian, who arouses the wrath of the fundamentalist.)

In any case, Duncan, choosing to live as an open homosexual, experienced from early youth what it was like to be the Other. And from the beginning he chose to make his homosexuality, his Otherness, the necessary condition of his poetry. As Ekbert Fass's capacious account of the early years demonstrates, the young Robert Duncan resolved to know himself *as evil,* to enter into the condition of Otherness as fully as possible. The poetry that issues from this project is political first of all simply in its refusal to legitimate *any* form of exclusion, its determination to unite light and dark, male and female. And secondly, this poetry is political in its insistence that the various parts of this broken world can and should come together, not in an ideal Monad, but rather as a system of rimes, with each integral unit echoing some (or all, or as many as possible) of the other units within the whole, which is in turn constituted only by these echoes. If we must apply a name to this (political *and* religious) position, I guess we could call it Mystical Anarchism. In the name of Mystical Anarchism, Duncan's poetry challenges Moloch itself. Against the state in all its forms, against dogma of all political and religious varieties, this poetry summons up the powers of love and renewal, which, Duncan defiantly insists, still move the sun and the other stars.

Notes

Introduction

1. Over the course of four days there were scheduled readings by 14 well-known and rising poets from the United States and Canada, plus contributions by some 60 more poets at three open readings that lasted into the night. Other events included dramatic presentations of poetry with musical accompaniment; poetry-writing workshops for both adult poets and school children; a panel on the state of current poetry including Hugh Kenner, Galway Kinnell, Denise Levertov, William Stafford, and Lewis Turco; a book fair with displays by 36 small presses; and panels and academic sessions including 89 papers and talks.

How Poets Learn

This article appeared in the *Puckerbrush Review* 8.1, Summer 1987, and is reprinted with permission.

The Public and Private Realms of Hill's *Mercian Hymns*

This article appeared in *Twentieth Century Literature* 34.4 (Winter 1988), 407–15, and is reprinted with permission.
1. Throughout the article I shall refer to Hill's prose-poems as "hymns."
2. In his "Introduction" to Hill's *Somewhere Is Such a Kingdom,* Harold Bloom comments that *"Mercian Hymns* is a kind of *Prelude*-in-little" (xxii).
3. Stenton observes that "the re-establishment of Mercian supremacy by Offa is the central fact in English history in the second half of the eighth century" (210).
4. Charles Thomlinson pointed out (in conversation, 17 April 1985) that Hill has sung this first hymn at poetry readings.

History, Mutation, and the Mutation of History in Edward Dorn's *Gunslinger*

This article appeared in *Sagetrieb* 6.1 (Spring 1987): 7–20, and is reprinted with permission.

1. Cf. Dyck, who reads *Gunslinger* as a "a treatise on the breakdown of classical logic" (611).

2. If *Gunslinger*'s humor contrasts with Olson's seriousness, nevertheless this stance toward the self echoes the older poet's assertion to the young Dorn that *"person"* is "not the same . . . as the individual as single" (*Prose* 3). Likewise Dorn's concerns with ontology, with the nature of human being, echo what Olson saw as the central question to ask about "person": "what, in fact, the critter, homo sap, is, as we take it, now" (*Prose* 6). In *Gunslinger* Dorn can be said to enact comically what Olson called for in "Projective Verse": "the getting rid of the lyrical interference of the individual as ego, of the 'subject' and his soul" (*Writings* 24).

Poetocracy: The Poetry Workshop Movement in Nicaragua

This article appeared in the *Telegraphy* 1 (1988): 25–32, and is reprinted with permission of *Telegraphy,* "a journal of art, poetry, reviews, interviews, and criticism."

The Sigh of Our Present: Nuclear Annihilation and Contemporary Poetry

1. For a more complete definition of "psychic numbing," see *Weapons* 100–110.

2. Think, for instance, of the widespread fear of extinction during the approach of the first millenium or the time of the black death in Europe. Also, the last two hundred years have produced such poems in English as Byron's "Darkness," Browning's "Childe Roland to the Dark Tower Came," Yeats's "The Second Coming," Eliot's *The Waste Land,* and Archibald MacLeish's "The End of the World," before the manufacture of atomic weaponry. Nor should I exclude the work of Samuel Beckett and Ted Hughes, both worthy of close study as apocalyptic writers.

3. For a brief discussion of poems written in response to nuclear proliferation from 1945 to 1963, see von Hallberg 129–33.

4. A partial list of titles from Levertov's works concerning annihilation includes "Say the Word" (a short story) and "Earth Balm" in *O Taste and See;* "A Vision" and "Living" in *The Sorrow Dance;* most of the poems in "The Age of Terror," Part V of *Candles in Babylon;* and Part II ("Prisoners") and Part V ("Of God and of the Gods") in *Oblique Prayers.*

5. I am thinking here of Derrida's statement: "One cannot be satisfied with saying that, in order to become serious and interesting today, a literature and a literary criticism must refer to the nuclear issue, must even be obsessed by it. This has to be said, and it is true. But I believe also that, at least indirectly, they have always done this. Literature has always belonged to the nuclear epoch, even if it does not talk 'seriously' about it" ("Apocalypse" 27).

6. For my account of Gunn's poem, see "How Nothing Has Changed: From Stevens's 'The Snow Man' to Gunn's 'The Annihilation of Nothing,' " *Poesis* 7.1 (1986): 23–34.

7. For a political example of this contemporary structure of thinking, as Derrida defines it, see Schell's discussion of the "rationality of irrationality" in U.S. deterrence policy, as a nuclear age strategy (Schell 204–05).

Gerald Stern's Mediation of the I and the I

1. Sukenick made frequent references to Olson in a lecture presented at Jagiellonian University in Krakow, Poland, in the spring of 1983. His comments on the Bossa Nova novel occur in *Surfiction*, edited by Raymond Federman (43).

"Free / of Blossom and Subterfuge": Louise Glück and the Language of Renunciation

1. See, for instance, Suzanne Juhasz, *Naked and Fiery Forms: Modern American Poetry by Women* (New York: Harper, 1976); Gilbert and Gubar; Margaret Homans, *Women Writers and Poetic Identity* (Princeton: Princeton UP, 1980).

2. I take the phrase from Gilbert and Gubar, p. xxiii; they are quoting from a 1935 letter by Louise Bogan in which Bogan refuses to edit an anthology of "female verse" because of her aversion to "corresponding with a lot of female songbirds." Gilbert and Gubar comment: "Obviously, as Gloria Bowles has pointed out, Bogan had internalized just those patriarchal interdictions that have historically caused women poets from Finch to Plath anxiety and guilt about attempting the pen."

3. Despite her bleak portrayal of heterosexual relationships, Glück's work never considers lesbianism as an option. Perhaps this reflects the thoroughness of what Judith Fetterly would call her "immasculation"—the extent to which she subscribes to a phallocentric value system.

4. Paul E. Garfinkel and David M. Garner, *Anorexia Nervosa: A Multidimensional Perspective* (New York: Brunner/Mazel, 1982) 10. This is not to deny that anorexia is *in effect* self-destructive; whatever it attempts, this condition remains a tragic pathology.

Adrienne Rich: Vision as Rewriting

1. For another look at Rich's dialogue with herself, including another major example of a later poem that revises earlier ones, see DuPlessis 135–39.

2. Judith McDaniel, concluding a commentary on this poem, describes the "movement away from this aesthetic toward an art that allowed a far more personal expression, [which] allowed her to take risks as a poet and a compassionate woman," as "Rich's essential transformation as an artist" (5).

3. Claire Keyes, writing on this poem and the volume in which it appears, focuses on these concerns as the "muted story" of Rich's early poetry, as opposed to the "dominant" (and dominated) story that "coincides with mainstream patriarchal values" (15–16). Keyes recognizes the masculinity of the poem's tigers and hints at their ineffectuality as an image of female power (22, 24). But neither she nor Rich lays out in detail the poem's own recapitulation of the dominant discourse and its muting of the subversive one.

4. It is especially interesting, in this light, that in defining *suture* in the context of Lacanian film criticism, Jane Gallop says that "suture, *like courtly love,* is the supplementation of an absence, the joining of a gap by representation" (45, emphasis added).

5. The possibility that Blake's poem might bear on Rich's in some way was first suggested to me by Phillip Arrington; it is strengthened by Rich's own recent citation of "The Tyger" as among the first poems she heard or read (*Blood* 169).

6. This move also helps define the relation between "Transcendental Etude" and the Beethoven poem. The "need to go through th[e] anger" manifest in the poems of the early 1970s is a matter of fidelity to reality, for "both the victimization and the anger experienced by women are real, and have real sources, everywhere in the environment, built into society, language, the structures of thought. They will (and they must) go on being tapped and explored by poets, among others. We can neither deny them, nor will we rest there" (*Lies* 48–49). But the not resting there, the shift in focus from oppression and its language to the dream of a common language and a community of women is a key point in the process of liberation. For more on this shift, which becomes a major theme in Rich's writing of the middle to late 1970s, see McDaniel 18, Whelchel 57, and Vanderbosch 115–16.

7. For an excellent explanation of these latter oppositions, see Altieri, "Symbolist Thought."

Concrete and Abstract Poetry: The World as Text and the Text as World

This article appeared in the *Visible Language* 23.1 (Winter 1989): 29–43, and is reprinted with permission.

The figures "Silencio" by Eugen Gomringer and "Extension 2" by Pierre Garnier were reprinted from Emmett Williams, ed., *An Anthology of Concrete Poetry.* Copyright 1968 by Something Else Press, Inc. Reprinted by permission of the publisher.

The figure "Julien Blaine the i-constructor" by Julien Blaine from *Concrete Poetry in France,* copyright 1981 by David W. Seaman, is reprinted by permission of UMI Research Press, Ann Arbor, Michigan.

"Geranium" is reproduced with permission by Mary Ellen Solt.

1. In the strictest sense, "concrete poetry" applies to the experimental visual texts of an international movement cofounded in the 1950s by Eugen Gomringer in Switzerland and the Noigandres group in Brazil. In their "Pilot-plan for Concrete Poetry," the Brazilian poets vaguely defined their work as productive of a "tension of word-objects in the time-space continuum," as creating a specifically linguistic ambiance, a "verbovocovisual" world fusing the advantages of verbal and non-verbal communication. Owing perhaps to the subsequent increase of many radically new shapes and forms of poetry and in manifestos embracing the fundamental principles of the movement, the term *concrete* was then generally adopted by anthologies and critical studies referring to many types of visual works. Since the 1960s concrete poetry has become a truly international movement, with a lively interchange of ideas around the world and active practitioners wherever poetry is being written. Décio Pignatari, Augusto de Campos, Haroldo de Campos, "Plan-pilote pour la poésie concrète," *Les Lettres* 31 (1963): 15–17.

2. As David Seaman has shown in his excellent historical study, *Concrete Poetry in France,* there were, of course, previous visual verse forms in France as in other countries, for example, the acrostic poems of Villon or Rabelais's "Dive Bouteille."

3. "La poésie visuelle exige du lecteur une position fixe et une stabilité végétale. / Ce soleil, au centre idéal du poème, éclaire en retenant." Pierre Garnier in *Les Lettres* 30 (1963): 17.

Ashbery and the Condition of Music

This article is part of the author's dissertation, copyright 1990 by Fred Everett Maus, reprinted by permission.

1. In focusing on indeterminacy as a crucial quality of Ashbery's writing, I share the concerns of Marjorie Perloff's fine study, *The Poetics of Indeterminacy* (Princeton: Princeton UP, 1981). The present paper was written before I saw Perloff's book, as an extension of my work on indeterminacy in musical interpretation. I have been gratified by the direct support Perloff's discussion provides for my interpretation of Ashbery, and by the close resemblance between her approach to an important literary tradition and my emphasis in musical analyses.

2. As Perloff has noted, Ashbery's early review of work by Gertrude Stein amounts to a precise description of traits common to Stein's writing and Ashbery's own style. According to Ashbery, "*Stanzas in Meditation* gives one the feeling of time passing, of things happening, of a 'plot,' though it would be difficult to say precisely what is going on." "The Impossible," *Poetry* July 1957: 251. The description is fine for much of Ashbery's writing as well.

3. It will be obvious that my comparison depends on a conception of instrumental music as a kind of abstract, indeterminate drama, rather than as a wholly nonrepresentational patterning of sounds. One virtue of such an account of music, apart from its verisimilitude, is precisely that it permits persuasive comparisons with other art forms.

4. Lawrence Kramer has discussed Ashbery's "polyvocality" in relation to musical polyphony in his *Music and Poetry: The Nineteenth Century and After* (Berkeley: U of California P, 1984) 203–21. Similar material appeared as an essay in David Lehman, ed., *Beyond Amazement* (Ithaca: Cornell UP, 1980). There is much to admire in Kramer's discussion. But his account of Ashbery's verbal polyphony, and of its musical affinities, is constrained by his focus on Elliott Carter's musical setting of "Syringa." Carter's setting uses two vocalists, suggesting a divided protagonist; Kramer finds such duality present already in Ashbery's poem, and not surprisingly the discussion moves to "Litany" and "Fantasia on 'The Nut-Brown Maid,' " in which dualities are explicit. But generally there is no reason to stress "twoness" over other multiplicities in Ashbery's polyphony. (For my purposes, "The Skaters" would provide a more useful extreme example than "Litany.") Further, a concentration on comparisons between Ashbery and Carter diverts Kramer's attention from the complex, indeterminate polyphony of older music, creating a misleading impression that Ashbery's musical affinities are specifically contemporary.

5. Nelson Goodman and Vernon Howard have written illuminatingly on the difficult notions of actual musical quotation and paraphrase. Goodman, "On Some Questions Concerning Quotation," *The Monist* April 1974: 294–306; Howard, "On Musical Quotation," ibid., 307–18. They discuss quotation between different musical works rather than within a single work. They show that the notions of musical quotation and paraphrases are puzzling and that the criteria for their application are unclear. Their arguments do not bear directly on my analysis, largely because I

am not concerned with *actual* quotation or paraphrase but with fictional or imaginary quotation. I could recast my claim in Goodman's terms as follows: the Haydn Sonata raises the question of whether certain passages metaphorically exemplify quotation, but it does not determinately resolve the issue. So expressed, my position is compatible with Goodman's and Howard's arguments.

6. I am indebted to Jonathan Kramer's essay "Multiple and Non-Linear Time in Beethoven's Opus 135" (*Perspectives of New Music* [Spring–Summer 1973]: 122–45), which offers valuable description of temporal complexities in music.

7. The topic of first-person and third-person perspectives in musical expression emerges clearly in Peter Kivy, *The Corded Shell* (Princeton: Princeton UP, 1980), though Kivy's conclusions are disappointingly simplistic. Edward T. Cone has written intriguingly of "identification" with the "persona" of a musical composition, in *The Composer's Voice* (Berkeley: U of California P, 1974).

Works Cited

Altieri, Charles. *Enlarging the Temple*. Lewisburg, PA: Bucknell UP, 1979.
——— . "From Symbolist Thought to Immanence: The Ground of Postmodern American Poetics." *Boundary 2* 1 (1973):605–41.
Anderson, Elliott, and Mary Kinzie, eds. *The Little Magazine in America: A Modern Documentary History*. Yonkers, NY: Pushcart, 1978.
Apollinaire, Guillaume. *Calligrammes*. Paris: Club du meilleur livre, 1955.
Ashbery, John. "Craft Interview." *New York Quarterly* 9 (Winter 1972): 14–15.
——— . *Houseboat Days*. New York: Penguin, 1977.
——— . *Self-Portrait in a Convex Mirror*. New York: Penguin, 1975.
Auden, W. H. Foreword. *A Change of World*. Ed. Adrienne Rich. Yale Series of Younger Poets. New Haven: Yale UP, 1951. Rpt. in Cooper 209–11.
Barthes, Roland. *Mythologies*. 1957. Trans. Annette Lavers. New York: Hill and Wang, 1972.
Berger, Charles. "Merrill and Pynchon: Our Apocalyptic Scribes." *James Merrill: Essays in Criticism*. Ed. David Lehman and Charles Berger. Ithaca: Cornell UP, 1983. 282–97.
Bernstein, Michael Andre, and Burton Hatlen. "Interview with Robert Duncan," *Sagetrieb* 4. 2 and 3 (Fall and Winter 1985): 87–135.
Berry, Wendell. *Collected Poems*. San Francisco: North Point, 1985. 350n.14.
——— . *Farming: A Handbook*. New York and London: Harcourt Brace Jovanovich, 1970. 207.
——— . *A Part*. San Francisco: North Point, 1980. 213.
——— . *The Unsettling of America*. San Francisco: Sierra Club Books, 1977. 207.
Beverly, John. "Poetry and Revolution in Central America." *The Year Left: An American Socialist Yearbook*. Ed. Mike Davis, Fred Pfeil, and Michael Sprinker. New York: Verso, 1985. 155–80.
Blaine, Julien. *Cette carte et autres*. Paris: Approches, 1968 (cited in Seaman).

Blaser, Robin. *Syntax*. Vancouver: Talonbooks, 1983.

Bloom, Harold. Introduction. *Somewhere Is Such a Kingdom*. By Geoffrey Hill. Boston: Houghton, 1975.

Bly, Robert. "Leaping Up Into Political Poetry." *Talking All Morning*. Ann Arbor: U of Michigan P, 1980. 95–105.

——— . *The Light Around the Body*. New York: Harper, 1967.

Bory, Jean-François. *Once Again*. Trans. Lee Hildreth. New York: New Directions, 1968.

——— . *Post-Scriptum*. Ed. Eric Losfeld. Paris: E. Losfeld, 1970 (cited in Seaman).

——— . "Veux." *Anthologie of Concretism*. Ed. Eugene Wildman. Chicago: Swallow, 1969.

Burkard, Michael. *Ruby for Grief*. Pittsburgh: U of Pittsburgh P, 1981.

Cardenal, Ernesto. *Zero Hour and Other Documentary Poems*. Ed. Donald D. Walsh. New York: New Directions, 1980.

Carter, Jared. *Millenial Harbinger*. Philadelphia: Slash and Burn Press, 1986.

Chopin, Henri. *Le dernier roman du monde*. Belgium: Cyanuur, 1970 (cited in Seaman).

Cixous, Hélène. "The Laugh of the Medusa." *New French Feminisms*. Ed. Elaine Marks and Isabelle de Courtivron. New York: Schocken, 1981. 245–64.

Clark, Katerina, and Michael Holquist. *Mikhail Bakhtin*. Cambridge: Harvard UP, 1985.

Clausen, Christopher. *The Place of Poetry*. Lexington: U of Kentucky P, 1981.

Cole, Richard. "The Last Days of Heaven." *New Yorker*, 27 August 1984: 36.

Cook, Albert. "Surrealism and Surrealisms." *American Poetry Review* 13, No. 4 (July/August 1984): 29–39.

Cooper, Jane Roberta, ed. *Reading Adrienne Rich: Reviews and Re-visions, 1951–81*. Ann Arbor: U of Michigan P, 1984.

Culler, Jonathan. *Structuralist Poetics*. Ithaca: Cornell UP, 1975, 1978.

Curtay, Jean-Paul. "Lettrism, Abstract Poetry, Mouth Symbols, and More. . . . " *Dada/Surrealism* 12 (1983): 81–89.

Davidson, Michael. "Archeologist [sic] of Morning: Charles Olson, Edward Dorn and Historical Method." *ELH* 47 (1980):158–79.

——— . " 'To eliminate the draw': Narrative and Language in *Slinger*." In Wesling, *Resistances* 113–49.

Derrida, Jacques. *Of Grammatology*. Trans. Gayatri Chakravorty Spivak. Baltimore: Johns Hopkins UP, 1976.

——— . "No Apocalypse, Not Now (Full Speed Ahead, Seven Missiles, Seven Missives)." *Diacritics: A Review of Contemporary Criticism* 14:2 (Summer 1984): 20–31.

Des Pres, Terrence. "Poetry and Politics." *TriQuarterly* 65 (1986):17–29.

———. "Self/Landscape/Grid." *New England Review and Bread Loaf Quarterly* 5.4 (Summer 1983): 441–50.

Dorn, Edward. *By the Sound.* Mount Vernon, WA: Frontier, 1971.

———. *The Collected Poems 1956–1974.* Bolinas, CA: Four Seasons Foundation, 1975.

———. *Gunslinger.* Durham, NC: Duke UP, 1989.

———. *Interviews.* Ed. Donald Allen. Bolinas, CA: Four Seasons Foundation, 1980.

———. *Some Business Recently Transacted in The White World.* West Newbury, MA: Frontier, 1971.

———. "Strumming Language." *Talking Poetics from Naropa Institute: Annals of the Jack Kerouac School of Disembodied Poetics.* Ed. Anne Waldman and Marilyn Webb. 2 vols. Boulder, CO: Shambala, 1978–79. 1:83–95.

———. *Views.* Ed. Donald Allen. San Francisco: Four Seasons Foundation, 1980.

———. *Yellow Lola, formerly titled Japanese Neon (Hello La Jolla, Book II).* Santa Barbara: Cadmus, 1981.

Douglas, Ann. "Descending Figure, An Interview with Louise Glück." *Columbia* Spring/Summer 1981. 116–25.

Duchesne, Juan Roman. "Testimonial Narratives in Latin America: Five Studies." *DAI* 45 (1984): 1414A. SUNY at Stony Brook.

Dugan, Alan. *New and Collected Poems, 1961–1983.* New York: Ecco, 1983.

Duncan, Robert. *The H. D. Book.* Comp. Michael Andre Bernstein. Published in chapters as follows:
Part I. Beginnings: Chapter 1. *Coyote's Journal* 5/6 (1966): 8–31; Chapter 2. *Coyote's Journal* 8 (1967): 27–35; Chapter 3. *Tri-Quarterly* 12 (Spring 1968): 67–82; Chapter 4. *Tri-Quarterly* 12 (Spring 1968): 82–98; Chapter 5, "Occult Matters." *Stony Brook* 1/2 (Fall 1968): 4–19; Chapter 6, "Rites of Participation, Part 1." *Caterpillar* 2 (January 1968): 125–54.
Part II. Nights and Days. "From the Day Book; excerpts from an extended study of H. D's poetry." *Origin* 1st ser. 10 (July 1963): 1–47; Chapter 1. *Sumac* I. 1 (Fall 1968): 101–46; Chapter 2. *Caterpillar* 6 (January 1969): 16–38; Chapter 3. *Io* 6 (Summer 1969): 117–40; Chapter 4. *Caterpillar* 7 (April 1969): 27–60; Chapter 5. *Sagetrieb* 4. 2 and 3 (Fall and Winter 1984): 39–85; Chapter 6, from Chapter 11. *Io* 10 (1971): 212–15; Chapter 6, section two. *Credences* 2 (August 1975): 50–52; Chapter 7. *Credences* 2 (August 1975): 53–67; Chapter 8. *Credences* 2 (August 1975): 68–94; Chapter 9. *Chicago Review* 30. 3 (Winter 1979): 37–88.

———. *Roots and Branches.* New York: New Directions, 1964.

Dunn, Stephen. "The Cocked Finger." *New England Review and Bread Loaf Quarterly* 5.4 (Summer 1983): 460–61.

DuPlessis, Rachel Blau. *Writing Beyond the Ending: Narrative Strategies of Twentieth-Century Women Writers.* Bloomington: Indiana UP, 1985.

Dyck, E. F. "P or Not-P? The Failure of Dichotomies." *Boundary 2* 6 (1978): 609–21.

Eagleton, Terry. "Myth and History in Recent Poetry." *British Poetry Since 1960.* Ed. Michael Schmidt and Grevel Lindop. Carcanet Press, 1972.

——. "The Revolt of the Reader." *New Literary History* 13 (1982): 449–52.

Edwards, Thomas R. *Imagination and Power: A Study of Poetry on Public Themes.* New York: Oxford UP, 1971.

Eliot, T. S. *The Complete Poems and Plays 1909–1950.* New York: Harcourt, 1962.

Fass, Ekbert. *Young Robert Duncan: Portrait of the Poet as Homosexual in Society.* Santa Barbara: Black Sparrow, 1983.

Finkelstein, Norman. "Robert Duncan: Poet of the Law," *Sagetrieb* 2. 1 (Spring 1983): 75–88.

Fish, Stanley. *Is There a Text in This Class?* Cambridge: Harvard UP, 1980, 1982.

Forche, Carolyn. *The Country Between Us.* New York: Harper, 1981.

Frost, Robert. *Complete Poems of Robert Frost.* New York: Holt, 1949.

Gallop, Jane. *The Daughter's Seduction: Feminism and Psychoanalysis.* Ithaca: Cornell UP, 1982.

Garber, Frederick. "Pockets of Secrecy, Places of Occasion." *American Poetry Review* July/August 1986.

Garnier, Pierre. "Soleil." *Les Lettres* 32, 1964.

Gilbert, Celia. *Bonfire.* Cambridge, MA: Alice James Books, 1983.

Gilbert, Sandra M., and Susan Gubar. "Introduction: Gender, Creativity, and the Woman Poet." *Shakespeare's Sisters: Feminist Essays on Woman Poets.* Bloomington: Indiana UP, 1979.

Ginsberg, Allen. *Howl and Other Poems.* San Francisco: City Lights, 1956.

——. *Plutonian Ode and Other Poems, 1977–1980.* San Francisco: City Lights, 1982.

Gioia, Dana. *Daily Horoscope.* St. Paul, MN: Graywolf, 1986.

Glück, Louise. *Descending Figure.* New York: Ecco, 1980.

——. *Firstborn.* New York: New American Library, 1968.

——. *The House on Marshland.* New York: Ecco, 1975.

——. *The Triumph of Achilles.* New York: Ecco, 1985.

Goldbarth, Albert. "Personal." *Ohio Review* 35 (1985): 72–73.

Gomringer, Eugen. *Die konstellationen.* Frauenfeld: Eugen Gomringer Press, 1963.

——. "Poésie concrète—panorama." *Les Lettres* 32 (1964): 8.

Gregg, Walter Wilson. *Pastoral Poetry and Pastoral Drama.* London: A. H. Bullen, 1906.

Hassan, Ihab. "Review." *New York Times Book Review* 9 September 1985.

Heyen, William. *The Generation of 2000.* Princeton: Ontario Press Review, 1984.

Hill, Geoffrey. "C. H. Sisson," *Poetry Nation Review* 39 (1984): 11–15.

———. *The Lords of Limit: Essays on Literature and Ideas.* New York: Oxford UP, 1984.

———. *Mercian Hymns.* London: Andre Deutsch, 1971.

Hitchcock, George, ed. *Kayak.* Issues 54–64.

Holden, Jonathan. *The Mark to Turn.* Lawrence, KS: UP of Kansas, 1976.

———. "Poetry and Commitment." *Ohio Review* 29 (1982): 15–30.

———. *The Rhetoric of the Contemporary Lyric.* Bloomington: Indiana UP, 1980.

Hoover, Paul. "Moral Poetry." *American Book Review* Nov.–Dec. 1984: 14–15.

Hughes, Ted. "Context." *The London Magazine* 1, No. 11 (February 1962): 44–45.

———. *Moortown Elegies.* London: Rainbow, 1978.

———. *Remains of Elmet.* London: Harper, 1979.

———. "Ted Hughes Writes." *Poetry Book Society Bulletin* 15 (September 1957): 1–2.

Ignatow, David. *Tread the Dark.* Boston: Atlantic-Little, 1978.

Jarman, Mark. "Contemporary Mannerism: American Poetry Slips into Something Comfortable." *Kayak* 54 (September 1980): 66–71.

———. "Generations and Contemporaries." *The Hudson Review* Summer 1985: 328–40.

Jimenez, Mayra, ed. *Fogata en la Oscurana.* Managua, Nic.: Ministry of Culture, 1985.

———. *Poesia Campesina de Solentiname.* Managua, Nic: Ministry of Culture, 1985.

———. *Poesia de las Fuerzas Armadas.* Managua, Nic: Ministry of Culture, 1985.

Jung, Carl. *Mysterium Coniunctionis.* Trans. R. F. C. Hull, 2d ed. Princeton: Princeton UP, 1970.

Kaminsky, Marc. *The Road from Hiroshima.* New York: Simon, 1984.

Kendig, Diane, trans. *A Pencil to Write Your Name: Poems from the Nicaraguan Poetry Workshop Movement.* Huron, OH: Bottom Dog Press, 1986.

Kern, Robert. "Clearing the Ground: Gary Snyder and the Modernist Imperative." *Criticism* 19 (1977): 158–77.

Keyes, Claire. *The Aesthetics of Power: The Poetry of Adrienne Rich.* Athens: U of Georgia P, 1986.

Kinnell, Galway. "Poetry, Personality, and Death." *A Field Guide to Contemporary Poetry and Poetics.* Ed. Stuart Friebert and David Young. New York: Longman, 1980.

Kooser, Ted. *One World at a Time.* Pittsburgh: U of Pittsburgh P, 1985.

———. *Sure Signs: New and Selected Poems.* Pittsburgh: U of Pittsburgh P, 1980.

Kumin, Maxine. *Our Ground Time Here Will Be Brief.* New York: Penguin, 1982.

Kuzma, Greg. "Rock Bottom: Louise Glück and the Poetry of Dispassion." *Midwest Quarterly* 24 (Summer 1983): 468–81.

Lawrence, D. H. "Poetry of the Present." *The Complete Poems.* Ed. Vivian DeSola and F. Warren Roberts. New York: Penguin, 1964.

Levertov, Denise. *Candles in Babylon.* New York: New Directions, 1982.

——. *Light Up the Cave.* New York: New Directions, 1981.

——. "Origins of a Poem." *The Poet in the World.* New York: New Directions, 1973, 43–56.

——. *Oblique Prayers.* New York: New Directions, 1984.

——. *Poems 1960–1967.* New York: New Directions, 1983.

Lifton, Robert Jay. *Death in Life: Survivors of Hiroshima.* New York: Basic, 1967.

——. *The Life of the Self: Toward a New Psychology.* New York: Basic, 1976.

Lifton, Robert Jay, and Richard Falk. *Indefensible Weapons: The Political and Psychological Case Against Nuclearism.* New York: Basic, 1982.

Lynen, John. *Pastoral Art of Robert Frost.* New Haven: Yale UP, 1960.

MacDiarmid, Hugh. *The Letters of Hugh MacDiarmid.* Ed. Alan Bold. Athens: U of Georgia P, 1984.

McDaniel, Judith. *"Reconstituting the World": The Poetry and Vision of Adrienne Rich.* Argyle, NY: Spinsters, Ink, 1978. Rpt. in Cooper 3–29.

Mallarmé, Stéphane. *Oeuvres complètes.* Paris: Gallimard, 1945.

Merrill, James. *The Changing Light at Sandover.* New York: Atheneum, 1983.

Milosz, Czeslaw. *The Witness of Poetry.* Cambridge: Harvard UP, 1983.

Molesworth, Charles. *Gary Snyder's Vision.* Columbia: U of Missouri P, 1983.

Moore, Honor. "Spuyten Duyvil." *New England Review and Bread Loaf Quarterly* 5.4 (Summer 1983): 626–33.

Nietzsche, Friedrich. *The Use and Abuse of History.* 1874. Trans. Adrian Collins. New York: Macmillan, 1949.

Olds, Sharon. *The Gold Cell.* New York: Alfred A. Knopf, 1989.

Olson, Charles. *Additional Prose: A Bibliography on America, Proprioception, & Other Notes & Essays.* Ed. George F. Butterick. Bolinas, CA: Four Seasons Foundation, 1974.

——. *Selected Writings.* Ed. Robert Creeley. New York: New Directions, 1966.

Ostriker, Alicia. *Stealing the Language: The Emergence of Women's Poetry in America.* Boston: Beacon, 1986.

Pape, Greg. *Border Crossings.* Pittsburgh: U of Pittsburgh P, 1978.

Perloff, Marjorie. Rev. of *The Collected Poems 1956–1974* and *Slinger,* by Edward Dorn. *New Republic* 4 April 1976: 22–26.

Peters, Robert. *The Peters Black and Blue Guide to Current Literary Journals.* Rochester, NY: Cherry Valley Editions, 1983.

Pinsky, Robert. *The Situation of Poetry.* Princeton: Princeton UP, 1976.

Poesia Politica Nicaraguense. Managua, Nic.: Ministry of Culture, 1986.

Pollack, Felix. "Elitism and the Littleness of Little Magazines." *Southwest Review* 61 (1976): 297–303.

Ponge, Francis. *Pièces*. Paris: Gallimard, 1962.

Pound, Ezra. *The Cantos 1–95*. New York: New Directions, 1956.

———. *Guide to Kulchur*. New York: New Directions, 1970.

———. *Literary Essays of Ezra Pound*. Ed. T. S. Eliot. New York: New Directions, 1968.

Rich, Adrienne. *Blood, Bread, and Poetry: Selected Prose 1979–1985*. New York: Norton, 1986.

———. *Diving into the Wreck: Poems 1971–1972*. New York: Norton, 1973.

———. *The Dream of a Common Language: Poems 1974–1977*. New York: Norton, 1978.

———. *The Fact of a Doorframe: Poems Selected and New, 1950–1984*. New York: Norton, 1984.

———. *On Lies, Secrets, and Silence: Selected Prose 1966–1978*. New York: Norton, 1979.

———. *Poems: Selected and New 1950–1974*. New York: Norton, 1975.

———. *Your Native Land, Your Life: Poems*. New York: Norton, 1986.

Richman, Robert. "Our 'Most Important' Living Poet." *Commentary* 74.1 (July 1982): 62–68.

Ruskin, John. *Fors Clavigera*. Vol. XXIX. London: George Allen, 1907.

Salmon, Andre, ed. *Le Guetteur Melancolique*. Paris: Gallimard, 1952 (cited in Seaman).

Santos, Sherod. "Near the Desert Test Sites." *New Yorker* 20 January 1986: 77.

Schell, Jonathan. *The Fate of the Earth*. New York: Avon, 1982.

Scholem, Gershom. *On the Kabbalah and Its Symbolism*. Trans. Ralph Manheim. New York: Schocken, 1969.

Seaman, David W. *Concrete Poetry in France*. Ann Arbor: UMI, 1981.

Shapiro, David. *John Ashbery: An Introduction to the Poetry*. New York: Columbia UP, 1979.

Shattuck, Roger. "Poet in the Wings." *New York Review of Books* 23 March 1978: 38–40.

Shipley, Betty, and Nina Langley, eds. *Meltdown: Poems from the Core*. Edmond, OK: Full Count Press, 1980.

Simpson, Louis. *An Introduction to Poetry*. New York: St. Martin's, 1972.

Simpson, Louis, and Al Poulin, Jr. "Conversation with Lou Simpson." Ed. Kate Hancock. *The World and I* 7 (1986): 335–37.

Sklar, Morty, ed. *Nuke-Rebuke: Writers & Artists Against Nuclear Energy & Weapons*. Iowa City, IA: The Spirit That Moves Us Press, 1984.

Snyder, Gary. *Axe Handles*. San Francisco: North Point, 1983.

———. *The Back Country*. New York: New Directions, 1968.

———. *Earth House Hold*. New York: New Directions, 1969.

———. *Riprap and Cold Mountain Poems*. San Francisco: Four Seasons Foundation, 1966.

————. *Turtle Island*. New York: New Directions, 1974.

Stafford, William. *Stories That Could Be True: New and Collected Poems*. New York: Harper, 1977.

Stenton, F. W. *Anglo-Saxon England*. Oxford: Clarendon, 1971.

Stern, Gerald. *Lucky Life*. Boston: Houghton, 1981.

————. "Notes from the River." *American Poetry Review* January/February 1979, 18–20.

————. *Paradise Poems*. New York: Vintage, 1984.

————. *The Red Coal*. Boston: Houghton, 1981.

Strand, Mark. *Selected Poems*. New York: Atheneum, 1984.

Talleres de Poesia, Antologia. Managua, Nic.: Ministry of Culture, 1983.

Turner, Frederick. *The New World*. Princeton: Princeton UP, 1985.

Vanderbosch, Jane. "Beginning Again." In Cooper 111–39.

von Hallberg, Robert. *American Poetry and Culture, 1945–1980*. Cambridge: Harvard UP, 1985.

————. " 'This Marvellous Accidentalism.' " In Wesling, *Resistances* 45–86.

Welchel, Marianne. "Mining the 'Earth Deposits': Women's History in Adrienne Rich's Poetry." In Cooper 51–71.

Wesling, Donald. "A Bibliography on Ed Dorn for America." *Parnassus* 5.2 (1977): 142–60.

————, ed. *Internal Resistances: The Poetry of Edward Dorn*. Berkeley: U of California P, 1985.

White, Steven F., trans. *Poets of Nicaragua: A Bilingual Anthology, 1918–1979*. Greensboro: Unicorn, 1982.

Whitman, Walt. *Leaves of Grass*. Ed. Sculley Bradley and Harold W. Blodgett. New York: Norton, 1973.

Williams, Emmett, ed. *An Anthology of Concrete Poetry*. New York: Something Else Press, 1967.

Williams, William Carlos. "Asphodel, That Greeny Flower." *Pictures from Brueghel*. 1962. New York: New Directions, 1967. 161–62.

Wormser, Baron. *Good Trembling*. Boston: Houghton, 1985.

Yates, Francis. *Giordano Bruno and the Hermetic Tradition*. New York: Vintage, 1969.

Young, Ian. "Poem Found in a Dime-Store Diary." Rpt. in *Structure and Meaning: An Introduction to Literature*. Ed. Anthony Dubé et al. Boston: Houghton, 1983. 579.

Zohar: The Book of Splendor. Ed. Gershom Scholem. New York: Schocken, 1963.

Contributors

LIONEL BASNEY, who teaches at Calvin College in Grand Rapids, Michigan, has published essays and reviews in *Eighteenth-Century Studies, South Atlantic Quarterly, Mosaic,* and *Sewanee Review,* and poetry in *Nimrod, Shenandoah, The Harvard Magazine,* and *The Country Journal.* He was awarded the Dyer/Ives Prize for poetry in 1987.

THOMAS E. BENEDIKTSSON received his doctorate from the University of Washington and is an associate professor of English at Montclair State College in New Jersey. His book *George Sterling* is part of the TUSA series, and his poems have appeared in *Ariel, Footwork, Paintbrush,* and *Journal of New Jersey Poets.* He is currently working on a study of Galway Kinnell's poetry.

RAND BRANDES has published articles on D. H. Lawrence, Ciaran Carson, Seamus Heaney, and Ted Hughes. He received his doctorate from Emory University, and is an assistant professor of English at Lenoir-Rhyne College in Hickory, North Carolina.

THOMAS B. BYERS is an associate professor at the University of Louisville, where he teaches American literature, modern and contemporary poetry, and interpretive theory. He is the author of *What I Cannot Say: Self, Word, and World in Whitman, Stevens, and Merwin,* and of essays and poems in *Arizona Quarterly, Modern Language Quarterly,* and *Poetry Miscellany* among others.

JOHN GERY is the author of a book of poems *(Charlemagne: A Song of Gestures)* and two chapbooks, and his poetry has been widely published. He has also published critical essays on John Ashbery, Ed Dorn, Alan Dugan, Thom Gunn, Italo Calvino, and Richard Wilbur. Holder of degrees from Princeton, University of Chicago, and Stanford, he is now an associate professor of English and coordinator of creative writing at the University of New Orleans.

ALAN GOLDING teaches American literature at the University of Louisville. Over forty of his articles and reviews, many concerned with poets in the Objectivist and Black Mountain traditions, have appeared in various journals and essay collections. His work in progress is *From Outlaw to Classic*, a study of the American poetry canon.

JEFFREY GENE GUNDY, whose M.A. and Ph.D. degrees are from Indiana University, is professor of English at Bluffton College in Ohio, where he has taught since 1985. He has published three poetry chapbooks and more than one hundred poems. His essays on teaching, contemporary poetry, and the quest for peace have appeared in a number of journals and such collections as *Teaching in the Small College* and *From the Heartlands: Photos and Essays from the Midwest*.

BURTON HATLEN is professor of English at the University of Maine and Fellow of the Institute on Writing and Thinking at Bard College. He has a Ph.D. from the University of California (Davis). His interests include Renaissance and modern American poetry, Marxist approaches to literature, sociolinguistics, and the teaching of writing. He is co-author of *George Oppen: Man and Poet* (1981); a collection of his poems, *I Wanted to Tell You*, appeared in 1988.

LYNN KELLER, who holds a Ph.D. from the University of Chicago, is associate professor of English at the University of Wisconsin-Madison, where she received the Chancellor's Distinguished Teaching Award in 1989. She is the author of *Re-Making It New: Contemporary American Poetry and the Modernist Tradition* (1987) and is currently working on a book on contemporary long poems. Several of her essays have appeared in journals nationwide.

DIANE KENDIG directs the Writers Series at the University of Findlay in Ohio, where she has taught English since 1984; she also teaches creative writing in the nearby medium-security prison. She has published two books of poetry and many individual poems, including translations from Spanish. She recently received an NEH Institute fellowship in translation.

HUGH KENNER, professor of English at Johns Hopkins University, is widely known for his writings on modern and contemporary literature. His books include studies of Wyndham Lewis, Joyce, Eliot, Pound, Beckett, and Buckminster Fuller. His trilogy on the "three provinces of literary modernism" includes *A Homemade World* and *A Colder Eye,* and was completed in 1988 with *A Sinking Island*.

DAVID T. LLOYD has a Ph.D. (English literature) and an M.A. (creative writing) from Brown University and also degrees from the University of

Vermont and St. Lawrence University. He directs the S. I. Newhouse Writing Center at LeMoyne College in Syracuse, N.Y., where he teaches modern literature and creative writing. He has published articles in such journals as *Ariel*, *Twentieth Century Literature*, and *Poetry Wales*, and his poetry and fiction have appeared in a number of journals in the U.S. and U.K.

STEPHEN MATTERSON completed his B.A. at Sunderland Polytechnic in England, and his Ph.D. at Sunderland and the University of Durham. He is the author of *Berryman and Lowell: The Art of Losing* (1988) and has a book on F. Scott Fitzgerald forthcoming from Macmillan. He also edited the Penguin edition of Melville's *The Confidence Man*. Since 1986 he has been Lecturer in American Literature at Trinity College, the University of Dublin, Ireland.

FRED E. MAUS holds an M.F.A. and a Ph.D. in music from Princeton, and an M.Litt. in philosophy from Oxford. He has written articles on nineteenth-century music for *Perspectives of New Music* and *College Music Symposium,* and his article "Music as Drama" in *Music Theory Spectrum* 10 (1988) is an exposition of the theoretical claims that underly his essay in this collection. He teaches music theory at Wellesley College.

MARY LEWIS SHAW, an assistant professor of French at Rutgers University, received her B.A. from the University of Arizona and her M.A., M.Ph., and Ph.D. from Columbia University; her dissertation is "Performance in the Texts of Mallarmé: The Passage from Art to Ritual." She has an article on ritual and art in *San Jose Studies* and one on "Apprehending the Idea Through Poetry and Dance" in *Dance Research Journal*.

PETER SIEDLECKI, who received his Ph.D. from SUNY Buffalo, is professor of English at Daemen College in Amherst, NY, where he has taught since 1965. He has also taught in the Attica State Correctional Facility since 1975 and has held Fulbright Senior Lectureships in Poland (1982–84) and in the German Democratic Republic (1988–89). His poetry has been published in numerous little magazines, and articles on Melville, Hawthorne, and John Fiske have appeared in European journals.

KENITH L. SIMMONS received her B.A. and M.A. from the University of Pittsburgh and her Ph.D. from the University of Wisconsin-Madison. She is an associate professor at the University of Hawaii at Hilo, where she teaches English literature and film. She has published on both of these subjects in a number of journals.

LORRIE N. SMITH holds M.A. and Ph.D. degrees from Brown University and teaches contemporary literature at St. Michael's College in Winooski,

Vermont. Her research interests include American political poetry and the literature of the Vietnam War, both subjects on which she has published extensively. She is co-editor of *America Rediscovered: Critical Essays on Literature and Film of the Vietnam War.*

LEONARD M. TRAWICK is a professor of English at Cleveland State University. He holds an M.A. from the University of Chicago and a Ph.D. in English from Harvard. His scholarly work includes *Backgrounds of Romanticism* and articles on Blake, Hazlitt, and other writers of the romantic period. His poems have appeared in a number of magazines, and he is author of a book of concrete poems (*Beastmorfs,* Cleveland State University Poetry Center, 1990). He is co-editor of *The Gamut,* a general interest journal, and editor of the CSU Poetry Center's series of contemporary poetry books.

Index